SELF-REFLECTIVE RENEWAL
IN SCHOOLS

SELF-REFLECTIVE RENEWAL
IN SCHOOLS

LOCAL LESSONS FROM A NATIONAL INITIATIVE

EDITED BY BRADLEY S. PORTIN, LYNN G. BECK,
MICHAEL S. KNAPP, AND JOSEPH MURPHY

Published under the auspices
of the National Education Association

Contemporary Studies in Social
and Policy Issues in Education:
The David C. Anchin Center Series

Kathryn M. Borman, Series Editor

Westport, Connecticut
London

Library of Congress Cataloging-in-Publication Data

Self-reflective renewal in schools : local lessons from a national initiative / edited by
Bradley S. Portin ... [et al.].
    p. cm. — (Contemporary studies in social and policy issues in education:
The David C. Anchin Center Series)
    Includes bibliographical references and index.
    ISBN 1–56750–663–1 (alk. paper)
    1. School improvement programs—United States—Case studies. I. Portin,
    Bradley S. II. Series.
LB2822.8.S45 2003
371.2'07—dc21
                                                                    2002072849

British Library Cataloguing in Publication Data is available.

Library of Congress Catalog Card Number: 2002072849
ISBN: 1–56750–663–1

First published in 2003

Praeger Publishers, 88 Post Road West, Westport, CT 06881
An imprint of Greenwood Publishing Group, Inc.
www.praeger.com

Printed in the United States of America

The paper used in this book complies with the
Permanent Paper Standard issued by the National
Information Standards Organization (Z39.48–1984).

10 9 8 7 6 5 4 3 2 1

To the memory of
Oscar Uribe
National Education Association

Contents

Preface

Entering the new millennium, the work of preparing all the children in our nation's schools for the world they enter holds the center of attention for our society. Nothing can be more important, and few undertakings more complex. This essential work of educating children happens in a particular context—an important and increasingly varied context—*the school*. For those who work in schools, who care about schools, or who wish to help schools serve young people better, it is essential to understand how schools examine and renew their service to children, while grasping the possibilities and limits of strategies that support the work of school renewal.

This book opens a window on this work through sharing the essential story of schools in nine states as they wrestled with a national school renewal initiative entitled *KEYS to Excellence in Your Schools*. An initiative of the National Education Association, KEYS aims, through the NEA's national presence and state affiliates, to offer every school in the country the means for examining and improving the school's effectiveness in educating children. As such, the initiative represents an important new agenda of school renewal and effectiveness by the largest teachers' union in the nation.

As explained throughout this book, KEYS can be thought of as a *tool* and a *process* rather than a *package*. The aim is to provide school staffs with systematic indicators of how they, as a school community, view their progress along thirty-five research-supported *indicators of school effectiveness*.

Broadly stated, the initiative offers a survey-based process for helping the school community appraise its progress and imagine improvements in five core areas:

1. Shared understanding and commitment to high goals
2. Open communication and collaborative problem solving
3. Continuous assessment for teaching and learning
4. Personal and professional learning
5. Resources to support teaching and learning

The story of each school's experience of KEYS, in relation to its local and state context, reveals how hard and how unique the work of school renewal is. Schools are complex places—with their own history, community, capacity, and challenge. Our aim in this book is to discover commonalities in the conditions that best support schools in this work, but also to tell their stories so that the uniqueness of each school provides its own lessons for readers. From the school's story, a journey richly described, other schools embarking on renewal can learn.

THE BOOK'S GENESIS

This collection of school case stories came to be through the commitment by the National Education Association to ground its initiation and implementation of KEYS in evidence and inquiry. Through its Division of Teaching and Learning, NEA commissioned a team of researchers in the field of school renewal to dig deep into the experience of schools in the first wave of KEYS implementation. Our charge was to tell their stories, both successes and struggles, in a way that would benefit both schools and the ongoing development of KEYS. The chapters in this book represent the results of this multi-year national study.

In supporting this work, the NEA has modeled what KEYS aims to provide for schools: a reflective and honest appraisal—of what is happening in schools—paralleling what the NEA initiative invites schools to do through self-reflective renewal activity. Through the NEA's partnership in the research, an important step has been taken toward understanding essential steps in the renewal of teaching and learning.

WHAT THE BOOK OFFERS

Because the volume presents the stories of school renewal activity in a variety of settings, people who work in schools—teachers, principals, and parents—will likely find a mirror for their own experience. For them, reading the experiences and learnings of others will help reveal where their cel-ebrations can occur as well as highlighting the issues that schools may encounter when embarking on similar journeys.

For those in the world of policy (e.g., district personnel, state education officers, legislators, and others), the nine cases portrayed in the following chapters bring light to an important, and not always examined, intersection between the policy environment and what happens in schools. The stories here reveal how the internal dynamics of renewal in schools can both enhance and subvert the achievement of policy goals, and, conversely, how policies can support or stymie the fragile work of renewal activity.

For the student of organizations, the cases here reinforce that *context matters* and help to show how context enters into the renewal equation. In addition, many of the cases reveal the capacities and resources—for leader-ship, courage to try new approaches, and self-reflection—that are vital to sustaining the work of renewal that schools undertake. Self-reflection sounds personal, and it is, but it is also organizational. How reflection, and conversations around reflection, occur and are sustained matters in shaping whether educators can move ahead in renewing their practice and their school to better educate students.

PREVIEW OF THE BOOK'S ORGANIZATION

The book is both the sum of nine stories and a larger whole. The context for these stories appears in Chapter 1 (KEYS and the Larger School Reform Movement in the United States). In that chapter, Murphy, Beck, Knapp, and Portin locate self-reflective renewal strategies within a larger history of school reform and describe the distinctive character of the KEYS Initiative. (Further detail about the study's methods, the thirty-five KEYS indicators, and the KEYS instrument appear in the book's three appendices.)

In Chapters 2 to 4, Bol and Stringfield (Tennessee), Jones and Louis (Minnesota), and Nettles (Maryland) tell the story of KEYS in schools within these three states. Taken together, these chapters show how the school staff's experience with KEYS was heavily dependent on forces and conditions outside the school.

In Chapters 5 to 7, Beck (California), Portin and Knapp (Washington), and Smylie (Illinois) present cases that reveal the powerful role played by a different set of conditions, largely internal to the school. In these cases, con-ditions, resources, and dynamics within the school interacted with the ini-tiative's nature to shape the school's response to KEYS.

Chapters 8 to 10, Teddlie (Mississippi), Borman (Florida), and Reyes (Texas) reveal what can happen when the external forces interact with the schools' internal capacity, thereby overshadowing renewal activity or set-ting the stage for staff to embrace renewal.

Finally, in Chapter 11, Portin, Beck, Knapp, and Murphy pull together what can be learned across all nine cases and present a way of conceptualizing the dynamics of self-reflective renewal in schools. From this analysis emerge insights regarding the school's institutional readiness for renewal and the conditions that may support it.

The cases represented in this book cover only nine states, and within them only one or a few school settings. There are many other renewal stories than those offered here. We make no claim to represent the experience of every school with KEYS, or any other school renewal strategy. Nonetheless, the range of conditions across these schools and the dynamics of their response to this initiative are suggestive of challenges that many, if not most, schools are likely to face. The reader will have to decide whether we got the story right.

ACKNOWLEDGMENTS

In preparing this book, we want to offer thanks and appreciation to the many individuals who helped it come to be. Our colleagues at the National Education Association have been tireless supporters and critical friends in the work. We want especially to acknowledge Rubén Cedeño, Tita Ferriol, Wayne Garrison, Ron Henderson, Romaine Hodge, Judith McQuaide, Jacques Nacson, Don Rollie, and Jeff Schneider. In addition, we are grateful for the contributions of others who worked in association with KEYS including those at state NEA affiliates, UniServ personnel, local teachers association personnel, school district staff, and others from the respective state offices of education.

As researchers, we were assisted by the support and insights of our colleagues at our universities who reviewed our findings and drafts of publications arising from the study; to John King for copy editing assistance; and, of course, for the important support from Marie Ellen Larcada, our editor at Greenwood Publishing Group.

Finally, this work could not have happened without the partnership and commitment of the schools across the country that participated. We especially thank the teachers, principals, district officials, and community members who opened the door on their experience of self-reflective renewal and gave us their time.

KEYS and the Larger School Reform Movement in the United States

Joseph Murphy, Lynn G. Beck, Michael S. Knapp, and Bradley S. Portin

In his famous 1976 article, Karl Weick painted a portrait of schools as loosely coupled systems. He argued that behind these loose linkages were schools that were characterized by unclear goals, a production function that was poorly articulated, and a near absence of accountability for organizational performance. Looking back over the last quarter century, it appears that Weick's portrait captured a system with historical roots nearly a century in length, but one that was on the verge of a massive overhaul.

As we have argued elsewhere (Murphy, 1991, 1996), the education system that Weick described has undergone profound changes in the last two decades. For better or worse, one purpose—enhanced student achievement—has ascended to the pinnacle of the goals hierarchy. While other objectives for schooling have hardly disappeared from the goals portfolio, on nearly every domain of the educational landscape student achievement stands out. At the same time, our comfort level in drawing connections between classroom and school conditions and student performance, in specifying the production function of schooling if you will, has risen dramatically. While there is much that remains to be learned, the knowledge base concerning factors that promote better schooling has expanded immeasurably over the last quarter century. Finally, accountability in a variety of forms has become a reality in the world of pre K–12 education. The ability of schools to ignore indicators of organizational and student performance or to deflect responsibility for those outcomes to families and youngsters themselves has been eroded considerably. Concomitantly, the spotlight on accountability-as-compliance has dimmed significantly. So, too, has the focus on the process dimensions of accountability. Rising in prominence are new forms of accountability, especially accountability for organizational outcomes and customer satisfaction.

When we compare Weick's analysis of a quarter-century past with the emerging story line chronicled earlier, evidence emerges of an industry in the throes of a major transition. And central to that transition at all points across the educational spectrum are efforts to reform or overhaul the existing system. Of particular interest for our purposes in this volume is that subset of reform initiatives that cluster under the rubric of school improvement, and among them, a class of school-based reform initiatives that emphasize a reflective process of school renewal. These initiatives target the school as a whole, and do so on the basis of different conceptions of the school, its *core technology* (teaching and learning), how it is managed and led, and how it connects institutionally to the society it serves.

This volume concentrates on a particular national effort to promote self-reflective school renewal: an initiative mounted by the National Education Association called *KEYS to Excellence in Your Schools*. Set in motion in 1996, the initiative seeks to promulgate a reflective renewal process in schools at all levels across the nation. The chapters in the book chronicle the entry of this renewal initiative into a variety of school settings across nine states over a three-year period from 1996 to 1999. The chapters represent a systematic attempt to learn about the way this kind of renewal approach plays out in individual schools, to inform educators and scholars, as well as initiative framers, including the National Education Association.

In this introductory chapter we set the stage for ensuing analyses by characterizing the larger national context in which the KEYS initiative and other school improvement initiatives reside and describing the nature of the KEYS initiative itself. To accomplish this, we first note how changing conceptions of education and educational institutions have worked their way through overlapping waves of school reform activity. Then, we highlight the range of approaches to reform that takes the whole school as the primary unit of change, and we locate self-reflective renewal initiatives among them. Finally, we lay out the intellectual roots of the KEYS initiative and describe its process, strategic assumptions, and the efforts (including the case studies presented in this book) made to understand its potential and limits.

BACKDROP FOR SELF-REFLECTIVE RENEWAL: THE CHANGING EDUCATIONAL ENTERPRISE AND THE SCHOOL REFORM MOVEMENT

The KEYS initiative has come into being in a changing educational enterprise subject to successive and overlapping waves of school reform activity over the last two decades. These larger environmental developments set the stage for self-reflective renewal strategies and have left their stamp on both the form that self-reflective school renewal takes and its prospects for constructive contributions to education and schooling.

The Changing Face of the Educational Enterprise

Surrounding school reform efforts of all kinds, three significant shifts are underway: in the technical core of schooling, in the organization and management of schools, and in the institutional relationship between schools and the communities they serve. Together, these changes set an overarching agenda for renewal of all schools, whatever the specific issues confronting any particular school. In addition, they point the way toward new roles and relationships among participants in the process of school renewal.

First, at the level of instructional practice—the technical core of schooling—radically different conceptions of learning and teaching are coming to dominate professional discourse and generate new forms of instructional practice. Rooted in new notions of knowledge and intelligence (derived from constructivist, sociological, and sociocultural thinking about learning) these conceptions depart sharply from long-established behaviorist ideas and have far-reaching consequences for teachers' work, the content of the curriculum, the students' role in classroom learning, and the production of knowledge. At a minimum, these ideas mean that school staff have a great deal of new learning to do, for their own schooling and professional training is unlikely to have prepared them for this kind of work.

Second, educators are calling into question widely accepted ways of managing and organizing schools. Forms of school organization and management that have been relatively unchanging across much of the last century are increasingly viewed as resting on industrial era premises that encourage fragmentation of effort, impose rigidities in the system, paralyze creativity and initiative, and divert effort from the most central purposes of schooling. In their place, educators and reformers are experimenting with ways to design and lead schools that enhance and differentiate professional roles, transform and distribute leadership, reduce hierarchy, emphasize collaboration among school staff, and seek the development of human resources.

Third, a new relationship between schools and the larger (generally immediate) environment is in the making as the public schools' quasi-monopoly comes into question and market controls over schooling become more accepted. On the assumption that this monopoly arrangement has made the schools complacent, unproductive, and insensitive to community needs and preferences, forces are underway that are realigning power and influence among professionals and the public. These forces encourage community members and parents as partners or, alternatively, consumers of educational services through arrangements that increase their choice in selecting a school, give them greater voice in school governance, or engage them as collaborators in the work of schooling.

Waves of School Reform Activity

Taken together, these changes have permeated an evolving school reform movement, which has gone through identifiable, yet overlapping waves of activity over the past two decades. While there is no simple way to distinguish one wave from the others, one can discern, in rough chronological sequence, three distinct sets of ideas, each with a characteristic perspective on the problem to be solved and the dominant mechanisms for solving it. Contemporary approaches to the renewal of schools can trace their intellectual roots to one or more of these waves. Furthermore, past waves of reform activity remain the context for the present. In particular, educators and other participants in schools often make assumptions about schooling, reform models, and the change process that reflect the thinking that predominated in one or more of these waves.

The Intensification Wave (1980–1987)

Reform activity in the early 1980s targeted low expectations and a presumed low quality of the teaching force, and sought to address these problems through system-wide prescription, much of it stemming from state government. There was a widespread feeling that, while seriously impaired, the educational system could be repaired by strong medicine. Accordingly, state mandates called for higher graduation requirements, the use of highly specified instructional models, and closely directed the allocation of resources. The driving forces for reform emanated from state government and other sources.

The Restructuring Wave (1986–1995)

Critics were swift to point out the shortcomings of intensification reforms on both philosophical and practical grounds. Arguing that such reforms did not quickly produce desired results, nor were they likely to, reformers called for a major overhaul—a restructuring—of the way schools were organized and governed. At that time, Elmore noted,

If we accept the existence of standard practices, and see their resilience as a symptom of organizational failure, then solutions seem to lie in fundamentally changing the organizational form of schools, the characteristics of the people who work in them, and the incentives under which they work. (1987, p. 66)

At the heart of this approach to the problem was the belief that educational improvement was contingent on empowering teachers to develop more effective approaches to their work, and to a lesser extent, on empowering parents as partners of educators. To enable teachers (and parents) meant basic changes in the organizational arrangements of schooling.

Accordingly, restructuring reform strategies sought to capitalize on the creativity and energy of individuals at the school-site level, rather than on the strong hand of government more removed from the locus of instruction. Restructuring reforms took various forms. Prominent among them were decentralization arrangements, emphasizing site-based management and shared decision making by stakeholders in particular school communities. Alongside these efforts was vigorous experimentation with the scale and design of the school program itself, led by intentional efforts to create vibrant small schools. At the same time, early versions of choice initiatives appeared for the first time, along with arrangements that increased citizen involvement in school governance, thereby introducing the market into the reform equation, and along with it, new ways of thinking about educational improvement.

The Reformation Wave (1992–present)

A third wave, less easily characterized, sought to marry ideas from the preceding two and build on them. While retaining the notion that school-site change and professional empowerment were important, this wave reasserted the role and presence of the district and state. This was manifest through attention to systemic change, broad consensus on content, performance, and, to an extent, opportunity-to-learn standards; and mechanisms that would hold students, teachers, and schools accountable for performance in relation to these standards. Alongside this standards-based reform activity, largely driven by government, were efforts of professional groups, in conjunction with arms of government (e.g., legislatures), to strengthen the teaching profession. At the same time, citizen and consumer-oriented reforms gained in legitimacy, and market influences began to work their way more prominently into reform designs through increased emphasis on chartering, radical deregulation, voucher arrangements, and home schooling. The reformation wave thus represents a time of considerable ferment— bringing considerable energy and a wide range of solutions and actors, as well as fundamental conflicts, to the fore in the educational enterprise.

SCHOOL-BASED REFORM AND SELF-REFLECTIVE RENEWAL

As the school reform movement has evolved, reformers have paid increasing attention to the school as a primary unit and locus of change. This argument builds from the idea that all formal education happens in schools, not in districts or states. On the other hand, approaches to the improvement of schooling that focus too narrowly on a specific aspect of the school (e.g., remedial classes for poor readers) risk ignoring larger forces in the school community that may be driving the supposed problem.

In this view of reform, only by addressing the school as a functioning system or community is there a good chance of dealing with the full range of immediate conditions that hinder learning and performance. This line of thinking highlights approaches to reform that are school-based and school-wide, seeking to energize and improve the functioning of individual schools through a variety of means.

Among the school-based, schoolwide efforts by educators to renew programs or practices, a range of strategies and strategic assumptions can be discerned. Most visible are name-brand approaches developed and popularized by highly visible reformers (e.g., Comer, Levin, Sizer, Slavin, and Hirsch) and often maintained through extensive nationwide networks. Less visible, but probably equally numerous, are the various locally developed approaches to strengthening school programs, each combining elements of governance, program structure, school culture, curriculum, and routines in ways that satisfy local interests and educational requirements (Shields & Knapp, 1997).

In recent years, a number of school-based reform approaches have been popularized and promoted through efforts by the federal government and others to encourage the adoption of comprehensive school reform models with proven ability to increase student performance. A research base has begun to develop, assembling evidence of these reform models in action (e.g., American Institutes for Research, 1999; Murphy & Datnow, 2002; New American Schools, 1999), along with mixed results regarding their efficacy (Berends, Heilbrun, McKelvey, & Sullivan, 1999). Several dozen such models made it onto an official list embedded in federal legislation as exemplars worthy of replication with federal assistance. But these represent only a fraction of the models and approaches that have been developed nationwide to revitalize the working of individual schools.

All of these models or approaches, whether legitimized by the federal government and well-known reform networks or home-grown in particular localities, share some important assumptions: (1) The individual school is taken as the central unit of reform; (2) the reform addresses the whole school and affects the school's program; and (3) school members take the initiative (though not necessarily sole initiative) to design and carry out the reform. But beyond these common features, the differences overwhelm the similarities.

School-based reforms vary on a number of important dimensions including: how much they prescribe what is taught and how teachers should teach it; how, and how much, they restructure time, staffing, and program; what allowance is made for student and parent choice, and for involving parents, not to mention the learners themselves, in school governance; how they approach decision making, planning, leadership, and problem solving; and what role they envision for external actors in helping the school staff embrace a new vision of their work (Shields & Knapp, 1997). Reforms further differ considerably in their core beliefs and mission regarding learning, teaching, and the purposes of schooling.

A central difference has to do with the emphasis placed on building within the school a productive and sustainable process for improving the school, as opposed to offering goals, curriculum structure, or organizational features—that is, the *content* of renewal activity—which might result from such a process. In particular, reform models and theories differ in how much they trust the staff members to evolve their own best solution to the challenges facing their school.

One strand of process-oriented reform places great emphasis on reflection, self-study, and data-driven deliberation among staff members about what their school needs, what it is accomplishing, where its strengths and weaknesses lie, and how to proceed to build a better school. The National Education Association's KEYS initiative, on which this book focuses, exemplifies such a model. In terms of the evolving school reform movement, described earlier, the data-driven reflective renewal approach embodied in the KEYS initiative is probably best understood as a restructuring effort. The initiative's model and its supporting architecture assume that what needs to be repaired is the organization of schools, that the structure of schooling often gets in the way of quality education and that through thoughtful work of teachers these barriers can be identified and removed. However, though largely a restructuring reform, the KEYS initiative also draws strength from some aspects of reformation ideology—for example, through its connection to powerful opportunity-to-learn standards and its acknowledgment of the power of professionals to collaboratively address organizational deficiencies.

THE KEYS INITIATIVE: INTELLECTUAL SCAFFOLDING AND STRATEGIC ASSUMPTIONS

The KEYS to Excellence in Your Schools initiative was undertaken by the National Education Association (NEA) as a means of enhancing the quality and performance of schools across the nation, based on demonstrated empirical connections between school conditions and student outcomes. KEYS represents the NEA's first effort to develop a school improvement initiative that rests on a measurable concept of school quality which, in turn, has demonstrable influence on student achievement.

KEYS is rooted in effective schools research—that is, scholarship conducted across the past two decades that seeks to identify environmental forces, organizational conditions, and school processes that impact student achievement. Research in this tradition generally has shown that high-performing schools share some common organizational conditions, independent of particular instructional and pedagogical strategies or preferences (Levine & Lezotte, 1990). Research on effective schools also reveals that these schools share a platform of values that support and bring meaning to the common organizational variables. The KEYS initiative framework builds directly on these ideas.[1]

Organizational Conditions

A variety of frameworks developed during the early part of the effective schools movement capture organizational conditions associated with school performance. For example, in their seminal review of the early work in this line of research, Purkey and Smith (1982) create a portrait of the *effective school* characterized by nine organizational conditions: (1) ample management authority at the school site; (2) instructional leadership capacity by the principal and others; (3) stability of the school staff; (4) curriculum articulation and organization that meaningfully connects what is learned across courses or grade levels; (5) schoolwide staff development, closely related to the instructional program; (6) parental involvement and support; (7) schoolwide recognition of academic success; (8) maximized learning time; and (9) support from the district central office. This review notes, as well, several characteristics of the organizational culture in effective schools, notably: collaborative planning and collegial relationships, a sense of community within the school, and order and discipline. More recent work has brought additional depth and clarity to our understanding of these school-level conditions that influence the work of teachers and students and that promote or hinder student performance (for a review, see Murphy, Beck, Crawford, Hodges, & McGaughy, 2001).

Core Values

Underlying the organizational conditions of highly effective schools are deeply held, common values. Murphy (1992) has identified four such core values emerging from effective schools research as key to sustained high levels of performance: (1) a belief in the educability of learners; (2) a focus on outcomes and equity; (3) a sense that the school is ultimately responsible for students' performance; and (4) commitment to consistency and coordination throughout the school community.

A Belief in the Educability of Learners

At the heart of the effective schools movement is an attack on the prevailing conception of student learning, summarized eloquently in the dominant aphorism of effective schools advocates: *all students can learn.* Historically, schools have been organized to produce results consistent with the normal curve, to sort youth into the various occupational strata needed to fuel the economy. The effective school movement helped push this dominant belief off of center stage. While the effective schools movement by and large failed to anticipate the constructivist cognitive models of learning that would be needed for the future, it did begin to underscore the importance of alterable, policy-manipulable variables and to direct the attention of academics and practitioners alike to the conditions of learning available in schools.

A Focus on Outcomes and Equity

For a variety of reasons, educators and the public in the United States have avoided serious inspection of educational outcomes, relying instead on community wealth and socioeconomic status, among other indicators, as proxies for the quality of a school. The effective schools movement challenged this prevailing view of assessing quality. Effective schools proponents realized that inputs and outputs were not necessarily linked (Finn, 1990), and they argued persuasively that rigorous assessments of schooling were needed and that one could judge the quality of education only by examining student outcomes, especially indices of learning. Equally important, they defined success not in absolute terms but as the value added to what students brought to the educational process. Finally, and most radically divergent from prevailing practice, they insisted that effectiveness depended on an equitable distribution of learning outcomes across the entire population of the school.

A Sense that the School is Ultimately Responsible for Student Performance

When quality education is defined primarily in terms of resources and student SES, when failure is an inherent characteristic of the learning model employed, and when the function of schooling is to sort children into occupational strata, responsibility for what happens to students lies less with school personnel and more with deficiencies in the students themselves and in the home/community environments in which they are nurtured. Effective schools researchers and practitioners rejected this philosophy and "shifted the focus of efforts to deal with poor academic performance among low income minorities from the child to the school" (Cuban, 1989, p. 784). Their attack on the practice of blaming the victim for the shortcomings of the school itself underscored the responsibility of the school community for what happens to the youth in its care.

A Commitment to Consistency and Coordination

One of the most powerful and enduring lessons from all the research on effective schools is that the better schools are more tightly linked—structurally, symbolically, and culturally—than the less effective ones. This finding suggests a strong explicit commitment among members of the school community to achieving this kind of coherence, rather than following the lines of least resistance, by which teachers operate independently of one another and with little attempt to align their efforts around common goals. Effective schools, by contrast, operate more as an organic whole and less as a loose collection of disparate subsystems. There is a great deal of consistency within and across the major components of the organization, especially regarding the teaching-learning process. Staff, parents, and students share a sense of direction. Components of the curriculum—objectives, materials, and assessment strategies—are tightly aligned. School staff share a common instructional language. Expectations for performance are similar throughout the school community; rewards and punishments are consistently distributed to students.

The KEYS Framework

Based on a comprehensive review of all of the work described previously, the National Education Association crafted the conceptual architecture that undergirds the KEYS initiative and developed an empirical base that supports it (Schneider, Verdugo, Uribe, & Greenberg, 1993). Specifically, KEYS directs attention and energy about school renewal to five general conditions—that is, the mixes of values and organizational features of schools—that have been found to be associated with exceptionally effective schools, namely:

• Shared understanding and commitment to high learning goals
• Open communication and collaborative problem solving
• Continuous assessment of teaching and learning
• Opportunities for personal and professional development
• Resources to support teaching and learning

KEYS Strategic Assumptions

To help schools develop and maintain these organizational conditions, the KEYS initiative has constructed a data-based strategy for school renewal. The strategy, as other process-oriented school reform approaches, relies on the internal initiative of school staff and assumes that, with appropriate forms of support, school staffs have the motivation and capability to substantially change the way they do their work and the outcomes of their efforts. The assumed starting point is some shared sense, however vague, that the school's program is not working as well as it could for some or all of its students, and also for members of its staff. Movement from that point forward, as this strategy conceives it, involves a process by which school staff gain understanding of the problem, develop a shared vision of where the school should be headed, and engage in activities that realize this vision in school structures, culture, and program. The process could lead to any number of outcomes.

The viability of the KEYS strategy rests on several premises. First, the KEYS process assumes that what makes a school effective is well understood and knowable. Building on the tradition of effective schools research, as noted earlier, the framers of the KEYS initiative identified empirically an expanded set of correlates of school effectiveness, the *35 Indicators of a Quality School* (see Appendix B), and demonstrated that schools with these attributes have high levels of student learning (Schneider, Verdugo, Uribe, & Greenberg, 1993). These correlates are all measurable, and survey instruments have been developed by the NEA for discovering whether, and to what extent, these correlates are manifested in a given school building.

Second, the process assumes that deliberative self-reflection by school staff about the school's structure, culture, and program, based on measures of the school's functioning, will provide both direction and motivation for locally determined plans to improve the school. By filling out a questionnaire, the staff and others produce data about the school that can then be compared to profiles of optimal functioning. The profile the school receives is a histogram for each of the thirty-five indicators of school success. The questionnaire data yield a score on each indicator showing how the school compares to a predetermined take-off point—the score level at which positive student achievement can be confidently predicted, according to the research on which KEYS is based (Schneider, Verdugo, Uribe, & Greenberg, 1993). Deliberation over the meaning of the measurements and how to improve them, assisted by external facilitation and support, leads to decisions about next steps and an action plan that is carried out over time. Periodic revisiting of the measurements (e.g., by readministering the instrument) can provide a benchmark against which to consider progress and further actions that might be necessary.

The ultimate contribution of such a process to school renewal rests on several more specific premises:

1. Engagement in a KEYS-style process is sufficiently motivating to sustain the interest and involvement of school staff over time.

2. Measurements of the school in relation to the thirty-five indicators are taken under acceptable conditions and reported back to the school in a timely fashion in a form that is understandable to them.

3. School staffs respond to the data in reflective, deliberative fashion and find in the data a sense of direction for their renewal efforts.

4. The right forms of school-based support (e.g., expertise, leadership, time for collaboration) are available for engagement in the process and in the resulting renewal activities.

5. When they want it or need it, school staffs engaged in the KEYS process have access to external assistance, especially from the local and state union infrastructure.

These assumptions can be thought of as a rough *theory of action* guiding the KEYS initiative. Several features of this theory of action are noteworthy. For one thing, the KEYS strategy places emphasis on a process of renewal rather than a directive for action—that is, outside the frameworks of the effective schools research it offers no prescriptions about the substantive direction that reform should take. That matter is left entirely to the school, and is assumed to vary across schools depending on the school's profile on the effectiveness indicators. This feature has both the virtue of a high degree of flexibility and adaptability, and the possible drawback of offering little or no guidance about what the school might try to do differently to realize better scores on the effectiveness indicators. While specific action is left to the school to decide, the profile of responses on the KEYS instrument does provide the school with marker points and direction for action. For example, a low score on KEY 24 (Academic programs are assessed) might naturally encourage a school staff to examine the assessment practices of their instructional programs.

Furthermore, the theory places a high reliance on the capabilities of the teachers' association infrastructure (e.g., district UniServ staff, support staff from the state affiliate offices). In some ways, this is a virtue given the pervasive presence of the teachers' association in most states and localities across the nation. At the same time, this may be a weakness given the limited capacity of some state affiliates, not to mention the fact that the primary expertise of many association staff lies in the traditional union territory of bargaining, addressing grievances, and otherwise engaging in member advocacy work rather than in guiding teachers' professional learning, developing new school structures, or helping with other likely targets of renewal activity.

Finally, the theory assumes that all involved have some sophistication with data and its interpretation. With full allowance that such sophistication can grow over time, there is still the possibility that quantitative data of the sort yielded by the KEYS process may not be sufficiently understandable to the participants to help them chart a direction for their course of action. This may especially be the case in the early stages of a reform process when there may be least clarity about in which direction to proceed.

The KEYS Instrument and Process

The 125-item KEYS instrument, administered to teachers, administrators, staff, and others in the school community (including parents and students, if the school decides to include these groups) yields data that characterize the organizational climate and health of the school. The instrument essentially functions as a broad-ranged needs-assessment survey, providing information on school qualities expressed in terms of organizational behaviors (see Appendix C: The KEYS Survey for an outline of the original instrument that was used in the cases in this volume).

In an individual school, the KEYS process begins with the decision by school staff to embark on the journey of self-reflection and renewal activity guided by the findings of the survey instrument. A design team is formed within the school, typically composed of several teachers and one or more administrators who are committed to seeing the process through. The team establishes plans for the administration of the survey, and after this has been done and forwarded to NEA, awaits feedback from the Association (or state affiliate). The return of the data (in graphical and other forms of display) provides the starting point for an intensive ongoing conversation among staff members about the strengths and weaknesses of their school and possible avenues for improving it. Though schools have enormous discretion in what they do in response to the process, a typical pattern is for staff members to form themselves into problem-solving task forces to address a selected number of areas where the instrument indicates that improvement is needed. After a period of time—as short as a year or a longer interval—the school may readminister the survey to track its progress on the indicators.

Throughout the process, but especially after the return of the survey data, staff members avail themselves of various sources of external assistance, chief among them, help from local and state union offices. The expertise of these units varies, as do the targets of improvement activity in the school. Through a matching process that relies heavily on the initiative of the school members and their particular needs, the staff develop and implement plans for approving the functioning of the school, addressing such areas as organizational development, restructuring, new approaches to instruction, more sophisticated assessment systems, and so on.

There are many possible variations on this pattern, and there is little to prevent a school staff from adapting the KEYS process to whatever purposes and conditions are most salient in the school. Thus, it is not only possible, but encouraged, for the process to subsume, or be subsumed, within other improvement activities underway in the school.[2]

UNDERSTANDING THE POTENTIAL AND LIMITS
OF SELF-REFLECTIVE RENEWAL STRATEGIES

Self-reflective renewal strategies raise many questions for reformers and scholars as well as initiative sponsors. In the case of KEYS, one can think of the implied theory of action as a set of assertions about schools' engagement in self-reflective renewal that are begging to be tested, explored, and confirmed or amended, based on evidence about response to this way of approaching school renewal. These assertions imply various questions, among them the following. What do school staff see in the process of self-study and reflection that draws them into it? Are some schools readier for this kind of renewal work than others, and if so, what makes them ready? In light of the fact that KEYS process is relatively content-free, where does the content for the school's renewal activity come from? How do school staff come to visualize new opportunities through the process of self-reflection? What is the quality of support for renewal available to schools and how do they access this support?

This book is part of the process of trying to answer these questions. From the inception of KEYS, the NEA has been keenly interested in learning how the KEYS process is working on all of the dimensions discussed earlier—the robustness of the underlying research base, the ability of the union to successfully negotiate the passage of KEYS to the school site, the skills of local school personnel to use the model productively, and so forth. In order to get some purchase on these issues, the NEA has engaged two lines of inquiry.

First, the Association mounted focus-group interviews that have included teachers, administrators, education support personnel, and parents associated with elementary, middle, and high schools participating in KEYS sites distributed across the country. Focus-group participants indicated that KEYS effectively directs conversation to the kinds of knowledge, tools, and resources that are required to promote student learning and achievement in our nation's public schools. Furthermore, the renewal process can, and has, afforded opportunities for stakeholders with differing perspectives and backgrounds to work toward a common vision for school improvement. Results from the focus groups also confirm that the context into which KEYS is introduced into individual schools influences its effects on school improvement activities.

Data obtained from focus groups also suggest that KEYS effectively empowers school staff. For example, survey results have served to clarify the otherwise chaotic organizational behavior patterns that exist in particular schools. In such instances, KEYS data have been used to identify barriers and diminished capacities, as well as to inform staff about inconsistencies between values and practices in the educational setting. Data from these focus groups also reveal that for school improvement efforts to be effective, a collective school leadership must be capable of making connections between KEYS and the larger curriculum and instruction issues facing schools.

These findings offer glimpses into the potential of a renewal strategy such as KEYS. A second line of inquiry, culminating in this book, has tried to develop more detailed, longitudinal pictures of the entry of KEYS into different kinds of schools facing a variety of challenges. Here, the NEA commissioned case studies of KEYS sites in nine states. This volume is dedicated to lessons uncovered in those cases. Specifically, the studies reveal the role played by KEYS in schools grappling with the difficult tasks of school improvement. More generally, the cases inform our understanding of school improvement at large, augmenting the knowledge base about factors that facilitate or hinder the difficult work of strengthening schools at the site level.

NOTES

1. Readers interested in the technical and statistical aspects of early KEYS survey research linking the social attributes of schools to student outcome variables are referred to Schneider, Verdugo, Uribe, and Greenberg (1993), and to Verdugo, Uribe, Schneider, Henderson, and Greenberg (1996).

2. We want to acknowledge the contributions of Wayne Garrison and Judith McQuaide from the National Education Association to this section of the chapter.

REFERENCES

American Institutes for Research. (1999). *An educators guide to schoolwide reform.* Washington, DC: Author.

Berends, M., Heilbrun, J., McKelvey, C., & Sullivan, T. (1999). *Assessing the progress of New American Schools: A status report.* Santa Monica: RAND Corp.

Cuban, L. (1989). The 'at-risk' label and the problem of urban school reform. *Phi Delta Kappan, 70*(10), 790–794, 799–801.

Elmore, R. F. (1987). Reform and the culture of authority in schools. *Educational Administration Quarterly, 23*(4), 60–78.

Finn, C. E. (1990). The biggest reform of all. *Phi Delta Kappan, 71*(8), 583–592.

Levine, D. U., & Lezotte, L. W. (1990). *Unusually effective schools: A review and analysis of research and practice.* Madison, WI: National Center for Effective Schools Research and Development.

Murphy, J. (1991). *Restructuring schools: Capturing and assessing the phenomena.* New York: Teachers College Press.

Murphy, J. (1992). School effectiveness and school restructuring: contributions to educational improvement. *School Effectiveness and School Improvement, 3*(2), 90–109.

Murphy, J. (1996). *The privatization of schooling: Problems and possibilities.* Thousand Oaks, CA: Corwin.

Murphy, J., Beck, L. G., Crawford, M., Hodges, A., & McGaughy, C. L. (2001). *The productive high school: Creating personalized academic communities.* Thousand Oaks, CA: Corwin.

Murphy, J., & Datnow, A. (Eds.). (2002). *Leadership for school reform: Lessons from comprehensive school reform designs.* Thousand Oaks, CA: Corwin.

New American Schools. (1999). *Working towards excellence: Examining the effectiveness of New American Schools designs.* Arlington, VA: Author.

Purkey, S. D., & Smith, M. S. (1982). Effective schools: A review. *Elementary School Journal, 83*(4), 427–452.

Schneider, J. M., Verdugo, R. R., Uribe, O., & Greenberg, N. M. (1993). Statistical quality control and school quality. *Contemporary Education, 64*(2), 84–87.

Shields, P. M., & Knapp, M. S. (1997). The promise and limits of school-based reform: A national snapshot. *Phi Delta Kappan, 79*(4), 288–94.

Verdugo, R. R., Uribe, O., Schneider, J. M., Henderson, R. D., & Greenberg, N. M. (1996). Statistical quality control, quality schools, and the NEA: Advocating for quality. *Contemporary Education, 67*(2), 88–93.

Weick, K. E. (1976). Educational Organizations as loosely coupled systems. *Administrative Science Quarterly, 21*(1), 1–9.

2

The KEYS Initiative in Memphis City Schools: A "Jump-start" on the Journey to School Restructuring

Linda Bol and Sam Stringfield

CONTEXT FOR THE CASE

Memphis, Tennessee, is the home of the blues, the birthplace of rock 'n' roll, and the unofficial capital of the Mississippi River delta. It was in Beale Street's blues bars that Elvis Presley sat and learned the rhythms and intonations that later made him famous. When Paul Simon sings that he is going to "Graceland," he is heading toward Memphis. B.B. King still performs at his own bar on Beale Street.

Less poetically, Memphis' leaders often describe theirs as the largest city in the *Mid-South*. The home of Federal Express, Memphis can probably justify its claim to being "the distribution capital of America."

The Memphis City Public Schools System's (MCS) 164 schools serve 116,000 students, making MCS one of the twenty largest school districts in the United States. Eighty-two percent of MCS students are African American, and 67 percent qualify for free or reduced-price meals. Educationally, Memphis combines the challenges of the Mississippi delta with those of an inner-city school district. Not surprisingly, MCS has a history of low achievement.

Throughout the 1990s, MCS has been a central player in America's efforts at educational improvement. Business and community leaders in Memphis were among the earliest and most enthusiastic adopters of Goals 2000. Those leaders' *Memphis 2000* program was developed and adopted in 1992. Their plan called for (a) broad-based community involvement in the six National Education Goals; (b) creation of a community-wide plan for achieving those goals; (c) developing a means of measuring progress; and (d) demonstrating readiness to create and support innovative education programs.

The city brought in a new superintendent, Dr. Gerri House, with a mandate for dramatic changes and improvement in student outcomes. Two of Dr. House's earliest assessments of her new system were that classroom teaching and district management strategies were mired in practices ill-suited to providing students with the skills they would need in twenty-first-century jobs, and that the within-district resources for the needed level of change were inadequate for the task. She began three associations that shaped Memphis' reform efforts throughout the decade.

To provide a district infrastructure to support the reform efforts, House collaborated with community leaders to launch Partners in Public Education (PIPE). PIPE, a nonprofit community foundation, provided funding for professional development facilities and activities.

Dr. House quickly began an association with the University of Memphis' College of Education, and particularly with the Center for Research in Educational Policy (CREP). Second, through CREP and its association with Johns Hopkins University, Dr. House led Memphis to become one of the initial New American Schools' *scale-up jurisdictions*. Beginning in the spring of 1995, MCS worked with six New American Schools (NAS) designs, and two other nationally disseminated whole-school reform designs.[1]

Dr. House contracted with a University of Memphis/CREP team to conduct a detailed assessment of the levels of implementation achieved by the eight reform designs in the thirty-four first-year schools. The assessment found that both organizational and classroom process change was happening in the thirty-four schools at a level greatly exceeding change in other Memphis schools (see articles in Datnow & Stringfield, 1997; Smith, Ross, McNelis, Squires, Wasson, Maxwell, Weddle, Nath, Grehan, & Buggy, 1998; Bol, Nunnery, Lowther, Dietrich, Pace, Anderson, Bassoppo-Moya, & Phillipsen, 1998). Armed with this knowledge, and frustrated at the slow pace of several other change efforts, Dr. House expanded the initial effort and invited several additional reform efforts into MCS. By the summer of 1997, Dr. House had mandated that all Memphis schools eventually associate with a nationally recognized whole-school reform design.

Dr. House had taken this last, bold step only after consultation with business and community leaders and, significantly, with the leadership of the Memphis Education Association (MEA). The MEA agreed to the move, believing it to be in the best long-term interest of both students and teachers.

The MEA administration was also aware that the NEA was piloting its own school improvement initiative: Keys to Excellence in Your School (KEYS). The local organization sent an extremely capable UniServ director to the KEYS national training. Upon her return, MEA requested that KEYS be a reform option available to Memphis' schools, and Dr. House agreed.

The newly trained UniServ director proved to be a passionate advocate for—and a skilled trainer in—KEYS. Fourteen MCS schools made commitments to KEYS. While the district made changes in school restructuring requirements, and these are described subsequently, it is worth noting that only one of the fourteen had dropped KEYS at the end of this case study, three years later.

The most KEYS-relevant change in Memphis' site-based restructuring efforts came in 1998. Dr. House and her leadership team concluded that the schools making the most rapid achievement gains tended to be associated with reforms that included specific reading curricula or curricula recommendations and supports. KEYS was one of the change efforts that did not include a reading curriculum. KEYS schools were required to revisit the issue of restructuring designs and to pick new, or at least additional, reform designs.

This unique history and structure in Memphis, combined with the flexibility of the KEYS national leadership, significantly shifted the Memphis component of this research project. Rather than conducting a three-year case study of a single school, the Memphis KEYS research team conducted a three-year study of fourteen schools in a single, rapidly changing district.

CONCEPTUAL UNDERPINNINGS

There were three central points to understanding the role of KEYS in Memphis. The first was the district's mandate that all schools engage in some form of nationally supported, site-based reform. The implicit conclusion drawn by Superintendent House was that the system could neither produce nor sustain the human capital necessary to reform 161 schools in a few years. However, if experienced, external change-sources could be tapped,[2] the reforms could be jump-started at all sites. Reforms could then be evaluated, and a locally successful subset of those reforms spread to all 164 schools.

Second, thirty-four of 164 schools had been in an initial, fully voluntary cohort. One hundred and twenty-seven schools had the benefit of watching thirty-four struggle with first-year implementation issues. When this larger group was asked to choose from a larger set of reform options, each had had the opportunity to learn about others' experiences with the general idea of reform and with several specific designs. The 130 schools had the opportunity to be better educated selectors of educational reform models.

KEYS was perceived by several schools as offering several advantages over other reforms. First, it had the obvious support of the local teachers' and principals' union.[3] Second, it had the support of a very active and well-known local UniServ director. An insider, not an outsider, or trainer, would lead the local work. Third, KEYS was obviously local-process driven. Each school's teachers and principal would complete a questionnaire, examine data, and participate in choosing actual interventions. Finally, KEYS was not prescriptive as were the other designs. Some faculty members were specifically reticent to participate in a relatively prescriptive curricular or process reform.

A final conceptual underpinning emerged in the later stages of the study and will be discussed in the final section of this chapter. That was that two significant strengths of the KEYS process were the ability to involve the full faculty and administration, and the focusing of the whole group on school-level problem solving. When the schools were required to choose an additional, content-specific, whole-school reform from a revised list approved by the MCS central administration, the KEYS schools had already focused on problems and possible options. While this had not been their original goal, the faculties had become well prepared to choose a new reform that was well matched to what the entire school had already agreed were each school's strengths and challenges.

KEYS SCHOOLS

Fourteen Memphis City schools adopted KEYS. Eight of these were elementary schools, three were middle or junior high schools, two were vocational technical centers, and one was a regular, comprehensive high school.

After adopting the KEYS initiative, the district mandated that all schools implement a restructuring model. Four elementary schools adopted the *Roots & Wings* model (Slavin & Madden, 2000), the three middle schools adopted the *Middle School* model, and the high school and vocational technical centers adopted *High Schools That Work* (Bottoms, Johnson, & Presson, 1992).[4] The remaining four elementary schools adopted four other models, namely *Accelerated Schools* (Levin, 1987), *Hand in Hand* (a local model developed by the schools' faculty, faculty at the University of Memphis, and the Memphis Arts council), *Multiple Intelligences* (Gardner, 1983), and *Voices of Love and Freedom*. Some schools adopted the model soon after implementing the KEYS initiative, while others adopted their model after having implemented KEYS from one to three years.

School profile data provide information about student demographics in the study schools (Memphis City Schools, 1997). Students are largely African Americans of low socioeconomic status who scored relatively low on standardized achievement tests. The percentage of African Americans for eleven of these schools ranged from 76 to 100 percent. Socioeconomic status is approximated by the percentage of students receiving free or reduced lunch. Between 55 and 97 percent of the students received free or reduced cost lunch. Few schools had total scores on the Comprehensive Test of Basic Skills that were above the fiftieth percentile, with several scoring below the thirtieth percentile at one or more grade levels. An exception to these demographics trends was observed at one elementary school. The majority of these students were white, did not receive free or reduced-price lunches, and scored very high on the standardized achievement test. It should be noted that this school is an *Optional School* (magnet) emphasizing enriched academics and requires achievement scores as one of its admission criteria.

THE STORY: FINDINGS AND INTERPRETATION

The findings, or story, of the success of KEYS in Memphis City Schools is organized around six research questions that guided the study. These questions were:

1. How do district and state contexts influence the outcomes?
2. What impact (political implications) has the local organization (MEA) had on the process of KEYS implementation?
3. How do the schools engage in the school improvement processes in response to the KEYS initiative?
4. How does KEYS affect organizational health?
5. How does the KEYS process affect learning and teaching?
6. How does the KEYS process affect valued outcomes?

Data related to each question is presented here.

The Influence of the District and State Context

The district context played a major role in the implementation of KEYS in Memphis City Schools. To say the district was ripe for school reform would be a gross understatement. Memphis has received national and international recognition and awards for being at the forefront of school restructuring efforts. The schools were not encouraged to implement any one specific reform, but were mandated to implement a school restructuring model from a list chosen by central administration. KEYS was introduced to the district during this period of transformation. Many schools embraced KEYS as a vehicle for school improvement.

Over half of the fourteen schools that decided to adopt KEYS did so in part because they believed it would become their major school restructuring model. The leadership at most schools thought that KEYS would qualify as their reform model even though it was not yet formally approved by the district. A year after the schools had adopted KEYS, the central administration formally declared that KEYS would not be considered a major restructuring model because it was seen as more organizational and process-oriented rather than academic in focus.

During the interviews, some respondents described being disappointed because they had selected KEYS to be their model. One school representative explained their reason for adopting KEYS as a reform model. "We looked at several initiatives but space, personnel, and equipment made it impossible to implement most other initiatives." They did not want a prescriptive model because they reported "a very diverse population and unique school."

Despite this initial disappointment after hearing that KEYS would not qualify as a major restructuring model, the district still supported the schools in their implementation of KEYS in addition to their major restructuring model and other reform efforts. Any efforts to improve education were encouraged, and KEYS was viewed as one of many beneficial programs to promote reform. Interview data revealed that the central administration, particularly the superintendent, was characterized as supportive of the KEYS Initiative. Some of the reasons for this perception were that the superintendent formally approved the KEYS implementation in the schools, attended KEYS meetings, provided release time for KEYS training, and was even a speaker at a national KEYS training session. Principals stated that the superintendent had made positive comments about KEYS, including the assertions that KEYS was valuable for selecting a school restructuring model and that KEYS was aligned with quality indicators endorsed by the district.

The state context appeared to have less influence on the implementation of KEYS. The people we interviewed talked about the support of the district, the local union (MEA), and the national union organization (NEA). However, the state organization (e.g., Tennessee Education Association, or TEA) and the state context more generally (e.g., state Department of Education) were rarely mentioned in our three years of interviews. One respondent noted that though the TEA approved of KEYS, they were not actively involved. This can partially be explained by noting that Memphis and the MEA were the first district and NEA local to work directly with NEA on KEYS. Previously, NEA had worked only through state associations.

The Impact of the MEA on KEYS Implementation

The MEA spearheaded the efforts to implement KEYS in Memphis City Schools, providing strong, steady, and enthusiastic support. Much of the success of KEYS can be attributed to this organization, and particularly, to the UniServ director in charge of KEYS. The positive relationship between the local union and the principals and teachers in these schools made the local educators willing to attend the first informational session about KEYS and then to adopt this initiative. Both principals and teachers alike are members of the MEA, which contributes to the acceptance of the organization and its endorsements.

During the within-school interviews, the MEA was described as very
supportive, providing leadership in "overseeing the initiative." Ms. Terrell,
the UniServ director in charge of KEYS, had made frequent visits to
schools to provide information, resources, and training, and to explain
KEYS results. "Terrell was a big support. She was there every time we
needed her." Another teacher said that, "With local and national help, Terrell actively supported the initiative." KEYS was considered to be "her
baby from the start."

Another activity sponsored by the MEA and NEA that helped to sustain
implementation of the KEYS initiative was a graduate-level course to KEYS
offered to committee members through the University of Maryland. The
class meetings were held at the MEA site, and teachers were offered college
credit for completing the course. Teachers, and one attending principal,
spoke very highly of this course. Having the teachers who attended the
course lead workshops and other faculty development efforts in their
schools facilitated capacity building. "We brought KEYS information back
to our school. We conducted the activities with our staff." The culminating
project in this course was the development of a school improvement plan.
A teacher observed that, "We had to write a school improvement plan in
the course which gave us a much better understanding of the expectations
and how to assess progress."

Terrell played a critical role in the early success of KEYS in Memphis City
Schools. However, in the final year of the study this UniServ director
resigned from her position to accept a position with the NEA. In her
absence, the momentum of KEYS appeared to stall. In the spring 2000
round of interviews, the participants commented that no one from the MEA
had visited their schools for KEYS purposes, and they had not had any
KEYS meetings or other KEYS related activities. The usual summer training session for KEYS did not take place in the summer of 1999. As a result,
KEYS may suffer in Terrell's absence because she was so involved in it.

Even though KEYS had lost some of its momentum due to the departure
of Ms. Terrell, school representatives indicated that a meeting was scheduled in the late spring of 2000, and they planned to attend. Representatives
from all but one school did attend the spring of 2000 focus-group meetings.
Their attendance suggested their willingness to continue with the KEYS initiative. When asked about the role of KEYS in their future plans, the vast
majority of school personnel said they would continue to implement KEYS.

A final, positive finding related to the impact of the local organization on
KEYS implementation was a change in perception about the teacher unions
in general. A broad range of teachers reported that they appreciated the fact
that the NEA sponsored KEYS and felt that "teachers could see their money
at work." The union was now being viewed differently because they were
involved in not only governance but also in programs designed to promote
school effectiveness. One teacher stated, "We see MEA in a different light.

It is now seen as a change agent, an organization to help us improve our schools and not just a union."

The Role of KEYS in School Improvement Processes

KEYS was viewed as an essential tool for initiating the school improvement process. Everyone we interviewed agreed that the major benefit of the KEYS Initiative was that it provided self-evaluation, a "self-study based on the effective school literature." The identification of strengths and weaknesses was the first step toward self-improvement. KEYS was said to have value as a "diagnostic tool," allowing you to "see where you are and work from there." Schools used the results from the KEYS survey to help them identify needs and priorities.

KEYS played a major role in the development of the formal school improvement plans required by the district. Beyond the fact that this plan guided each Memphis school's improvement efforts, it was also important because it was one part of the overall, formal evaluation of the principal and school. All of the schools used KEYS to help develop their district-mandated School Improvement Plans. Respondents volunteered that there was a great deal of overlap between their school improvement plans and their action plans, which were developed as part of the KEYS Initiative. The purpose of both plans is to identify areas that need improvement and plan strategies for realizing this improvement. As one principal noted, her school used "their action plan and KEYS strategies to write their School Improvement plans." In other schools the KEYS action plans were also used to guide Title I plans and the regional accreditation board evaluation report.

One crucial question about the implementation of the KEYS Initiative in Memphis City Schools was its relationship to the fourteen schools' subsequent restructuring model. As described earlier, most schools that adopted KEYS believed it would be their restructuring model and were disappointed to later learn that the district administration would not approve KEYS as a restructuring model. Schools were then faced with a decision of what new model to select after they had already implemented KEYS. To help us understand this process, we asked respondents to describe the alignment of KEYS with these restructuring models, noting any similarities and differences.

Respondents in eight schools described how KEYS either aided in the selection of their restructuring model or facilitated the transition to implementing another model. KEYS was said to be "perfect for helping select a school design" because it is a "self-analysis," identifying strengths and weaknesses. Using data gathered in KEYS, schools found that the subsequent selection process could be guided by data. One principal asserted that KEYS helped them decide on their model (Voices of Love and Freedom) because there was a "match in philosophy." "KEYS pinpointed the deficits and Voices addressed these deficits." Teachers in schools subsequently choosing Roots and Wings made similar comments. In terms of facilitating the transition to another model, a coordinator said they would be able to "jump right in," easing the difficulty of transition because of similarities between the models. Some programs or activities sparked by KEYS but aligned with the new models were already in place, further facilitating the transition.

Other responses to this question emphasized the similarities between KEYS and the restructuring models. One of the two most frequently noted similarities was the reliance on family and community support to improve education. A second was a focus on assessment, not just of their students but of their overall progress toward school improvement. A focus on open communication among all stakeholders, high expectations for students and their achievement, and the removal of barriers to learning were also noted as similarities between KEYS and the various restructuring models

Although participants cited the benefits of KEYS for self-assessment, the development of school improvement plans, and the selection and transition into the school restructuring designs, in later interviews we found that staff were feeling more and more overwhelmed with trying to implement their new restructuring designs as well as other programs and initiatives.[5] In some cases, the KEYS initiative was put on the back burner as they struggled to fully implement their restructuring models. The restructuring models had to take precedence because they were being held accountable by the district for implementation of these models.

Schools differed in their response to these competing demands. Some schools no longer focused on KEYS and a few considered dropping it entirely. Most other schools adopted a more adaptive strategy for maintaining KEYS in the context of seemingly competing models and programs. Rather than treating KEYS as an isolated or separate entity, they integrated it into their model and other initiatives. It is considered one of the many strategies used for school improvement, part of a whole reform package. "We will continue to use KEYS but more as one program that is integrated, interwoven with other reform strategies." Others noted that integration was possible because of the similar outcome goals between KEYS and other reforms. A KEYS principal stated, "Everything we do removes barriers to learning." One KEYS coordinator described this alignment in more detail.

As the KEYS coordinator and instructional facilitator, I frequently refer to the KEYS manual for guidance in bringing all the programs together. In particular, I focus on the parental involvement and professional growth parts of the manual. KEYS facilitates implementation of the restructuring models . . . tells you how to pull it all together and have personnel in the right places. (KEYS coordinator)

It appears that the implementation and success of KEYS in environments of apparently competing initiatives depends on the schools' perception of the role of KEYS and their ability to integrate it with other initiatives.

The Effect of KEYS on Organizational Health

KEYS had a positive effect on organizational health by improving communication, alignment of aims and practices, teamwork, and general school climate. These themes were often addressed in tandem when respondents described changes in their schools since KEYS was implemented. For example, one coordinator characterized the faculty as "more motivated" and "collaborating more," resulting in a general improvement in school climate. Another coordinator said that the faculty "needed to come together as a team," and be provided with "more opportunities for open communication."

Realizing the need for change and becoming organized to initiate change was another major benefit for the organizational health of the school. Resistance to change can be a major barrier to school reform, and KEYS helped break down this resistance. KEYS was accepted in part because teachers and principals were not coerced into adopting it. According to one coordinator, their school would not have been able to decide on a model if it were not for KEYS. "KEYS enabled them to reach consensus" after faculty completed the team-building exercises.

In order to improve communication, team building, and morale, faculties began by completing the team-building activities and exercises provided in the KEYS manual. For example, they completed the Style of Communication Inventory and other exercises aimed at *connectivity, collaboration,* and *congeniality.* In some schools teachers were divided into teams in order to address indicators targeted by their schools. They became the experts on these topics, developing strategies for improvement and informing other faculty. As one coordinator stated, "KEYS-related activities got even the reluctant, previously uninvolved teachers involved. They got involved without even knowing it." Similarly, another coordinator noted that the teachers are "more active" and that "there is a whole different atmosphere" which has "greatly improved our school."

KEYS not only provided information to schools about what indicators were in need of improvement but also about strengths in the schools. Part of what KEYS provided was a "celebration of successes" which improved morale. Some participants talked about needing to remind themselves of what they did well and not simply focus on what was negative. One principal said that the faculty "now have a better image of themselves and a better public image." Part of this "better public image" was supported by the MEA and NEA by providing resources for school brochures, videos, posters, banners, and other ways to inform the community about programs in their schools. In addition, NEA/MEA sponsored the attendance of a few KEYS committee members to national conferences, where they were invited to discuss their KEYS related activities.

The Effect of KEYS on Learning and Teaching

Perhaps the largest contribution of KEYS to the improvement of teaching was in the provision of professional development opportunities. One principal said, "Teachers are attending more workshops, regionally and nationally," and that teachers keep "personal staff development logs." Other respondents told us that KEYS was consistently incorporated into their faculty meetings. "Our staff development includes inservice for KEYS during the faculty meetings." Faculty were participating in KEYS workshops, and some were attending the courses offered by the University of Maryland and organized by the NEA/MEA. Teachers seemed to be participating in and taking more responsibility for their own professional development. The professional development opportunities would logically make an impact on classroom teaching. Teachers learned new strategies that they took back to their schools and classrooms.

An important benefit of KEYS was that it tended to instill a sense of the need for change. KEYS promoted a climate of reform in these schools. This was promoted through participation in workshops, conferences, and other professional development activities. Just as important as learning new skills and strategies was the sense of efficacy and confidence gained by teachers. "KEYS improved instruction largely by giving teachers more confidence."

Another respondent talked about using "professional development to build capacity." Teachers are sent to national conferences and "then come back and teach other teachers." Building capacity was also a common theme when we asked about the benefits of the KEYS sponsored course offered by the University of Maryland. A more comprehensive model of professional development would also encompass collaboration and teamwork among teachers. As described in the preceding section, KEYS was said to promote this kind of collaboration and teamwork. Collaboration among colleagues combined with capacity-building results in a "community of learners" who also rely on one another for professional development.

The Effect of KEYS on Valued Outcomes

When considering the effect of KEYS on valued outcomes, we are undoubtedly most interested in the impact of KEYS on students. Ultimately, the success of all school reform initiatives must be evaluated in terms of their effects on students, most importantly student achievement. However, it was not possible to quantitatively disentangle the impact of KEYS from the host of other reforms that were simultaneously being implemented in these schools. The most notable of these was the implementation of the major school restructuring designs in Memphis City Schools (e.g., Roots and Wings).

What we can discuss are the indirect effects of KEYS on student outcomes. Most of these indirect effects were addressed earlier in the context of school improvement planning, the selection of school restructuring models, organizational health, and professional development opportunities. However, there are other indirect effects that have not yet been discussed in this chapter.

The first of these was increased parental and community participation in the schools. KEY indicators in need of improvement across nearly all schools were those associated with parental and community involvement. Schools targeted these indicators for intervention and focused their efforts on promoting community participation. The specific kinds of activities and programs aimed at increasing their involvement included more parent meetings, open houses, workshops, community events, and communication with parents in the form of newsletters, bulletins, phone calls, and even door-to-door canvassing. Part of parents' exposure to KEYS was through completing the KEYS survey and serving on School Leadership Councils.

As a result of these efforts, parents and other community members were described as more involved with the school in general. One principal stated that the "PTSA is becoming more active," whereas another said more parents now attend the monthly meetings. Support from business adopters and other community organizations was reportedly on the rise. Their sponsorship was demonstrated in the form of increased donations, volunteers, publicity, and other resources. That is not to say that schools are satisfied with the level of community participation, but many have seen some improvement.

A second, indirect outcome was the focus on improving assessments. This was another KEY indicator that many schools targeted for intervention. Assessment referred not only to student assessment but also assessment of academic programs. For improving student assessment, schools were developing more authentic or performance-based assessments that were aligned with both district standards and their major restructuring models. Some school representatives talked about the need for assessments to be "more relevant for students," especially with the "increasing diversity of the student population." For improving program assessment, participants relied on data to identify program priorities. KEYS was one source of data used in the decision-making process.

The final valued outcome not previously addressed was the use of KEYS data and planning in grant development. While some KEYS members decided not to focus on KEY indicators that required substantial additional resources, members in other schools decided that they would attempt to obtain these resources by writing grants. For example, one school leadership team wrote a proposal to become a *21st Century Classroom* school.

Another developed a proposal to more adequately support full implementation of their restructuring model. The effect of these efforts on students has been indirect, but may be leading to overall school improvement.

IMPLICATIONS FOR REFORM AND SCHOOL IMPROVEMENT

Seven implications for school reform can be derived from our study of the KEYS implementation in fourteen Memphis City Schools. Each is discussed next.

First, KEYS can play a clear facilitative role in moving schools toward meaningful restructuring. In school after school the research team heard very positive statements from both teachers and principals regarding the value of KEYS as a school change agent.

Second, the specific values perceived by local educators included: (a) focusing the full faculty on core goals and objectives; (b) a greatly increased, faculty-wide focus on goal-relevant data; (c) aligning of the entire school's professional development planning and allocation with each school's new, concrete, widely endorsed school goals; and (d) much more open communication and coordination among all professionals within the school. These are all changes that align with characteristics of High Reliability Organizations (HROs), whether in industry (Roberts, 1993) or in education (Stringfield, 1998); collectively they could be expected to enhance any school's chances for success in any subsequent change effort.

Third, the KEYS success in Memphis was due in large part to a combination of the enthusiastic support of two consecutive presidents of the Memphis Education Association and the tireless work of one of the MEA's UniServ directors. The local UniServ director attended trainings in Washington, DC, provided workshops in Memphis, arranged for a graduate-credit university course to focus on KEYS, and was in near-constant contact with the fourteen participating schools.

One potentially important artifact of MEA's dissemination of KEYS was that a range of teachers and administrators stated that they were proud that KEYS was an NEA/MEA sponsored activity. Teachers and principals volunteered that KEYS was a clear example of a return on their investment of union dues.

Fourth, the other clearly critical player in the rapid dissemination of KEYS was the school district. Early in the tenure of Superintendent House it became clear to all of Memphis' educators that school reform was going to be the district's singular focus. Schools that had no history of involvement in any type of coordinated reform efforts began seeking out diverse reform options. It is unlikely that fourteen schools would have sought out KEYS (or any other single reform) absent a crystal clear signal from the district that reform was nonnegotiable. The superintendent attended KEYS trainings and voiced full support for the union's initiative.

Fifth, KEYS played a role in Memphis that was not anticipated. A year after the introduction of KEYS at fourteen sites, the superintendent mandated that all schools not working with one of a limited set of reforms would have to add such a reform at their site. Restructuring designs on this more restricted list were universally less open-ended than was KEYS.

Principals and teachers made two responses, both of which should be interpreted as encouraging to KEYS supporters. First, although schools would have been free to have dropped KEYS and simply substituted a different reform, only one did. The remaining thirteen schools continued their associations with KEYS and the KEYS processes. Second, teachers and principals in the substantial majority of the fourteen schools stated that participation in KEYS had provided their schools with excellent preparation for choosing subsequent school improvement steps, including the choice of a reform from the superintendent's list.

Schools either chose a follow-up reform because it addressed issues highlighted through KEYS, or because the faculty saw the follow-up as the most KEYS-like of the available options. The research team rarely heard a teacher or principal telling us that the KEYS experience had not been valuable, even though schools were being required to add other reform designs. Educators appeared to view KEYS as an excellent jump start to reform.

Sixth, local educators did not view KEYS as a specific reform per se. The Memphis research team has been told in national meetings that some schools in other locations became stuck after they received their KEYS questionnaire data. Perhaps it was because there was so much reform and restructuring happening across the city, or perhaps it was the activist Uni-Serv director, but for whatever reason, Memphis' schools seemed to have little difficulty connecting their KEYS work to specific school improvement planning activities. As they moved forward, the educators continued to reference KEYS, and did so without getting stuck at a planning-no-action stage. They seemed to see KEYS as a set of self-assessment and possible-direction finding activities, rather than as a full school improvement model, and the educators were comfortable with KEYS playing that role.

Our final observation regarding the role of KEYS in reform concerns the sustainability of KEYS or any other process over time. As more states publish report cards of schools' progress, we are provided increasing opportunities to note that most schools are involved in five to fifteen special projects or promising programs at any given moment. Some of these, such as *Reading Recovery* or the sponsoring of a Girl Scout troop are clearly bounded. Others, such as participation in the federally funded *Comprehensive School Reform Demonstration* (CSRD) projects involve whole faculties. Keeping any one effort from being totally eclipsed in such a cacophony of competing initiatives is quite a challenge. Absent a very active, highly involved UniServ director, it is unlikely that all fourteen Memphis schools would have sustained a commitment to KEYS.

Being just another flash in the school reform pan is clearly not a goal of NEA's KEYS project. Faculties at fourteen schools told the Memphis research team that KEYS was not only valuable but also a major source of practitioner pride in their union. Sustaining the KEYS initiative in any school or school system will almost certainly require several achievable but currently rare steps on the part of the NEA and its local affiliates. The first will be the identification of enthusiastic coach/trainer/cheerleader UniServ directors. Second will be the provision of initial and ongoing training for those directors. Third will be organized systems of within- and cross-school peer supports for teachers and principals.

Each of those steps is challenging, and each has associated costs. Yet the Memphis KEYS experience indicates that through this effort, benefits can accrue to both the participating schools and the NEA.

NOTES

1. The five NAS designs included ATLAS Communities, Audrey Cohen College System of Education, Co-NECT Design, Modern Red Schoolhouse, and Roots and Wings. For descriptions of each design, see Stringfield, Ross, & Smith (1996). The two non-NAS designs were Accelerated Schools and Paideia schools. All eight, together with the larger design of the Memphis Restructuring Initiative are described in Stringfield, Datnow, Herman, & Berkeley (1997). For more on the Memphis Restructuring Initiative, see also Smith, Ross, McNelis, Squires, Wasson, Maxwell, Weddle, Nath, Grehan, & Buggy (1998); Bol, Nunnery, Lowther, Dietrich, Pace, Anderson, Bassoppo-Moyo, & Phillipsen (1998); Ross, Sanders, Wright, Stringfield, Wang, & Alberg (2001).

2. See Nunnery (1998) for a discussion of the effects of local vs. externally developed reforms.

3. In Memphis City Schools, the teachers and principals can both join the MEA. Also note that Tennessee is an open shop state, meaning that no one is required to join, or pays to, any union. Membership is voluntary.

4. See also the High Schools That Work website, http://www.sreb.org/programs/hstw/hstwindex.asp

5. Note that teachers in the initial thirty-four MRI schools expressed similar rates of anxiety after one year of implementation (Stringfield & Ross, 1997).

REFERENCES

Bol, L., Nunnery, J., Lowther, D., Dietrich, A., Pace, J., Anderson, R., Bassoppo-Moyo, T., & Phillipsen, L. (1998). Inside-in and Outside-in support for restructuring: The effects of internal and external support on change in the New American Schools. *Education and Urban Society, 30*(3), 326–358.

Bottoms, G., Johnson, M., & Presson, A. (1992). *Making high schools work.* Atlanta: Southern Regional Education Board.

Datnow, A., & Stringfield, S. (Eds.). (1997). Special Issue: The Memphis Restructuring Initiative. *School Effectiveness and School Improvement, 8*(1).

Gardner, H. (1983). *Frames of mind: The theory of multiple intelligences*. New York: Basic Books.

Levin, H. (1987). Accelerated schools for disadvantaged students. *Educational Leadership, 44*(6), 19–21.

Memphis City Schools. (1997). *School profiles*. Memphis, TN: Author.

Nunnery, J. (1998). Reform ideology and the locus of development problem in educational restructuring. *Education and Urban Society, 30*(3), 277–296.

Roberts, K. (1993). *New challenges to understanding organizations*. New York: Macmillan.

Ross, S., Sanders, W., Wright, P., Stringfield, S., Wang, L., & Alberg, M. (2001). Two- and three-year achievement results from the Memphis Restructuring Initiative. *School Effectiveness and School Improvement, 12*(3), 323–346.

Slavin, R., & Madden, N. (2000). Roots & Wings: Effects of whole-school reform on student achievement. *Journal of Education for Students Placed At Risk, 5*(1 & 2) 109–136.

Smith, L., Ross, S., McNelis, M., Squires, M., Wasson, R., Maxwell, S., Weddle, K., Nath, L., Grehan, A., & Buggy, T. (1998). The Memphis Restructuring Initiative: Analysis of activities and outcomes that affect implementation success. *Education and Urban Society, 30*(3), 298–325.

Stringfield, S. (1998). Organizational learning and current reform efforts. In K. Leithwood & K. S. Louis (Eds.), *Schools as learning communities* (pp. 255–268). Lisse, Netherlands: Swets & Zeitlinger.

Stringfield, S., Datnow, A., Herman, R., & Berkeley, C. (1997). Introduction to the Memphis Restructuring Initiative. *School Effectiveness and School Improvement, 8*(1), 3–35.

Stringfield, S., & Ross, S. (1997). A "reflection" at mile three of a marathon: The Memphis Restructuring Initiative in mid-stride. *School Effectiveness and School Improvement, 8*(1), 151–161.

Stringfield, S., Ross, S., & Smith, L. (Eds.). (1996). *Bold plans for school restructuring: The New American Schools designs*. Mahwah, NJ: Lawrence Erlbaum Associates.

3

Unions, Politicians, and Educators: The Case of KEYS in River Bluffs Elementary, Minnesota

Lisa M. Jones and Karen Seashore Louis

It's the lives of our kids in a political battle . . . and that's exactly what it is.
—*River Bluffs Elementary School Teacher*

The story of KEYS in Minnesota, as reported by union employees and school personnel, requires an analysis of the state and local contexts in which the program was implemented. After an initial rocky start, KEYS took off in the school that we focus on, but was ultimately derailed by larger political initiatives that distracted both the state's union employees and the school district itself. In this chapter we present these political initiatives in the context of a specific school, but the experiences of River Bluffs do not differ markedly from those of other Minnesota schools and districts that became involved in the program's pilot phase. Our data focus on KEYS and the changing roles of individual participants and the union, paying attention to local history and context, changes in stance or expectations about union roles, changes in actual practice or behavior, and the linkage of the KEYS efforts to national, state, and local reforms. As a result, our chapter emphasizes the effects of organizational factors and the external educational policy environment on efforts to create a teacher-directed change effort focused on teacher practice.

THE CHANGING TEACHER UNION ROLE AS A KEY CONTEXT

Traditionally, teacher union agendas have targeted acceptable working conditions for teachers rather than emphasizing professional standards and development that could facilitate student academic performance (Bascia, 1997). The current state and national political environment challenges union leaders to shift their efforts to school reform agendas that focus on students rather than teachers' work lives. These challenges arise as conflicts between policy makers' expectations of reform outcomes and local union interests. Critics argue that unions need to view teachers as partners within schools rather than as employees of the school district with limited responsibility for quality (Kolderie, 1985). Should unions continue to maintain their status quo agenda, increasingly, reform advocates and policy makers will perceive them as irrelevant to change efforts.

Kerchner, Koppich & Weeves (1997) argue that a reinvention from a management-labor mind-set to a "united mind workers" organization allows unions to maintain their relevance. Moreover, the national debate on school reform has often challenged teachers' unions to act as effective change agents to enhance the quality of American public education. The relatively recent move by the national teacher unions to embrace the industrialized concept of *new unionism* can be examined against a history of changing union-management relationships within the private sector, which began in the late-1970s to early 1980s.

New unionism refers to shared decision making (including authority and responsibility), a commitment to service improvement, flattening the hierarchy, and the professionalization of teaching. A key feature of the transformed relationships between union representatives and management involves the collaborative initiation of change, which is the main focus of this investigation. Complex environmental, technological, and financial pressures operating within a politically charged atmosphere have forced management and labor to both reconsider and redesign their traditional roles and relationships. Successful companies have found they need to adapt to changing conditions and avoid behaviors that put organizational growth and survival at risk (Mahoney & Watson, 1993). Efforts to reform the role of teacher unions from within also occur in a volatile context. Lieberman (1997), for example, contends that the lack of competition in the public sector removes the pressure on the NEA and AFT to change. Competition in the private sector forces union representatives and management to redesign their relationships to succeed in an aggressive market.

In fact, much of the reform effort, including most state legislation, has focused on teachers as objects of reform, rather than as partners in reform. Recent 1998 Pennsylvania initiatives, as in many states, focused on improving the quality of those who teach: pre-service teachers must maintain a 3.0 undergraduate grade point average, and the best math and science student should be certified to teach without traditional college of education course-work ("NEA's New Unionism," 1998). Similarly, a 1995 Chicago school reform package passed by the Illinois state legislature included an eighteen-month moratorium on teacher strikes and removed from collective bargaining several professional workforce issues such as class size. Clearly, these two salient actions by policy makers reflect a growing discontent with the status quo efforts of teacher unions that focus on quality of work rather than quality of professional issues.

Nevertheless, new unionism in public education has emerged as a major initiative within many locals across the country. Traditions within the Chicago Teachers' Union (CTU), an AFT affiliate, and the Milwaukee Teachers' Education Association (MTEA), a NEA affiliate, illustrate the expanded role of the union in its programmatic commitment to educational quality. The CTU argues that pursuing bread and butter issues gives teachers needed security, but at the same time it has become more involved in sponsoring professional development. The CTU has played a more active role in selecting new teachers for the system, and has helped to implement programs for beginning teacher mentoring and induction. Similarly, the MTEA established self-improvement programs for teachers such as annual lectures, speakers, and continuing education in specific content areas to improve instructional quality (Lowe & Fuller, 1998).

NEA president Bob Chase suggested that local unions should unite with school districts to improve low-achieving schools throughout the nation. These schools, labeled *F schools,* are characterized by overcrowded classrooms, lack of educational materials, inadequate or deteriorating physical plants, low SES students, and high absenteeism among students ("NEA President Highlights," 1998). Chase's comments suggest that the F schools contribute to a decline in student academic performance. Local unions vary in their support of this trend. Some have refused to allow teachers in individual schools to work outside the union contract (e.g., on more after-school programming for students) even when the school staff unanimously agreed to do so. Other locals have supported contract waivers. Still others have worked with school boards and central administrators to reform incentive and compensation systems completely to support professional work. For example, the local union in the Robbinsdale, MN, school district established a new incentive system similar to the Saturn Car Company. Rather than a focus on merit pay plans, the contract requires teachers to submit skill portfolios every five years, which may result in significant bonuses (Bradley, 1998). Similarly, in Minneapolis the contract provides for increasing oversight of new teachers plus mandatory and detailed demonstration of competence prior to receiving tenure (Minneapolis Federation of Teachers and Minneapolis Public Schools, 1999). In Chicago, the CTU supports school-initiated contract waivers allowing teachers to work beyond their thirty-three-hour negotiated workweek on school improvement and professional development activities.[1] In Glenview, Illinois, the Glenview Education Association created a professional compensation system that linked salary and stipends to work roles and responsibilities rather than to hours worked. All of these local changes reflect a shift from a seniority system of financial reward to incentives that rely on performance quality.

In summary, the emergence of a new unionism that focuses on a collaborative rather than adversarial relationship between labor and management is aligned with increased quality and productivity in both the private and educational sectors. This does not mean, of course, that there has been a uniform transition. Currently, national teacher union leaders are still calling on local affiliates to adopt these changes within their communities—in other words, to bring the new unionism home in a palatable way to members. The priorities reflect an emphasis on shared decision-making authority, professional development, redesigned pay and incentive structures, and collaborative efforts to align teachers and administrators in school improvements that target student success rather than simply the quality of a teacher's work life. The next sections describe the ways in which one such nationally organized change effort (KEYS) affected school initiatives at an elementary school in Minnesota.

FUNCTIONS OF KEYS

The schools in this study used the KEYS instrument as well as the KEYS process of collaborative training and technical support. KEYS aims to serve three functions. The first is technical. KEYS seeks to stimulate and guide research-based local school improvement. A second function is political and organizational. NEA expected KEYS to increase the role of state and local associations in school improvement and to increase collaboration between association representatives and school and district administrators by focusing on a concrete school improvement activity. A third function of KEYS is cultural and symbolic. As an initiative to improve schools and promote more collaborative and productive relations between the union and district and school administrators, KEYS may help reshape public perceptions of the NEA and its affiliates in the image of the new unionism. In addition, KEYS could help in reshaping the nature of responsibility within the union itself, reallocating the role of change agent from the national and state associations to the local affiliates and individual schools.

THE STORY

> The history is that assessment was facilitated and left to lie. We helped our people forget about it.
>
> —*UniServ Director*

Our story begins with the context surrounding the implementation of KEYS at a local elementary school. First we describe the overall state and community context in which this school is located. Next we discuss the school's rationale for engaging with the KEYS pilot work. The third section describes the problems—both internal and external—experienced with the deployment of the assessment and the political context that affected the ongoing use of KEYS. We then introduce a new stream of information that emerged, during our investigation, as a critical factor in affecting the outcomes of our case: the state's educational policy initiatives and environment. A summary section provides overall results of the assessment.

State and Community Context for the KEYS School

Introducing KEYS in Minnesota

Bob Robinson,[2] a UniServ director in Minnesota, heard about KEYS at a number of national conventions, and persuaded others in the Minnesota Education Association (MEA) office that the state should become an early participant. The program also fit with the MEA's desire to press forward with a reform agenda package at a time when merger discussions were being initiated with the Minnesota Federation of Teachers.[3] While the state association staff was agreeable, the initiative continued to be championed by Bob, who was part of the national training cadre. Six of the eleven UniServ directors volunteered to participate and were trained by NEA.

In spite of Bob's enthusiasm, the introduction of KEYS proceeded slowly in Minnesota. Each of the six involved UniServ directors, along with Bob, made presentations to local union representatives. Interest was muted, but the UniServ directors continued to spread the word among their local districts to find schools that met their criteria of readiness. Open information sessions generally elicited limited attendance. In several cases, individual schools volunteered, but in most cases the UniServ directors spent time talking to teachers and building administrators to find appropriate pilot sites. Local elected union representatives were supportive, but there was little strong sponsorship of KEYS. Each school sought support from the superintendent (and sometimes the school board) after an initial decision to become involved. By the end of 1997, ten buildings had volunteered throughout the state.

A typical example is the first school that we selected for a case study. Carnation Elementary School is located in an inner-ring suburb that is experiencing rapid growth in low-income and immigrant children. The UniServ director targeted the school for participation because he viewed the principal as effective in "running his own shop" rather than responding to every new initiative from outside. In addition, the district was supportive of site-based management and had a tradition of promoting innovation. In this case, with the blessing of the local union executive committee, the Uniserv director approached the principal and the building staff to see if they were interested. Once the building had agreed, the district staff was informed. As with many of the initially contacted schools, Carnation entered the program with enthusiasm, but later interviews indicated that the KEYS effort had been put on the back burner. According to one informant, "a very fine principal in the school reacted to the results of the KEYS survey with the view that, 'well, we flunked,' and shelved it. It had a negative psychological effect."

As we entered the second year of case study data collection, we therefore decided to shift our focus to an elementary school that appeared to have the strongest continuing interest in working with the KEYS process to develop their own improvement programs: River Bluffs Elementary.

The School and Its Context

River Bluffs Elementary is located in Brookville, a community of slightly more that 20,000 people that is located 25 miles southeast from the Twin Cities. The Brookville school district, with 5,271 students (prekindergarten–12), manages nine schools and is situated in a modestly growing community. Most newcomers commute to the Twin Cities, but have chosen the small-town lifestyle afforded in the city. It is important to note that one-half of the total state population lives in the Twin Cities metro area. By comparison with the rest of the state, semi-rural/small town Brookville is rather urbanized; by comparison with a major metropolitan area, it might be classified as semi-rural. There are currently no reported students in the district with limited English proficiency, but state data indicate that the number of immigrants in this part of the state is low. The dropout rate for the district is 1 percent, 12 percent free and reduced lunch, and 3 percent minority population.

The district mission statement identifies a commitment to excellence for all learners in the community. "It is our hope that each learner's potential is developed to the fullest. We believe in lifelong learning, and are constantly exploring new ways to improve our educational offerings" (Brookville district website).[4]

River Bluffs Elementary School is located on the western edge of the Brookville community. Built in 1988, the building serves 588 first through sixth graders with an additional 150 prekindergarten students. Approximately 7 to 8 percent of the student population receive free or reduced-price lunches. The school's students are predominantly white and middle class— their parents are part of the community that champions the local schools. Principal Art Peterson commented on the strong community support felt in the school district, "We're fortunate because our community has always supported our schools. And, so we are fortunate to teach in a district like this. We have strong support."

The relatively large staff has frequently tried to develop a family feeling within the school. However, despite goodwill and strong community support, River Bluffs Elementary School has its share of internal difficulties. Some of the issues that create tension and prevent the development of a unified staff include competition for space with early childhood and community education programs are housed in the same facility. While perennial, these tensions do not focus on programmatic issues, but competition for valuable resources. In addition, building leadership to support teachers has been weak: there had been three principals at River Bluffs Elementary between 1991 and 1997, which contributes to a sense of inconsistency in planning and goals, according to all participants.

Keys to Excellence in Your Schools (KEYS) first attracted the attention of River Bluffs in early 1997 (see Table 3.1 for the time line of events). The UniServ director, Bob, shared the KEYS information with a teacher at the school. The incorporation of KEYS into the school's discussions about improvement was essentially teacher-driven: a group of teachers presented the program to the school board and superintendent within the context of planning for professional development.

The Rationale for KEYS

According to the informants, two critical events stimulated River Bluffs staff members' interest in using the KEYS assessment to help with strategic planning: (1) principal turnover; and, (2) an antagonistic governor who engaged in teacher bashing. The principal who had recently come to River Bluffs, Art Peterson, suggested that it was important to develop a plan that

TABLE 3.1 Chronology of Important Events Related to the KEYS Process at River Bluffs Elementary School

Early 1997	Late 1997	Feb. 1998	Fall 1998	1999	2000
"Vision Planning" began	KEYS results scrapped	Survey given again	Focus groups	State graduation standards implemented	State union takes stand on standards

1997		1998		1999	2000
1991–97 Principals changed 3 times	1997 Statewide meeting for interested schools	Spring 1997 KEYS survey given	Feb. 1998 $12,000 from state union	1998–99 NEA-MFT merger	1999 UniServ director assigned elsewhere

could provide some planning stability to direct the future of the school—an antidote to the administrative uncertainty of the 1990s. The school staff believed that KEYS would prove useful as an assessment tool that would guide strategic planning and create consensus.

But KEYS also provided the staff with a public relations tool to demonstrate a commitment to school improvement. Former governor Arne Carlson frequently criticized educators during his eight-year tenure as the state's chief executive. A staunch supporter of government-financed vouchers for private schools, his comments demoralized the educational community in Brookville and River Bluffs Elementary. Carlson repeatedly commented that the only way to improve elementary and secondary education in the state was to provide state-supported vouchers for parents to send their children to private schools (as he had done). Teachers at River Bluffs talked a great deal about the ongoing barrage of negative commentary from the state's chief executive. They believed that the governor saw teachers as "the enemy" and blamed them for what he perceived as poor academic performance. The governor said "you gotta fix, you gotta fix . . . the schools." Thus, River Bluffs Elementary began the school improvement planning process.

Planning and Implementation at River Bluffs

Vision planning, the River Bluffs staff's term to describe strategic planning, became the foundation for a school improvement program that would, ultimately, include KEYS. It was during the initial vision planning phase (which coincided with Art Peterson's assumption of the principal's position) that MEA UniServ director, Bob Robinson, presented KEYS to a River Bluffs teacher. Impressed with the KEYS instrument, the teacher shared it with other River Bluffs teachers and both school and district level administrators.

The vision planning activities were part of a district-wide effort. Each school in the district was mandated to have an improvement committee, and it was this committee at River Bluffs that became attracted to the survey's capacity to provide baseline data to determine future directions in the ongoing improvement process. Staff expected that KEYS would enable them to further identify both strengths and needs, as well as allow them to monitor their progress over time. They were also enthusiastic about getting support from Bob to push them forward in their understanding of the KEYS process.

River Bluffs was the first school in the state to administer the assessment to the certified staff. The teachers and principal chose not to use the survey with other stakeholders because they felt that they were just beginning to understand how KEYS could be used. Other schools in the district knew of River Bluffs efforts and remained interested in both the process and results, but did not choose to join in the effort.

As in the case of Carnation Elementary, when the KEYS survey results were released, the staff felt demoralized by information suggesting that they had failed, a perception based on scores below the KEYS take-off point. One staff member noted that it was "very intimidating for some staff members." Because of his other responsibilities, Bob Robinson was not available for consultation during the period immediately after the results were received. It is impossible to fault Bob for his inability to follow up in a timely fashion. According to our previous analysis (Louis, Smylie, Jones, & Seppanen, 2000), unobserved directors uniformly report "survival in regular duties comes first." Confused about the findings, which (as intended) produced results that pointed toward areas in which the school was less successful than it believed, the staff viewed KEYS "in a negative light." In the absence of sustained technical assistance in working through the results, the survey findings provided the staff with neither an adequate baseline by which to measure future improvement nor a clear direction for the school to follow in the planning process. Robinson continued to be distracted with other responsibilities, and was unable to do any follow-up activities around interpreting the KEYS survey. As he (and others) pointed out, "[KEYS] is more like a hobby than a real job" for overextended union representatives.

Principal Art Peterson was relatively new to the school at the time when KEYS emerged. Accustomed to a turbulent, accountability-based administrative model apparent in the school district in which he had been employed previously, he was unfamiliar with the issues unique to River Bluffs Elementary, which were more subtle and emotional. Teachers were hurt by the KEYS results and withdrew from active participation in talking about how to use them. Art encouraged teacher leadership but, according to him, struggled in its implementation. He led the staff in a discussion about the KEYS results in an attempt to develop some concrete objectives for the vision planning process, but felt himself at a loss to help move his staff because he also didn't understand the implications very well. Peterson noted, "The other piece was just the language of the survey and the interpretation of the survey after the first go around. It just wasn't understandable."

Bob, meanwhile, became aware of River Bluffs' disappointment with the KEYS process when he met a teacher at another local meeting. He convened a panel of representatives from several of the schools that administered the survey to discuss the results and their implications. The school staffs believed they failed, but the facilitation by Bob helped them understand that KEYS was not intended to produce pass-or-fail results, but rather to point to areas on which schools might work. The connection with the state Uni-Serv director became a critical piece in the use of the KEYS assessment. Peterson told us, "He went to school for it [KEYS] and he just really had an excellent background and was able to translate that to us and to the staff."

Reenergized by Bob's panel discussion, the participants returned to River Bluffs Elementary with a desire to use what they learned for their ongoing improvement planning process. The KEYS survey was administered again in February 1998 (to obtain up-to-date information) and focus groups facilitated by Bob enabled the team to reassess the KEYS results and determine concrete improvements in practice. The staff learned that they needed to work on collaboration with one another in a more systematic way and develop a plan for student reading improvement. Teachers celebrated the following day with a breakfast meeting that allowed them to exchange the ideas generated in their smaller focus groups with the larger staff.

Building on their renewed enthusiasm, River Bluffs Elementary staff leveraged the KEYS results to acquire an independent $12,000 grant from the MEA Foundation for Excellence for the remainder of the 1998–1999 and the 1999–2000 school years. The grant was useful for the staff to meet and design an improvement plan, and stimulated the school to conduct focus groups with a variety of stakeholders around improvement goals. It allowed the team to arrange for substitutes for both the certified and non-certified staff so they could participate in professional development and to address the KEYS results, which indicated a need to develop a more collaborative environment in the school. The grant stipulated that teachers and staff were expected to provide time for professional development without pay—a requirement that was endorsed by both the state and local affiliate. Minnesota legislation provided school-based professional development funds that were initially used to supplement the grant. River Bluffs teachers and administrators felt that they were well positioned to develop a detailed improvement program that incorporated KEYS results with additional data that they had collected on their own.

Trouble on the Horizon

Shortly after the planning effort was back on track in River Bluffs, two external events occurred that were to have significant long-term effects on the incorporation of KEYS. First, in 1999 the Minnesota legislature finally passed a new set of graduation standards that were expected to affect the curriculum from elementary school through high school. *The Profile of Learning* required each student to complete performance packages in a wide variety of areas—both traditional content and subject matters, but also new areas such as citizenship. The standards and packages were mandated, but not the way in which districts should meet them, or how they should judge whether a student's performance was adequate. The ambiguous nature of The Profile of Learning has been controversial both in and outside of Minnesota. The initial discussions around the legislation promised significant assistance from the state for the development of exemplary packages and for training for teachers in how to teach to the new show what you know standards. However, as is often the case, the consequences of the legislation for practice turned out to be significantly more complicated than state officials anticipated. In every district across the state, money available for professional development was funneled into the standards development and implementation process. River Bluffs was no exception, and the funding from the state to support long-range planning based on KEYS was almost immediately diverted to support the new state mandates.

The most unfortunate problem emerged after the merger when the union was forced to confront an intense political issue for their constituency: accountability. Early interviews with educators and union representatives revealed that the graduation standards recently imposed upon the educational system forced a major shift in focus away from KEYS and toward implementation of the new standards. Teachers in River Bluffs believed, at the time of the early interviews, that they would revisit KEYS after they became comfortable with the graduation standards. They expressed frustration and tension over the state-driven mandates that force teachers to spend more time on paperwork.

The most recent series of interviews illustrate the frustration educators continue to experience with the state's graduation standards. Mary, a River Bluffs teacher said:

I think we went through so many years with our previous governor where public education in Minnesota was put down, we're battling back from that perception. Now we have the accountability coming down in lots of different ways and it's not coming, necessarily from educators, it is coming from outside people and it's just real difficult for teachers at this point. I think it is taking a lot of their [the union's] energy.

At almost the same time, the two largest Minnesota teacher unions—the Minnesota Education Association (affiliated with NEA) and the Minnesota Federation of Teachers (an AFT affiliate) chose to merge with one another. While the merger was supported by both national unions, it created enormous internal disruptions in union operations, ranging from the merely irritating (moving offices) to the very delicate (reorganizing the lines of reporting and activities between two staffs that were of different size and previously competitive). During this period, Bob Robinson, the union employee who was working most closely with KEYS, was promoted to a new position in the state office. Not surprisingly, although the MEA had been very supportive of KEYS in principle, there was limited energy in the new Education Minnesota (the name of the merged union) to focus on the implementation of a relatively small pilot program. The KEYS tool, which was initially viewed within the MEA as providing a means to involve the union in the process of school improvement, "fell off the map" under the dual pressure of internal politics and the need for Education Minnesota to present a united front around the onerous graduation standards. As a Uni-Serv director (other than Bob) reported: "The NEA-AFT merger interrupted everything. The progress was put off. It is unfortunate."

THE FUTURE OF KEYS IN RIVER BLUFFS ELEMENTARY

> When I even talked about it, should we revisit KEYS? No, one person
> was very adamant saying, "the staff will not go for it."
> —*Linda, River Bluffs teacher*

On the other hand, it seems unlikely that River Bluffs will use the KEYS tool in the near future. The process requires additional staff time and funding and needs hands-on union involvement. However, the respondents believe that KEYS helped build collegial relationships within the building and they trust this collegiality affects kids, directly. Diane referred to the effects of KEYS in the following statement:

Even though we may not address KEYS again . . . KEYS was just one part of how we were looking at ourselves. We did a vision planning piece and all of the other components. It was just one piece of the puzzle. So, even though that piece might be taken out or not revisited, it doesn't mean that the other parts will not keep going. But, time is crucial. The one thing the grant did do for us it gave us time for some planning and some staff development pieces.

THE STORY: A RECAP

KEYS became important to the River Bluffs Elementary staff because it helped them identify specific areas where they needed improvement: collaboration and communication. Art Peterson stated, "Intuitively, we knew that this was what we needed, but KEYS helped tell us that. . . . It was the whole staff versus a committee telling us . . . it came from outside, it made it easier to carry us forward, and it added affirmation."

The MEA grant provided a substantial boost to the effort to use KEYS at precisely the point where renewed interest in improvement planning occurred. While it didn't fund the entire effort, it encouraged staff to participate since teachers would not be required to participate in professional development activities only as overload. The typical problem of "burnout" for volunteers in a school reform effort was, thus, blunted.

Another important component of KEYS is the collaboration that developed between teachers and administrators. Peterson remarked: "KEYS brings teachers, staff and administration together . . . not administration bringing stuff to teachers, not top-down, but does offer teachers and administrators the ability to work together for change, and a new direction for the school."

The confidentiality of the KEYS survey encouraged people to respond honestly about their school. Thus, teachers felt less threatened by a confidential survey than a public meeting, which further stimulates collaboration between administration and staff. KEYS provided an explanation for needed changes and encouraged the staff to structure its own path to achieve those changes. On the other hand, both teachers and the principal are critical of the KEYS instrument. In addition to Art Peterson's frustrations in trying to communicate the meaning of the survey to his teachers, Deb noted that, "It doesn't work for people like custodial staff, who have a lot to contribute to school improvement."

The use of an assessment tool to identify strengths and weaknesses combined with the collaborative planning efforts of teachers and administrators influenced the school's climate. Encouraging risk-taking seems important to the staff of River Bluffs Elementary School in forging their plan for school improvement. Mary, a teacher who has taught for thirty-three years commented, "We aren't stagnant. . . . Sometimes it gets uncomfortable, but risk-taking and change are hard."

Given that there were endemic and unaddressed problems within the school building, the KEYS process was viewed as helpful in overcoming barriers to talking: "I think it did break down the barriers between professional staff and non-certified staff so that we all feel part of the same team rather than so separate. It's brought those groups together within the building. So, I think that was a positive outcome" (Mary).

Funding to support professional development becomes increasingly critical to the KEYS process because teachers believe the assessment process adds to their already-full workload. Optimistically, the River Bluffs staff stated that KEYS could provide some level of continuity to their school improvement process by allowing them to benchmark their process. They believe that KEYS could be used to see what they have accomplished and identify additional challenges. In other words, KEYS becomes a tool in a continuous improvement process. Realistically, however, unless external support is available, the chances of KEYS becoming a permanent part of the River Bluffs improvement story are slim.

THE STORY IN RETROSPECT: AN ANALYSIS

Our analysis of the River Bluffs experience will focus on the three dimensions that we identified at the beginning of this chapter, which we have previously used to analyze the implementation of KEYS at the state level (Louis, Smylie, Jones, & Seppanen, 2000).

Technical Problems with KEYS in River Bluffs

Aside from issues related to the interpretation of the results, one compelling complaint from all involved was language and useability. The language of the instrument did not translate well for noncertified staff, and the results were not interpretable among the professional staff without more guidance than they initially received. The goals of the process included encouraging the involvement of all school staff in the school improvement process. However, respondents remarked that the language was intimidating and somewhat threatening for the custodians, cooks, and other noncertified staff in the building. The language was "very teacher friendly" but isolated non-teachers from the school improvement process. Mary stated, "There were so many questions on there that you couldn't answer if you weren't in the classroom. It didn't make sense, either. Being as we're now a union including professionals and non-professionals, it seems that piece has to reflect that. I would have hated to not be a teacher and try to answer some of those questions." The staff coped with this by deciding not to re-administer the survey during the second round until the language changed.

As noted previously, the NEA KEYS survey results delivered to the River Bluffs staff were also intimidating. They did not understand the benchmarking process that labeled some factors in their schools as needing remediation (below the take-off point), and didn't give themselves credit for those results that were identified as ready for take off. Because they didn't understand how to translate the results into their planning process, the initial administration of the survey proved not to be useful. Only later intervention by the tireless (but distracted) MEA representative who assumed responsibility for supporting the KEYS effort in Minnesota pulled the staff back into an enthusiastic effort to use KEYS for their own purposes.

The resource of time is particularly problematic. Teachers suggest they are already *stretched thin* and *burned out* not only from their workload. In Minnesota, the emotional burnout from fighting the public's perception that they are not performing their jobs well was probably more important. They could not see how KEYS could help them change how the public perceives them, although they did, with the union's support, use the KEYS results to attract more funds for school improvement planning. Linda said:

Anything you are working on—contacting legislators, meetings, etc.—when the pieces are added on to what you already have to do, something falls behind. We need to focus on the classroom and kids. Most of us would be open for change if there is a solid reason, not just change for change's sake. We need time and resources to implement change well.

Another technical problem arose when Bob's role with the union changed. He played a critical part in the implementation of the KEYS effort at the local site and facilitated a process that informed the River Bluffs staff about the meaning of the results. Deb commented that: "Bob was willing to come out on his own time. This was critical because he helped us interpret the assessment and how to translate it into professional development activities. His coming out and helping us really got us going." When Bob became less available because of his new duties, the apparently crucial role of external facilitation disappeared.

Political Dimensions of KEYS in River Bluffs

The best intentions (and attention) from the union could not erase the impact of turbulence in the political system. The negative perception about KEYS results that were distributed before the school-planned intervention was minor compared to the ongoing problems the staff face in negotiating a contentious political world: "Everything we do is driven by the political system—everything—from the dollars we give to the classroom, to what's mandated" (Linda).

Clearly, the implementation of KEYS did not occur in an isolated environment free from the constraints of an external political monolith—the state of Minnesota. The interpretation problems were apparently manageable, but it was the volatile political environment that presented with a great degree of conflict that derailed the KEYS process. Two major events occurred in the political landscape that forced the emphasis away from KEYS: the state Profiles in Learning plan, and the national and state AFT-NEA merger.

Two key themes concerning graduation standards emerge in this statement. First, it appears that the accountability issues raised in the state of Minnesota also are a function of former governor Carlson's animosity toward public education. Second, the Union's energy has been directed away from the school improvement process toward an ongoing discussion and effort with the state legislature, governor's office, and the administration regarding the graduation standards. Recently, Education Minnesota distributed a survey to its membership to determine their feelings and perceptions about the graduation standards. Thirty-nine percent of the respondents stated that the plan should be abolished. The remaining "50-something percent wanted changes in the Profiles" (school union representative, Linda). The state union board decided to work with policy makers to ask that changes be made because "that is what the membership wanted."

The school staff believes it is the union's role to navigate the political waters and work for teachers. Unfortunately, that leaves little time for the union to focus on implementing an improvement process at the site level. As Linda commented, the union itself must grapple with the other important issues that confront education such as future retirements:

As I think about the union's piece with school reform and all those—the profile has taken a big piece but also another big piece that they're working on right now is how are we going to replace a third of our working force that's going to leave in the next five years. What changes are going to be needed to bring people into the profession and that's going to be a huge piece and that's also going be a high priority within the union. (Linda)

Deb reflected on the national political landscape and the role the union must play:

I think it goes way beyond just Minnesota. Every presidential candidate I'm listening to is gonna "reform education" How can you reform it with every political candidate? I do think they are getting in the way of what we should be doing in the classroom. But, I don't think that is going to change and I do think Education Minnesota has to spend its time putting out the fires. That's number one priority because we live and die by what happens in that legislature. It's their number one job to be our voice in the political system. (Deb)

Although educators rely on the union to work with policy makers, teachers involve themselves proactively in the political process at the state level. Coping with this conflict consumed the River Bluffs staff members as well, distracting them from their own priorities in planning for their own school: "We have a group of teachers that are up lobbying today. They're out talking to legislators and this is our local piece doing it because it is so vitally important. Every level within the state has to talk with our political system because it drives everything we do" (Mary). Teachers and administrators at River Bluffs must also cope with the demands imposed upon them by the legislature—as is the case with the graduation standards. Essentially, the standards require them to use classroom time to administer various academic achievement-oriented tests. Teachers have realigned their efforts to target the requirements of Profiles in Learning.

"I think what the philosophy of KEYS would be . . . for people to determine what's most important for them to change within their school system or within their school environment" (Art Peterson). This comment underlies some of the frustrations the River Bluffs staff expressed with a political system that imposes change. Aggravated by the top-down nature of politically driven school reform apparent across the United States, teachers said they feel demoralized and criticized by a system that does not understand the nature of their work. One teacher put it succinctly with the statement, "I keep wondering, what do they think we've been doing for the past many years?"

Cultural Conflicts: Who Is Responsible?

One major issue that faced River Bluffs and other districts involved with KEYS concerns different perspectives on where the energy for school reform emerges. Deb stated that, "People are still looking for the magic silver bullet and forgetting that they still need to do the heavy lifting after they get results."

This comment is compelling because someone provided it from the state union office, and it contrasts sharply with the comments at the school site that the union should be responsible for contacting teachers and administrators and promoting change. This raises an important issue about any sort of school reform or improvement programs: where does the responsibility lie? Deb stated that:

We really haven't had anybody that ever called and said, "Where are you in this process?" Or, "What do you need from us?" We are totally . . . and I'm sure if we called somebody there would certainly be some help. But, there has not been any follow-up . . . I think it's more critical for someone from the state to contact the local. Just because we are so busy in our daily lives of doing what we're supposed to do here. And, this is an extra piece. And so to keep that moving forward, you need a little bit of outside energy or you need communication from them to say, "Here's whom you can call. Please call any time." I think it has to be extended both ways but if you don't get that initial communication from them, it's not going to happen the other way. (Deb)

The reality for River Bluffs Elementary School is that change requires effort on multiple fronts, but the ways in which the different actors should work together in a "new union" framework is unclear. It requires an investment of critical resources such as time and money. It requires commitment from the union and the staff. However, KEYS remains another improvement tool in an already-full toolbox. "We need more than the tool. You need somebody who is facilitating it. I think you need training in it and you need resource people. We know that if true systemic change is going to come, it has to come through research and resources. So, we need time as educators to do some of that ourselves. That's where this next piece has taken us" (Mary).

Local union members need time and support to change their ownership of the school reform agenda. One of the problems discussed earlier is that the results demoralized the River Bluffs staff. If this occurs in a school that enjoys strong support from the local community and is less "under the gun" than other districts in the state regarding remediation and performance, it suggests that the passive school culture of "they're doing this to us; we don't have control" is difficult to change. Even relatively advantaged schools such as River Bluffs lack the internal capacity to work together to interpret the data and establish plans for future training. Various participants commented: "We need to talk about using the results before the assessment even begins. It is part of the process. We need to talk about how to analyze the results and incorporate the results into regular work. . . . There might need to be some pre-training with a small committee, but I think, eventually, the message would have to go out to everyone. Why, and what, and what impact will it have?"

A remaining cultural issue raised at the union level is how the "new union" reform efforts, which are based on administrative-teacher collaboration, occur. Bob Robinson summarized his experience working across the state saying that, "In an ideal world, administration shouldn't drive it. The reality is that it does. Administration is expected to be leaders . . . building a leadership team."

Art Peterson was acknowledged as an administrator who sought collaboration, and individuals at the site did not express frustration with the role of the principal in the process. Perhaps that occurred because teachers presented KEYS to the staff. Although the River Bluffs Elementary principal struggled with teacher leadership, he did create an environment in which teachers felt comfortable to introduce a new idea. Nevertheless, neither he nor the teachers had previous experiences that would help them guide a participatory planning process.

IMPLICATIONS AND SUMMARY

KEYS is an important symbol of NEA's commitment to school improvement. It signals recognition by the union that its members and the schools in which they work can and should be improved. It demonstrates concern and acceptance of some responsibility for the quality of schools and student learning beyond a concern for protection of its members.

The state and local actors we interviewed uniformly pointed to KEYS as a symbol of the union's efforts to become involved with school improvement. Union employees in Minnesota viewed KEYS as a vehicle for and symbol of union partnership with management in school reform. What it symbolizes is that "we are going to be full partners in this with the community, with the school district administration, and all the players in the school." To several UniServ directors, KEYS symbolized a return to "the old days," before collective bargaining, when the NEA's mission focused more specifically on school reform and quality. Said one director, "Actually, we're going back to our roots, when . . . we were a professional association."

In this chapter, we have reviewed principles of new unionism and the prospects that KEYS, a school improvement initiative of the NEA, might fulfill three functions consistent with those principles. Drawing on relevant literature and initial findings of case studies of KEYS, we suggest that while KEYS content and processes are consistent with research on effective schools and change processes, the ability of KEYS to promote school improvement is likely to be hampered by a number of factors. Our analysis raised questions about the adequacy of preparation and support, role alignment, and follow-through. Further, our analysis suggested that implementation might be made more difficult by the general nature of indicators and goals for improvement they imply. While worthwhile and important to support change generally, KEYS risks being pushed aside by better-defined initiatives related more specifically to the substantive needs and interests of schools, such as graduation standards.

Finally, we argued that KEYS could serve a symbolic function to help reshape perceptions and enhance the legitimacy of the NEA inside and outside the union. We described how KEYS is a potentially potent symbol of NEA's commitment to and responsibility for school improvement, of transcendence beyond its members' and its own self-interests, and of an emphasis on local, professional determinism. At the same time, we cautioned that the symbolic value of KEYS might depend over time on NEA's ability to make good on the initiative's prospects for promoting school improvement and political and organizational change. In other words, the symbolic value of KEYS may depend on the union's ability to "walk the talk."

While KEYS has many noteworthy features and the potential to help NEA move in the direction of new unionism, its ability to surmount these obstacles will depend on the political and financial support it receives from the national organization and its state affiliates. This may involve revision of some of the broad elements of KEYS to make it more relevant and meaningful to schools and school districts that struggle with immediate, specific, substantive concerns.

At this point, KEYS remains on the margin. Our examination of KEYS at one site in Minnesota suggests that until it becomes better integrated into and supported by the NEA, and until the NEA can develop a constituent base for it, KEYS potential to promote principles of the new unionism through school improvement is unlikely to be realized.

NOTES

1. Teachers may, but are not required to, seek additional pay for the extra work.
2. Pseudonyms are used for all individuals and schools.
3. The AFT has had a stronger school reform agenda than has the NEA. The MFT and the MEA subsequently became the first state union to merge. The single union is now known as Education Minnesota.
4. We do not include the website URL in our references in order to preserve the school's anonymity.

REFERENCES

Bascia, N. (1997). Invisible leadership: Teachers' union activity in schools. *Alberta Journal of Educational Research* (43), 2–3, pp. 69–85.

Bradley, A. (1998, February 25). A better way to pay: Project studies innovations in teacher compensation and seeks to spur more people to try new models. *Education Week*, pp. 29–31.

Chase, B. (1997, February 5). *The new NEA: Reinventing teacher unions for a new era.* Speech delivered to the National Press Club, Washington, DC.

Kerchner, C. T., Koppich, J. E., & Weeres, J. G. (1997). *United mind workers: Unions and teaching in the knowledge society.* San Francisco: Jossey-Bass.

Kolderie, T. (1985). What if teachers could work for themselves? *Equity and Choice* 1(3), pp. 75–79.

Lieberman, M. (1997). *The teacher unions: How the NEA and AFT sabotage reform and hold students, parents, teachers, and taxpayers hostage to democracy.* New York: Free Press.

Louis, K. S., Smylie, M., Jones, L., & Seppanen, P. (2000). The role of unions as leaders for school change: An analysis of the 'KEYS' program in two states. In K. Riley and K. S. Louis (Eds.), *Leadership for change: International perspectives.* London: Falmer.

Lowe, R., & Fuller, H. (1998, April 1). The new unionism and the very old: What history can tell Bob Chase and his critics. *Education Week*, pp. 46–50.

Mahoney, T. A., & Watson, M. R. (1993). Evolving modes of work force governance: An evaluation. In B. E. Kaufman & M. M. Kleiner (Eds.), *Employee representation: Alternatives and future directions* (pp. 135–168). Madison, WI: Industrial Relations Research Association.

Minneapolis Federation of Teachers and Minneapolis Public Schools. (1999). *Teacher contract 1999–2001: Respect, responsibility, results.* Minneapolis: Minneapolis Federation of Teachers.

NEA president highlights one year of new unionism. (1998, February 18). *Education Week*, p. 9.

NEA's new unionism taking hold, Chase says. (1998). *Education Daily, 31*(29), pp. 1–3.

4

Building a School Community Using KEYS: The Shoreview School in Maryland

Saundra Murray Nettles

The first stop on the Shoreview High School (SHS) website gives the visitor a virtual tour of the campus, with its two-story building erected on thirty-six acres in the early 1960s. One of three high schools in a small city on Maryland's eastern shore, the real SHS is a well-maintained school with nearly 1,300 students and over 100 faculty and staff members. The school's curriculum features advanced placement and college level courses in calculus, the sciences and social sciences, and foreign language; a little over half of the students go on to four-year colleges. The student body is racially diverse: 65 percent of its students are white, 30 percent African American, 5 percent Asian, and 1 percent Hispanic. Sue Johnson has been the principal since the 1997–98 school year.

Another stop on the website is labeled "S.I.T." For some years, SHS has had a SIT, or School Improvement Team. However, as the title of a 1997 SIT document noted: "It's broke, but how do we fix it?" Efforts to reconsider the function and role of the SIT began under the leadership of the outgoing principal and continued with the new administration. In the spring of 1997, the ten-member SIT met with faculty at another high school in the city and discussed that school's experience with Total Quality Management and shared decision making. After further discussion at a SHS professional day, the faculty decided that shared decision making was worth further exploration. In the fall of 1997, the SIT chose KEYS and a set of organizational development processes developed by the Maryland State Teachers Association as the approach to undertake shared decision making to improve the school.

But adoption and effective implementation of new processes at the school level is a complex phenomenon that can be facilitated or hindered by multiple factors pertaining to the organization and to the innovation. As reviewed by Gottfredson and colleagues (1997), features of the organization linked to effective implementation include school climate, leadership of the principal and central office staff, level of school resources, and organizational capacity. Implementation is particularly problematic in schools that rate poorly on these indicators. Features of the innovation include effective teacher training and participation in the process of change.

This chapter describes how a local school adopted KEYS and the roles that the state and national associations played. Concurrent outcomes of the process and how the district school board influenced them are also considered. The period covered is from February 1997, when the initial meeting on KEYS was conducted at the state association offices, until July 1999, when the school adopted another framework for reaching its goals.

The findings are reported as a narrative organized according to cross-site research questions and themes. The narrative is a detailed account that incorporates quotes from respondents and documents and researcher interpretations drawn on concepts of organizational development.

THE PROCESS OF KEYS IMPLEMENTATION AND ADOPTION AT THE STATE AND LOCAL LEVEL

After the KEYS process was announced, state teachers association officials, including the executive director, and representatives from the national association formed a joint work group that met over a three-month period in early 1997. At the first meeting the consensus was that the KEYS process would be incorporated into the state association's existing school reform efforts. Subsequent meetings focused on likely first sites, measures of success, and budget issues (there was nothing in the state association's budget for KEYS).

By mid-1997, after meetings of focus groups from the larger joint work group, an initiative titled Improving Maryland Schools (IMS) emerged as the appropriate mechanism for KEYS. An MSTA/NEA initiative, IMS is a process-oriented series of work sessions planned collaboratively with individual schools. The curriculum was developed after consultation with several organizations, including the NEA, the Maryland State Board of Education, the Maryland Association of Colleges for Teacher Education, and others.

Four modules constitute the curriculum. For example, the "100 Series" includes seven modules, the core of which is *Decisionpoints,* a consensus-building process using the sixty-two categories that the NEA National Center for Innovation identified in KEYS research. The *300 Series* includes a module, *Using KEYS,* which introduces participants to the KEYS instru-

ment that assesses schools on thirty-five of the sixty-two indicators introduced in *Decisionpoints*.

The IMS director took on the task of recruiting schools to participate,
contacting state association directors, UniServ staff, and district officials
across the state. Among those that the IMS director met with was the assistant superintendent of [a Maryland county] public schools, who in turn
advised Johnson, the incoming principal of Shoreview High School, that an
upcoming event put on by the state association, the annual Leadership
Training Retreat, would be a vehicle for professional development on
decision-making processes. An added incentive was that the 1997 retreat
would be at a university located near the school; the Shoreview faculty
would not have to incur travel expenses.

HOW THE SCHOOL ENGAGED IN SCHOOL IMPROVEMENT PROCESSES IN RESPONSE TO KEYS

This school's response to the KEYS Initiative can be understood in terms
of four overlapping processes. First, the participants engaged in activities
that built the school's organizational capacity for understanding such an
initiative. Second, at critical junctures, the principal and others exercised
leadership in support of self-reflective school improvement. Third, the participants made judicious use of data to guide their improvement efforts.
Finally, the participants adapted the KEYS framework as a new and more
sophisticated vision of the school's future emerged.

Building Organizational Capacity

The faculty who first engaged in KEYS—and, indeed, the school as a
whole—lacked the capacity as a collective to undertake a reflective improvement process. The Leadership Retreat helped them build this capacity by
teaching them how to be a team and giving them useful decision-making
tools. Thereafter, in the early months of KEYS implementation, they
widened the scope of the improvement process by expanding the School
Improvement Team, looking to KEYS as both instrument and ongoing
process, and developing explicit procedures for schoolwide decision making.

Learning to Be a Team

The 1997 Leadership Training Retreat was a residential program organized into schools (for example, Advocacy, Organization Development for
Association Leaders). Each participant or team of participants from a
school registered for one school. In addition to the institutes, there were ple-
nary sessions featuring conversations with officials from the national and
state associations on focal issues, such as quality and student achievement.

Eighteen faculty members and principal Johnson participated in the school, Leadership in School Improvement. The state association's IMS director conducted the school with presentations by staff and executives of county affiliates. The curriculum included modules from IMS intended to introduce skills needed for participatory decision making. For example, participants engaged in a game, *Systems Thinking, Systems Changing,* which simulates the development of a continuously improving learning environment. Also included in the curriculum was participation in Decisionpoints, described earlier, and an introduction to the KEYS survey.

The state's reform of assessment, the *Maryland School Performance Assessment Program,* was a salient issue. In the leadership training retreat, evidence was presented regarding the positive relationship between KEYS indicators and performance on the state assessment, at that time given in the 3rd, 5th, and 8th grades to rate school academic performance. The assessment was of concern to the school's faculty because the state department of education planned to extend the assessment through the *High School Improvement Program.* The high school assessments would cover four academic areas (English, science, mathematics, and social studies) and, beginning in fall 2001, 9th grade students would have to pass tests in order to graduate. The tests would also gauge school performance.

I attended the retreat in the course of selecting a site for the KEYS case study. My field notes included observations of the SHS staff. These observations indicate signs of engagement: many questions were asked about fine points of the process; there were requests for explanations; and the group had lively, extensive discussions about how to use various tools.

The retreat, coupled with the KEYS/IMS curriculum, was a potent combination. The training energized the faculty members who attended, as apparent in a history of the SIT noted earlier. This document, prepared by members of the SIT after attending the retreat, was couched in terms of processes taught at this meeting. The document called for "widening the circle," to encompass other "stakeholders." An example of an event that grew out of this concern was a meeting between those who attended the retreat and three members of the SIT who had not been at the training. At the meeting, the retreat group reported on concepts learned and the KEYS survey, discussed potential new roles for the SIT and, as the following quote from the document revealed, used a lesson from the retreat in decision making.

After discussing the plan to "widen the circle" to board administrators, [a SIT member] raised concern about communicating with them before addressing the entire faculty. The group came to consensus ("Can you live with it?") about the issue and decided to move forward with the lunch meeting. Members of the group felt that this meeting would alleviate staff concerns that these plans for improvement might not be endorsed by the superintendent.

Widening the Circle

Prior to KEYS' introduction, there was a movement underway toward expansion of the SIT. That movement began during the 1996–97 school year under the leadership of Johnson's predecessor and Johnson herself. The 1996–97 SIT had begun looking at different models of shared decision making, and toward the end of the school year, Johnson had asked the faculty to form teams based on faculty concerns.

After the retreat and subsequent meetings of participants, two major events occurred to widen the scope of the school improvement process. First, the SIT was expanded from ten to eighteen members including the school administrators, one representative from each of the faculty action teams (Instruction, Student Behavior Management, Student Attendance, Student Activities, Technology, Facility, and Human/Staff/Public Relations), the department heads, and two facilitators. School board representatives attended SIT meetings, as well, advising the SIT as to district policies and procedures regarding a range of issues. The SIT and action teams were to meet monthly. Action teams were the primary mechanisms for extensive faculty participation. Approximately 70 percent of the faculty participated in action teams during the first year.

The second event was a one-day simulation of *Systems Thinking/Systems Changing* on a Saturday in late September 1997. The entire faculty was invited; roughly a third of the faculty who had not attended the leadership retreat participated. The superintendent was present during part of the day. One of the state association facilitators led the workshop, along with the two SIT facilitators. Handouts included a flowchart outlining the IMS Systems Thinking process and a listing of the KEYS indicators.

The KEYS survey was administered on November 6, 1997, and the same state association facilitator who had facilitated the day-long training in September conducted a workshop on Decisionpoints. The Decisionpoints tool is in the form of four decks of cards; each deck corresponds to a topic in school improvement. Participants engage in a consensus-building process to select options contained within each deck. By most reports, the consensus-building exercise was disturbing to some members of the faculty, primarily because areas of conflict about options emerged and the process orientation of KEYS/IMS was questioned.

Understanding KEYS as Both an Instrument and an Ongoing Process

To gain a sense of the ways that faculty understood the KEYS process I interviewed twelve teachers, all members of the School Improvement Team, the day after the KEYS instrument was administered. Five of the teachers had attended the retreat. Two meanings of KEYS emerged. About half of the respondents (evenly divided between those who had attended the LTR and those who had not) understood KEYS to be an instrument. The following comments are illustrative.

> It's a barometer that brings success.
>
> These are the elements for a school to be successful and meet the needs of the students and community. These are things that need to evolve. You have to end up with the thirty-five indicators.
>
> A starting point—trying to find out perceptions of where we are. Very good indicators, right on.
>
> Initially a study was done with some schools. Looked at them to see what they had in common. The common thread was where we are in relation to successful schools. If KEYS points in the direction to promote more learning, I'll accept it because students are interested in education.

The other group of respondents viewed KEYS as a process. Again, the comments were evenly distributed between those who had attended the retreat and those who had not.

> It seems that you're trying to empower teachers, support them to implement changes for better education for students. Lots of focus on team building (if we're ever going to be a team, we are one now and need to get goals established).
>
> We survey our school community to establish what the current status is. We see where we want to go. The whole process is designed to make this a better place for students to learn.
>
> KEYS is to recognize our weaknesses and strengths, improve communication in the building.

At this early stage in the KEYS/IMS process, the faculty members I spoke with believed that commitment was strong, but that there were pockets of resistance and cynicism. The following comments capture this sense:

> Overall commitment is strong, but there are a few resistors in key positions. Some resistors want it but are cynical.
>
> I foresee difficulties bringing people on board. However, it's OK if we see progress.
>
> I am very committed, but the time is going to be a large problem for me and other faculty members. The faculty is very committed.

Developing Explicit Procedures for Making Decisions

One of the most important actions a group has to take is formulating processes for decision making and communication. Minutes of the 1997–98 SIT indicated that the team addressed questions about the decision-making process (who, for example, made final decisions for the school?); developed procedures for communication between the action teams and the SIT; received reports from action teams; and referred to the teams problems suggested by faculty or specific tasks that needed follow-up.

For example, the SIT developed an Issue Referral Form. The following example from one of the Instruction Action Team meetings illustrates the activities involving the referral:

We received an Issue Referral Form requesting a clarification of guidelines (if they exist) for how students doing a teacher practicum may be utilized. It was suggested that [name of teacher] be contacted for information. She let us know that she did not know or have a list of rules. Mr. [name] was also contacted and he is not in charge either. Questions that we need to consider at this point are: (1) Who is in charge? (2) Is there an existing set of guidelines? If so, what are they? (3) Do we need anyone's approval to set up our own guidelines?

Faculty continued to have opportunities for skills development in the course of identifying approaches to decision making. For example, the SIT decided to develop a sociogram, one tool identified in the Systems Thinking/Systems Changing simulation, depicting the relationships in the school and community. This task was referred to the Human Relations Issue Team in the October SIT meeting and was completed by December 1997.

Exercising Leadership for Reflective School Improvement

In a letter to the SHS faculty prior to the 1997 Leadership Training Retreat, the newly selected principal wrote:

As you know, my leadership style is one of collaboration and input. I have and will continue to welcome your input. Please consider stopping by school this summer to share any ideas that you may have. I want to hear from you; what you consider effective and areas that you feel need improvement. I am also interested in talking with each of you about your role in the school improvement process as we restructure the school to become more efficient.

Comments from interviews in fall 1997 revealed that faculty noted a change in the locus of decision making. The words of one teacher captured this sense: "How decisions are made is changing. More site-based. I see that working, but we're all learning; seems to be lack of communication; decision making is being handled with action teams. I'm not sure this is widely accepted in the county, but it is in the school."

Indeed, the site-based process was unfolding under the leadership of the principal, the SIT facilitators, and the chairs of the action teams. Throughout the school year, meetings were conducted as scheduled, and SIT members attended regularly. (Action team attendance fluctuated, however.) An infrastructure of procedures for handling suggestions and concerns was put in place. An increasingly smooth, constant flow of transactions occurred between individual faculty members, action teams, the SIT, and school and district administrators. The bulk involved school climate issues ranging from procedures to address student parking violations (guided by the Facilities Action Team) to a successful proposal, initiated by the Instruction Team, to change the administration of the county's criterion referenced test. Parent and community involvement in the SIT and action teams was limited, however, and a persistent topic of discussion.

The vision of collaborative leadership expanded when the principal and a member of the SIT participated in a KEYS course offered at the University of Maryland during the spring 1998 semester. The course, taught by faculty from the College of Education, included lectures, practical exercises and readings on systems thinking as developed by Peter Senge in *The Fifth Discipline* (1990), model building, instruction, collaboration and communication, professional development, and assessment. Both participants were enthusiastic about the KEYS course. They were particularly influenced by their reading of *The Fifth Discipline* and its vision of a learning community, and others on the faculty were attracted to the idea. During the spring semester, a teacher attended a week-long workshop on *The Fifth Discipline*. Subsequently, he wrote a proposal to the Waters Foundation for a half-time school improvement facilitator to integrate systems thinking in the SIT and in the classroom. The proposal was funded (about $48,000) and the facilitator, a member of the SIT, was to begin her responsibilities in fall 1998. One of the goals of the grant was to develop systems thinking within the SIT and in classrooms.

At the end of the 1997–98 term, Johnson expressed an interest in the action teams becoming action research teams, or inquiry teams. However, she knew that teachers were particularly concerned about student behavior; she believed that the route to alleviating discipline problems was through improvement of instructional strategies. In her view, she would "have to be more specific in evaluation and feedback to teachers ahead of time." Overall, she felt that the school was "slowly moving in the direction of seeing and understanding systemic change," but that the school improvement process was "not a quick fix."

Using Data to Guide Change

At the 1998 MSTA Leadership Training Retreat, the SIT requested and received customized training toward development of the School Improvement Plan required by the county. The teacher who attended the KEYS course used materials from *The Fifth Discipline Fieldbook* (Senge, Roberts, & Ross, 1994) to facilitate Shoreview School sessions. By then, five parents were engaging in decision making for the school. They also participated in the process of creating a school improvement plan, along with twenty-two teachers.

Led by the SIT facilitators, the process entailed drafting a mission statement and developing a time line; compiling for teacher review packets of suggestions for goals, objectives, and strategies; facilitating consensus on the emerging mission statement and plans; compiling syntheses of lists generated by action teams; and presenting drafts to stakeholders and the faculty as a whole. The SIT used a working document, *Goals and Strategies for Shoreview High School,* which included data from the KEYS survey, Middle States commendations and recommendations, an activity (*Reach for the Stars,* in which participants envision the ideal school), and the report card of the Maryland School Performance Assessment Program. In the *Goals and Strategies* document, data were grouped in four categories: personal development, social development, safe and supportive environment, and academic development. The bulk of KEYS indicators were in the social development and personal development categories.

The KEYS survey had been administered nearly a year before, in November 1997, and in February 1998, the IMS director interpreted the data, which showed that the school had reached the take-off point on one of the thirty-five KEYS indicators (see Appendix B), "the school uses teacher-made tests to assess students." In the time between receiving the feedback and the October deadline for submitting the plan, the school and SIT leadership gained a firmer understanding of the use of data to guide change through participation in the KEYS course and the 1998 leadership training retreat.

Concurrently with sorting of data into the categories of the *Goals and Strategies,* the SIT finalized the school mission: "It is the mission at the Shoreview High School to provide a safe, supportive educational community which fosters academic, social, personal, aesthetic, and physical development, as well as life-long learning for all students."

Action teams then contributed objectives, strategies, measures, and time lines pertaining to five goals:

- Increase student achievement.
- Improve and create methods of communication between and among all stakeholders.
- Improve student support services.
- Improve the school learning climate.
- Improve the physical plant.

The plan was developed by mid October. Progress toward the student achievement goal was to be measured by several indicators, including milestones reached, professional development sessions completed, and data generated. For this goal, for example, among the eleven strategies listed in the School Improvement Plan were the following:

1. Strategies submitted by the Technology Team

- Training staff on effective research using the Internet
- Training staff on use of Grade Book Plus to compile accurate student data

2. Strategies submitted by the Instruction Team

- Assisting parents of foreign language students on study skills specific to each discipline
- Developing a math modeling course
- Compiling samples of High School Assessment activities to share within departments
- Research successful cross-curricular programs.

Overall, the bulk (40 percent) of the strategies concentrated on the goal of improving the school learning climate. Strategies to increase student achievement and improve the physical plant each accounted for 15 percent of the total strategies included in the plan, while improved communication and student support services accounted for 21 percent and 8 percent of the total strategies respectively.

The school newsletter announced the plan on the front page of the October 1998 issue. A new action team, the Career Planning and Continuing Education Team, was created, and minutes for the SIT were posted on the Shoreview High School website. As in the previous school year, a sizeable majority of teachers participated in school improvement through the SIT or the action teams. The school improvement facilitator/systems thinking coach began half-time duties with funding from the Waters Foundation. She produced a matrix of systems thinking activities and applications in social studies, science, math, and school organization. The matrix included existing systems thinking activities and identified plans such as one for developing a math course in systems thinking and math modeling. The district created two positions whose duties included coordination of the county and state grants to local schools seeking to implement the learning goals. As of the October 1998 SIT meeting, the Board of Education SIT coordinators attended the SIT meetings. Again, the school improvement process was underway.

Adapting to a Different Framework

By midterm, there were signs that the school improvement process was shifting direction. One of the SIT members said, "I think we have an interim system that works. We shouldn't be totally wed to this system, on the SIT team's ability to see the system. We need to focus on student achievement. Everyone's coming to that realization, as opposed to last year when we could not see that for all the little problems."

Although attendance at the SIT remained consistent, minutes of the meetings recorded expressions of concern about lessened attendance at action team meetings and complaints from teachers that participation in action teams was not part of their jobs. In January 1999, a teacher submitted a proposal for a staff retreat to enhance staff unity. According to the rationale for the proposal, some of the staff were lukewarm about site-based management; communication was centered in departmental planning areas, not in a central faculty room; and faculty were often critical of professional development sessions. There were other, more pointed concerns about the school improvement process. In the words of one instructional leader, the state association was "more concerned with how to do school improvement; not with how to make changes at the classroom level."

The KEYS/IMS process that began with the 1997 Leadership Retreat indeed proved to be an interim framework. At the March 1999 SIT meeting, the Board of Education coordinators presented, as part of a countywide dissemination effort, the framework for school improvement endorsed by the district. The framework was the National Study of School Evaluation (NSSE) School Improvement and Planning Framework. The presentation included a comparison of the NSSE framework and the Systems Thinking/Systems Changing simulation, a component of the Improving Maryland's Schools that the SIT used extensively. Also included were comments on additional needs to be addressed in future school plans.

At the April SIT, the principal led a discussion of the plan to be formulated for the 1999 to 2002 school years, explaining that the current plan did not address instructional goals. She stressed the need for alignment of the local school improvement process with the state reform efforts:

We are all aware of the Maryland State Department of Education's constant push for educational reform and improvement in our schools. The functional test was part of this, then came the MSPAP, and in a few years the Core Learning /goals will become the High School Assessment Standards. One problem in implementing these changes is how to get the reform movement into the classrooms. One avenue that the Department of Education is relying on is school improvement teams in each school. Every school in the state should have one, and partial funding (through grants) for these teams comes from the Department. Although SITs like to think of themselves as being autonomous, they are really just a part of a state network of educators working toward the same goal—school improvement.

Further, she emphasized that the classroom was the locus of school improvement: "What each of us does with the students in our classroom during our 50 minutes per day is the most controllable educational factor we have."

The SIT decided to include one of the Skills for Success[1] in the future plan, and in selecting a specific instructional goal, to use information from the KEYS survey, the Middle States, Maryland Core Learning Goals, and a list of barriers to student success compiled by the faculty. The Board of Education SIT coordinators provided written guidance to the action teams as to how to develop new goals.

The plan for the 1999–2001 school years was completed by the end of April and distributed to the SIT at its May meeting. The new plan included four goals:

1. Improve student achievement.
2. Students will be educated in a safe, supportive educational community.
3. Improve and create communication among all stakeholders.
4. Improve the school learning climate.

Each goal was defined by objectives, strategies/activities, persons responsible, time line, documentation, estimated resources and funding source, management plan, and milestones. Thus the new plan was more detailed that the 1998–99 plan.

The goal to improve student achievement included an instructional goal based on one of the Skills for Success: "Students will self-assess their own learning strategies and identify ways they can strengthen their learning." Another objective was to develop a math modeling course, but systems thinking was not mentioned. At the May meeting, the team agreed to focus on learning skills as topics for the professional day activities for the coming year. One of the two SIT facilitators ended her term according to the bylaws. The incoming facilitator had been closely involved in the SIT process for the entire year.

During the summer, five faculty members participated in a School Improvement Workshop led by the Board of Education representatives. The transition to a new framework was complete.

OUTCOMES

There is no simple means for gauging the outcomes of the KEYS process at Shoreview High School. While one may consider concurrent changes in the school's performance (including attendance, test score gains, and disciplinary referrals, which have improved during this time period), these allow one only to establish the direction of change in measures of the school's performance, for which there may be many explanations.

Participation in KEYS offers one important source of explanation for changes in the school's organizational health during this time period. Put another way, the changes in the dimensions of school functioning to which

KEYS indicators relate—and which KEYS is designed to address—are likely to have contributed to the improving profile of school performance, through the enhancement in shared understanding and commitment to high goals, attempts to increase open communication and collaborative problem solving, engagement in continuous assessment for teaching and learning, attention to personal and professional learning, and investment of resources to support teaching and learning.

Concurrent Gains in School Performance

The Maryland State Department of Education uses a formula to compute an indicator of overall school performance, the school performance index (SPI). The SPI includes the attendance rate ADS (average distance from satisfactory), the retention rate ADS, and performance on Maryland Functional Tests ADS in reading, math, writing, and citizenship. School Performance Indices were 97.84, 98.23, and 98.34 for 1996, 1997, and 1998 respectively—in other words, a modest gain.

The 1998 Shoreview High School proposal for Safe and Drug-Free School funding attributed a decline in disciplinary referrals to collaborative efforts in the school improvement process. The totals for disciplinary referrals were 2,683, 3,169, and 2,432 for the 1995–96, 1996–97, and 1997–98 school years respectively.

Organizational Health

Table 4.1 presents the concurrent effects on organizational health according to KEYS indicators for (1) the 1997–98 school year and fall 1998, when the KEYS/IMS process was implemented; and (2) spring of 1999, when the shift to a new school improvement process occurred. While the changes noted in the table cannot be solely attributed to the KEYS/IMS process, engagement with this process clearly contributed to these developments in the school.

Shared Understanding and Commitment to High Goals

Indicators in this category pertain to stakeholder commitment to long-range continuous improvement, clarity and explicitness of goals for achievable educational outcomes, and stakeholder beliefs that all students can learn.

A shared view of student potential apparently preceded KEYS. The Middle States evaluation at the start of the 1996–97 school year cited the school as having a "rigorous program that encourages students to take upper level, AP, and other college level courses" as well as the school's "effective programs for remediation, mainstreaming, and ESOL." The predominant

TABLE 4.1   Effects on Organizational Health, by Categories of KEYS Indicators

Effect Type

According to KEYS Indicators	1997–1998	Fall 1998	Spring 1999
Shared understanding			
1. Parents and school employees are committed to long-range continuous improvement.	*Faculty: SIT members strongly committed as indicated by attendance at meetings and interview comments. 82% of faculty involved in SIT and action teams.	*Faculty: SIT members very committed. Parents: Five involved in '99 LTR.	Faculty commits in writing to instructional goal.
2. Central and building administrators are committed to long-range continuous improvement.	*Strong commitment: Principal attended LTR, KEYS training, KEYS course. Asst. Principals attended SIT meetings. Central: Superintendent attended KEYS training; BOE representatives at every SIT meeting.	*Strong commitment: Principal reinstated faculty meetings. BOE appointed two SIT coordinators who attended school SIT meetings.	—
3. Goals to achieve educational outcomes are clear and explicit.	*Action team formulated goals, as evident in documents.	*Comprehensive, explicit goals presented in School Improvement Plan for 1998–1999.	*Comprehensive, explicit goals (including instructional goal) detailed in School Improvement Plan for 1999–2002.
5 & 6. Educators, parents, students believe all students can learn.	*Beliefs expressed through slogans, art, displays in building, application for Minority Achievement Grant.	School Improvement Plan includes strategy of using state Minority Achievement Grant funds to increase awareness of achievement and cultural diversity.	Faculty began to examine data on minority achievement.

TABLE 4.1 Continued

Effect Type

According to KEYS Indicators	1997–1998	Fall 1998	Spring 1999
Open communication and collaborative problem solving			
4. All involved in improving education.	Faculty, administrators (see KEYS 1, 2) Parents and students on action teams.	See 1997–98.	See Fall 1998.
12., 13., 14., 16., 17. Removal of barriers to learning.	Instruction Action Team identified instructional issues through faculty survey.	Used KEYS survey and other data to develop School Improvement Plan.	Faculty generated list of barriers to student success; used data to develop School Improvement Plan.
32., 33., 34., 35. Two-way, nonthreatening communication; communication within climate for innovation.	S.I.T. and action team agenda and minutes posted in main office; school improvement communication procedures established; faculty aware that they have a voice at school and district levels.	Development of school website; faculty perceives overall improvement in communication.	—
Continuous assessment for teaching and learning			
18.–26. Frequency and quality of assessment.	Instruction Action Team/SIT proposed and granted approval for improvements in test-taking conditions for district criterion referenced tests.	Instruction Action Team develops proposal to facilitate academic transition from middle school to high school. Proposal addressed assessment issues. School Improvement Plan addresses assessment issues.	School Improvement Plan addresses assessment issues.
27.–29. Selection of instructional materials.	—	—	Instruction Action Team begins to identify best practices.

TABLE 4.1 Continued

Effect Type According to KEYS Indicators	1997–1998	Fall 1998	Spring 1999
Personal and professional learning 11. School is overall learning environment.	Applied for and received foundation grant to infuse systems thinking in classrooms and school organization; decreased disciplinary referrals. Action teams introduce projects to improve school environment.	Developed matrix of systems thinking activities. Action teams continue projects to improve school environment.	—
30.–31. Ongoing, consistent staff development in problem solving, leadership, and communication; staff development is state-of-art practical experience.	Leadership Training Retreat; other KEYS related in-services; KEYS course at University of Maryland; KEYS workshop on parent/community involvement.	Leadership Training Retreat; MSTA Symposium: A Journey to School Improvement.	Workshop on School Improvement; Coalition for District Excellence.
Resources to support teaching and learning 7.–9. Adequate space, supplies, support services.	Applied for and received state funds for school improvement goals: Minority Student Achievement Grant, Safe and Drug-Free Schools Grant.	—	—
10. Psychological and social work services available.	—	Behavior Management Team began making contacts with outside social services agencies that might assist students.	—

*Researcher assertion based on evidence from multiple data sources.

—Not addressed by SIT.

theme in faculty interviews conducted at the outset of KEYS implementation can be summed up in the words of one teacher: "I do believe every student can learn, but they don't learn the same things in the same ways." Concern for minority achievement emerged in the first year of KEYS/IMS implementation; explicit attention to achievement of subgroups of the student population was apparent by the end of the 1999 school year.

As noted earlier, views were mixed concerning the potential commitment of staff to the shared decision-making process. From 1997 to 1999, as the state reform in high school assessment became increasingly salient, commitment was high, as indicated by the extent of overall faculty involvement and attendance at SIT meetings. Increasing the involvement of parents in the school improvement process was ongoing, but commitment from the district and building administrators was high from the outset.

Goal statements become more explicit from the start of KEYS/IMS to the implementation of a different framework. Development of an explicit goal for instruction occurred during that period.

Open Communication and Collaborative Problem Solving

The eleven indicators in this category address stakeholder involvement in identifying and removing barriers to learning and the existence of two-way, nonthreatening communication between types of stakeholders. According to faculty interviews, prior to KEYS/IMS implementation the structure of decision making resembled the traditional mode of top-down administration. As the KEYS/IMS process was implemented, faculty, district representatives, building administrators, and a small but growing group of parents became actively involved in cooperative, public problem-solving efforts. Barriers to instruction were identified during 1997–98, and as the transition to the county-wide framework was occurring, barriers to student learning were identified prior to the development of an instructional goal.

Continuous Assessment for Teaching and Learning

This category includes indicators that address the use of diverse methods to assess students, instructional materials, and the overall academic program.

When KEYS/IMS was first introduced, faculty interviews revealed a variety of viewpoints concerning the way the school used information. However, the predominant responses alluded to the influence on assessment and curriculum of national standards, county criterion referenced tests, and the impending state assessment. During the 1997–98 school year, the SIT proposed and was granted Board of Education approval for improved conditions for students taking the county criterion referenced tests. Only one of the indicators pertaining to assessment (KEY 23: Assessments take into account student background) appeared in the *Goals and Strategies* document that was used to prepare the 1998–99 school improvement plan.

However, assessment issues were covered in both the leadership retreat and the KEYS course at the University of Maryland.

Assessment issues were addressed in the plan. For example, the Technology Team contributed an objective to familiarize the staff with *Grade Book Plus,* a computer program to compile accurate student data. The Instruction Action Team identified a strategy to have teachers model in classrooms aspects of the impending state High School Assessment. In the 1999–2001 plan, for example, strategies associated with the instructional goal included assessment of student progress in learning-to-learn skills and student self-assessments.

Personal and Professional Learning

KEYS indicators in this category pertain to the school as an overall learning environment for employees and students; ongoing, consistent staff development in decision making, problem solving, leadership, and communication; and ongoing staff development that is high priority, state of the art, and practical.

Most first-year activity focused on improving the school climate. Minutes for action teams described discussions of many issues and ideas for resolving them. Some projects were launched. For example, the Human Relations Action Team initiated casual days to raise funds for community projects; the Technology Action Team conducted workshops for faculty in computer use; and the Facilities Action Team implemented a policy concerning parking violations. As noted previously, staff development in decision making and other processes was extensive in the first year, but was less frequent during the second year.

The Middle States evaluation commended the school for its "experienced, dedicated, knowledgeable, involved staff," but recommended that "all staff members develop their own professional development program and avail themselves of easily accessible graduate study and in-service training opportunities." Both of the school improvement plans included strategies for staff development sessions on diverse topics.

Resources to Support Teaching and Learning

KEYS indicators in this category pertain to adequate space, supplies, support services, and psychological and social work services. The Middle States evaluation identified several resource needs that predate the KEYS process, including extensive improvements in the physical plant systems (e.g., heating, ventilation, roofing, handicapped accessibility) and the need for expanded guidance services. These recommendations, along with data from KEYS and other sources, were used to formulate explicit resource related objectives in the school improvement plan for 1998–99. However, during both years of the study, additional resources were assembled.

DISCUSSION

The foregoing evidence of engagement in and understanding of the KEYS/IMS process indicates that the school's SIT adopted the reform strategy and was actively implementing it. Immediately after training, the SIT began using skills acquired during training, and about seven weeks after training, had engaged the assistance of a state association facilitator who provided further guidance in a day-long workshop that was open to all the faculty. By the time of the KEYS survey in early November 1997, barely two months had passed since the initial leadership training.

Three factors explain this strong initial implementation of KEYS. First, many faculty members were ready to engage in some form of shared decision making, although there was uncertainty as to which strategy to choose. This readiness coincided with the ongoing efforts of the state teachers association to recruit sites for KEYS implementation and SHS's decision to take advantage of a training opportunity.

Second, the training by the state association presented KEYS within a clearly defined curriculum that integrated the process of change with skills development in that process. Participants in the leadership retreat could see where KEYS research and the survey fit in the overall curriculum and how they could make use of KEYS to move the school forward. The initial lessons were reinforced by facilitators from the state association and, within the school, by the reflective, enthusiastic leadership of the principal and faculty members who attended the retreat. The two SIT facilitators, in particular, championed the process.

Third, engagement in training was extensive at the outset. The 1997 leadership retreat offered four full days, or twenty-four hours of training of a critical mass of faculty (roughly 23 percent). From this group there emerged internal change agents, including the two faculty members selected to facilitate the SIT. Six weeks later, a full-day Saturday session offered another opportunity, this one open to all faculty who wished to participate. Other professional development occurred through the KEYS course, sessions in which KEYS data were interpreted, and a customized series of experiences at the 1998 leadership retreat.

Engagement in KEYS contributed to the overall health of the school as an organization, as evident in the SIT/action teams initiatives taken on the thirty-five KEYS indicators. The school, showing an upward trend in the already high state index of school performance, made strides in its goal of shared decision making, undergirded by public, explicit procedures.

Owens (1998) explains that the healthy organization accomplishes its goals, maintains its internal functioning, and adapts adequately to its environment. Thus, in view of the increasing need to align the school improvement process to district and state reform goals, the SIT's adaptation to a different framework for school improvement can be considered another indicator of organizational health. The shift was facilitated by the stable infrastructure developed concurrently with KEYS implementation; the compatibility of the new framework with the systems thinking approach embodied in the IMS; and leadership of the principal, the SIT facilitators, and the Board of Education representatives.

The ease with which the SIT made this transition, coupled with the explicit map of the correspondence between the new and old frameworks, suggests that the basic components of the school improvement process are generic. Portin and colleagues (1998) described the KEYS strategy as "noticeably content-free, that is, it offers virtually no prescriptions about the substantive direction that reform should take." The SHS case suggests that adoption of innovation and effective organizational development can be facilitated through a structured process, coupled with extensive training in group problem-solving processes, approaches that consider the school as a complex system, use of assessments, and options for effective strategies to achieve explicit goals. In this case, the state association offered these elements, and the school—with guidance and support from the school district, building administrators, SIT facilitators, and the national association— made a strong start toward realizing its vision of shared decision making.

NOTE

1. The three Skills for Success identified by the Maryland State Department of Education (MSDE) include Learning to Learn, Thinking, and Communication.

REFERENCES

Gottfredson, D. C., Fink, C. M., Skroban, S., & Gottfredson, G. D. (1997). Making prevention work. In R. P. Weissberg (Ed.), *Issues in children's and families' lives* (Vol. 4): *Healthy children 2010. Establishing preventive services* (pp. 219–252). Thousand Oaks, CA: Sage.

Owens, R. C. (1998). *Organizational behavior in education.* Boston: Allyn and Bacon.

Portin, B. S., Knapp, M. S., & Murphy, J. F. (1998, October). *School-based reform through reflection: Partnership between the teachers association and the school.* Paper presented at the annual convention of the University Council for Educational Administration, St. Louis, Missouri.

Senge, P. M. (1990). *The fifth discipline: The art and practice of the learning organization.* New York: Doubleday.

Senge, P. M., Roberts, C., & Ross, R. B. (1994). *The fifth discipline fieldbook: Strategies and tools for building a learning organization.* New York: Doubleday.

5

KEYS in California: The Case of Wallace High School

Lynn G. Beck

In 1998, teachers and administrators at Robert Wallace High School in a small city near Santa Barbara, California, decided that KEYS, a reform initiative of the National Education Association, offered them a workable format for pursuing improvement. This chapter tells the story of the unfolding of their efforts. It is organized in the following way. I begin with a brief consideration of the state and association contexts surrounding the adoption and implementation of KEYS at Wallace. This is followed by a longer narrative in which I attempt to tell the story of change efforts at this site. I conclude the chapter with reflections upon lessons about KEYS and change learned by the educators at Wallace and by me as I have sought to glean insights from this research.

THE STATE CONTEXT

During the 1980s, California was, in many ways, a model of statewide reform. Under the leadership of the State Superintendent of Public Education, Bill Honig, working with a set of community and education leaders, the state crafted a robust set of frameworks that "provided a general sense of desired education practice" (Cantlon, Rushcamp, & Freeman, 1991, p. 72). These frameworks identified competencies that every student in California should demonstrate as he/she moved through the educational system and, in broad strokes, painted a picture of the knowledge and skills youngsters should acquire at the different educational levels. Hailed as "more comprehensive than those in any other state" (Cantlon et al., 1991, p. 72), California's frameworks emphasized "teaching for thinking and under-standing [that was] not compromised by a countervailing emphasis on mastery of basic skills" (Porter, Archbald, & Tyree, 1991, p. 31) and, during the 1980s, were quite influential in shaping state and district policy and school and classroom practice.

During his time as the state superintendent, Honig had managed to effect a reasonably strong consensus around policy and practice. When he left office in 1992 under a cloud of a conflict of interest indictment, a vacuum existed—one that various sides strove to fill. Republican governor Pete Wilson, embracing a conservative educational agenda, and his constituents advocated a number of initiatives that made their way onto ballots. Several, including Proposition 187 and Proposition 227, were approved by a majority of voters, while others (including Proposition 174 and Proposition 8)[1] were unsuccessful. Regardless of their political fate, the presence of these education related initiatives on ballots and the intense, emotional campaigns surrounding them catapulted education into public consciousness. Administrators and teachers were pressured by advocates of different perspectives who looked to them for ammunition to support particular points of view.

In the midst of the turmoil generated by campaigns for and against different initiatives, State Superintendent Delaine Eastin, Honig's successor, attempted to build her own agenda. High standards with a focus on critical thinking, performance assessments, deregulation, and incentives for reform leading to high performance were among her themes. Efforts to translate these themes into policy and practice met with only limited success. Strong, well-organized conservative groups led campaigns to shift the focus of schooling away from critical thinking toward basic skills. And an effort to implement a statewide performance assessment, the California Learning Assessment System (CLAS) Test, lasted only one year, brought down, in part, by shortcomings in the implementation process and, in large measure, by opposition from politicians, parents, and some educators who were uncomfortable with many aspects of the test. Efforts at *incentivizing* high performance were, in many ways, overtaken by attempts to create strong disincentives for lack of performance. The Public Schools Accountability Act of 1999, for instance, established a statewide accountability system that holds each school accountable for making gains in student achievement each year. If a school fails to meet its annual growth target after the first full year of implementation, an external evaluator "shall solicit input from the parents and legal guardians of the pupils in the school" (California Department of Education, 2002, p. 5) to ensure that members of the school community are aware of the school's progress. If the school continues to fail to meet its growth target after a second year, the state superintendent shall "assume all the legal rights, duties, and powers of the governing board . . . , [and] shall reassign the principal of that school" (California Department of Education, 2002, p. 8). In addition, the state superintendent is required to take action that might include school reorganization, employee transfers, or even closure.

Reform agendas in California faced additional challenges in the form of expanding school-age populations and limited resources to serve them. In the 1999–2000 academic year, California's school-age population topped out at over 6 million children, the largest enrollment of any state in the United States[2] (California Teachers Association, 2000a). Adding to the complexity of simple increases in the numbers of students were two realities. First, large numbers of these students tend to be poor, non-white and non-English speaking, and located in crowded urban areas. Second the state lacks trained teachers and facilities to serve these youngsters.

THE ASSOCIATION CONTEXT

Begun in 1863, the California Teachers Association (CTA), with a membership of more than 295,000 people, is the largest organization of working men and women in the state. In part because of its size, the association delivers most of its services through four regional offices. The vast majority of CTA members are educators including almost 95 percent of California's public school teachers and other certificated personnel. Historically, CTA has been a major force in shaping California's educational landscape. It has sponsored important legislation such as Proposition 98, a law guaranteeing that schools and community colleges receive a minimum amount (around 40 percent) from state and local property taxes) and defended this legislation in 1993 in a major judicial showdown with the governor and legislature (*CTA v. Gould*). The association has also been a vocal participant in debates surrounding all statewide initiatives with implications for educators.

The activities of CTA at the state level have been matched by activities of many of the regional offices and local chapters. Routine issues such as salary negotiations consume much of the time and energy of local and regional leaders and staff. In areas attempting major reform initiatives such as Los Angeles and San Diego, association leaders and members have played major roles in shaping the direction of the reforms. Local associations have sponsored several major teacher strikes with the full support of the state association. And in cases where city, state, or district officials have attempted major reorganization of schools, local association leaders have persistently and consistently fought for protection of teachers and their rights (e.g., Glass, 1989).

In California, the state teachers association has certainly been an active reactor to various pressures including ballot, gubernatorial, and legislative initiatives. In the late 1990s, it also took a proactive stance. In 1997, for instance, the association approved a comprehensive *Blueprint for Educational Excellence* (California Teachers Association, 2000b), a policy document that articulates legislative goals for ensuring continuous improvement in all schools in the state. In 1999, in turn, the association began an extensive project entitled *CTA for the Next Century*. This project involved a series of data collection activities designed to help association leaders to identify areas of strategic focus to guide planning, policy development, and resource allocation in the next century.

THE SITE CONTEXT

Located in the southern end of a city of approximately 100,000 people living near Vandenburg Air Force Base about forty miles from Santa Barbara, Robert Wallace High School draws students from the unincorporated area of the city. Enrollment during the 1998–99 school year for grades 9–12 was over 2,300 students. During this academic year two-thirds of the student body was white; one-third was Latino. The remaining students were Asian, American Indian, Black, and Latino.

During the 1997–98 academic year, 196 of Wallace's students were children of migrant workers, and 129 were resource students. Sixty-two of the graduating seniors matriculated to a four-year university. Two hundred and fifty-three students enrolled in the local community college. During this year, standardized test scores and other data indicate that 72 percent of Wallace's students were performing at average levels. Twenty-seven percent were considered low performers, and 1 percent rated as high performers. These figures change when the performance of minority students is considered. Within this group, 3 percent were high performing, 36 percent were average, and 62 percent fell into the low range.

In 1997–98, Wallace had a certificated (teaching) staff of 102 including 14 special education instructors, 1 full-time psychologist and 1 part-time psychologist, 2 ROP instructors, a part-time librarian, and a part-time athletic director. Its management/governance structure divides leadership between two separate groups. A site-based management team composed of administrators and a small number of teachers handles the day-to-day decisions within the site. A shared-decision-making team (which includes parents) is responsible for larger policy decisions. Wallace High School appears to be an active site that enjoys a fair amount of support from the surrounding community.

KEYS AT WALLACE HIGH SCHOOL

Wallace High School is not a site with a great deal of interest in change. Principal Jon Arnold laughingly notes that Wallace had "the world's longest pregnancy" with block scheduling, for teachers and administrators studied and planned for this scheduling innovation for three years only to decide—at the "eleventh hour"—that "we don't really want to do this." This attitude, he says, is "pretty typical" of this site. Interestingly, though, KEYS as a vehicle for change was enthusiastically received at this site.

The idea of KEYS was introduced to Wallace in the spring of 1998 after Arnold and School Improvement Coordinator Anna Robb attended the training session sponsored by the NEA and Region 3 of the state teachers association. Arnold and Robb reported leaving the training session "all fired up." They returned to Wallace and met with the entire faculty to report on KEYS and encourage its adoption. Both stated that they believed KEYS would be an effective tool at Wallace because "it was data-based" and "it afforded choices to faculty." Their explanation of this reform and enthusiasm for it carried the day with faculty who voted overwhelmingly to adopt KEYS. During my initial visit to this site, I interviewed six teachers and asked each about the adoption of this reform. Three of the faculty referenced the fact that KEYS provided "data" that could guide decisions. Every respondent noted that the choices afforded faculty by the structure of KEYS were attractive to them and their colleagues. One also stated, "Anna really carried things with her enthusiasm"—a sentiment echoed by two others.

The adoption set the stage for two years of implementation, which I recount next. In these years, the KEYS Initiative was sustained, despite changes in the configuration of its supporters, although the momentum and direction of the initiative changed somewhat over time.

The Implementation of KEYS: Year One

Administered in late spring 1998, the KEYS survey was taken by faculty, most classified staff, students participating in student governance, and a small number of parents.[3] Results were returned during the summer and reviewed first by Robb, Arnold, and several other members of the site-based management team. (Those who worked with KEYS data during the summer of 1998 became a de facto KEYS Implementation Team and paid special attention to the unfolding of this reform.) Robb and Arnold took the lead in sifting through the data and designing what Robb called "a user-friendly" way to present them. (Essentially Robb and Arnold created a set of charts that mapped Wallace's scores on the various indicators and compared them to the take-off points identified by NEA.)

Early in the fall of 1998, Robb and Arnold presented the charts to the faculty. Some discussion about the results occurred at this time. Then, following a format that had been suggested to them during the KEYS training session, Robb and Arnold suggested that faculty identify five indicators that should receive priority attention during the 1998–99 academic year. (Their plan was to encourage the faculty to work on five or six indicators each year. If this plan were followed, the site would have addressed all of the indicators over a five-year period.) They also invited each teacher to choose an indicator committee on which to participate. The entire process was quite open ended—facilitated, but not orchestrated, by Robb and supported by Arnold. Both reported encouraging faculty to select indicators where "Wallace was near the take-off point" and to consider those on which they, as teachers, could make a difference. In the main, faculty did select indicators where Wallace's score was near the score that NEA had identified, to be the priorities for the academic year. The indicators chosen were:

- KEY 31: Staff development is an ongoing, high quality, state-of-the-art, practical experience for all school employees.
- KEY 32, 34: There is two-way, non-threatening communication between school administrators and others. There is two-way, non-threatening communication among teachers.
- KEY 20: The school uses teacher-made tests to assess students.
- KEY 28: Instructional materials are selected based on appropriateness to student needs.
- KEY 7: Space is adequate within the school building.

When I visited Wallace in March 1999, Robb and Arnold expressed some concern about teachers' decision to address KEY 7 since this is "not one teachers could really control—at least not quickly and directly." Both reported, though, that teachers felt strongly about this issue, and they believed that the process needed to have integrity—that teachers' choices needed to be "real." I had an opportunity to meet with two members of the committee working on this indicator during my visit in March 1999, and both indicated that they also realized that, in the words of one, "tackling space was a real stretch." Both reported, though, that they felt that this was an important issue and wanted to "tackle it."

Robb's position as School Improvement Coordinator enabled her to press for the establishment of structures that would enable teachers to move ahead with work on KEYS indicators. Time allocated for staff development was carefully set aside for committee meetings, and each group met several times during the 1998–99 year. With the assistance of Robb who helped to structure these meetings, each group elected a facilitator and recorder and created a strategic action plan for their group. This involved identifying goals and actions to address those goals, establishing a time line and budget, and allocating responsibility for "next steps."

Early in the process of implementation, a reporting "stream" was established by the KEYS Implementation Team. Each of the committees reported to the principal, the KEYS team, and the larger site-based management team. After reviewing the results of each committee's work, someone (usually Arnold or Robb) reported back to the committees, commenting on areas such as budgetary needs, constraints, and options. Two respondents indicated that this reporting stream resembled a "dialogue" more than a formal reporting structure and stated that it represented a satisfying and nonthreatening way for them to interact with the leadership team.

Robb reported that, during the first few months of KEYS at Wallace, she had some slight misgivings about the entire process because faculty groups had difficulty organizing themselves. She and three other individuals with whom I spoke also indicated that implementation had slowed down a bit because of the many initiatives that California Schools were "handed" by the state.[4] Robb, supported by colleagues on the KEYS team, took the lead in assisting the faculty to overcome both of these potential roadblocks. As alluded to earlier, when she saw that faculty were struggling with self-organization, Robb intervened and provided each committee with a structure and a specific task in the form of an action plan. When it became obvious that the various demands from the state were distracting faculty and threatening to interrupt KEYS planning, Robb, Arnold, and one other member of the KEYS Implementation Team worked to figure out the "alignment" between KEYS efforts and these other initiatives. The third member of this trio, a teacher who is very talented with graphics, created a set of visuals to demonstrate this alignment. These were shared with the entire faculty by Robb, who regularly proclaimed, "KEYS can help us accomplish these things. It plays right into the work we need to be doing." Apparently both of the interventions were successful. When I visited Wallace in March 1999, all committees had completed action plans, and several had begun implementing certain features of them. In formal interviews, three individuals carefully explained the ways that KEYS could and would help Wallace address various state demands and mandates.

I was able to visit Wallace in late April 1999, to participate in a professional development day devoted to KEYS and the KEYS group. Planned by Robb, the schedule for the day allowed for a brief business meeting, followed by presentations from the five KEYS groups and by extensive discussion of the work that each group was doing.

The first group had worked on KEY 31 (Staff development is an ongoing, high-quality, state of the art, practical experience for all employees). After a brief, informal analysis of staff development needs, this group presented options for addressing these needs. Of those presented, the one eliciting the most interest from other faculty was the possibility of taking courses at a nearby community college (paid for by the district). Options related to site-specific professional development (such as on-site technology training and CTA/NEA sponsored work related to KEYS) received little attention.

The second group had worked on the two indicators (KEY 32 and 34) dealing with establishing "two-way, non-threatening communication" at the site. Of all groups, this one had taken the most action to implement their ideas. Their plans included creating an in-house newsletter and an e-mail protocol for responding to memos and sponsoring faculty and staff social events. Members of the committee had begun to implement their plans. One teacher had enthusiastically started an in-house newsletter. The group had designed and piloted an e-mail protocol, and they had sponsored a number of social events already. Faculty applauded these efforts.

I was anxious to hear the next two reports because they dealt with issues more directly linked to instruction. The report from the third group focused on their efforts to address KEY 20: "The school uses teacher-made tests to assess students." I had expected this group to focus on tests aimed at assessing student learning that were constructed by Wallace teachers and was surprised that this group concentrated on standardizing tests across departments so that better decisions about student placement could be made. Following this presentation, faculty engaged in a long discussion about issues of the complexities of placing freshmen appropriately. The fourth group had dealt with KEY 28: "Instructional materials are selected based on appropriateness to student needs." Like the preceding group, this committee focused on placement. Essentially, they recommended instituting a system of testing to determine reading levels of incoming freshmen and purchasing a research-based reading program and training several faculty in the use of this program. Again, the conversation following this presentation focused on problems with "freshmen placement."

The final group to present represented the committee working on KEY 7: "Space is adequate within the school building." With great passion, presenters began with dramatic data about the overcrowding at Wallace, noting that the enrollments in feeder middle schools seemed to indicate that the problem would only get worse. Referring to the Columbine School tragedy, they then noted that, if this happened at Wallace, the logistics of moving youngsters out of the building and bringing emergency aid in were likely to be problematic simply because the halls could not easily accommodate everyone. Group representatives presented a plan for a major campaign for a new high school. At the end of the presentation, one spokesperson did note that they would be willing to consider "short-term" strategies for alleviating overcrowding such as creative scheduling that brought students to school in shifts. However, they were clear about their commitment to push for a new school. This group received much applause and many affirmations. The work of the various committees and the response of the larger faculty to the various presentations suggested several things about the first year of KEYS implementation.

I concluded my investigation of the first year of KEYS at Wallace with a number of structured and semi-structured interviews. Conversations with two parents who were members of the school Decision-Making Team, extensive interviews with Robb and Arnold, and a thoughtful conversation with Jill Freeman, a member of the regional CTA staff, were among the most informative. The parents had been present for the presentations of the KEYS committees, and both indicated that they were pleased with the apparent enthusiasm the reform had generated. At the same time, they appeared to be suspicious of the ultimate usefulness of a teacher-driven approach to school change. Indicating that they were concerned that every child learn "basic skills," one parent expressed his belief that a "straightforward, no-nonsense" approach by teachers would most likely lead to student achievement. The other parent agreed with her colleague and added that she was frustrated that parents were not more involved in the school.

Robb and Arnold indicated pleasure over the apparent enthusiasm of the faculty, reminding me (and, it seemed, themselves) that participation in these groups had been one of the few activities that had elicited enthusiasm across the entire faculty. They also recognized, however, that there was much work to be done. Both were aware that faculty were focusing, for the most part, on issues that were only indirectly linked to major changes in teaching and learning. Their hope for a greater focus on instruction centered on two things. They believed that the research underlying the KEYS instrument was correct in its assumption that the creation of conditions for effective teaching and student learning would help to promote both and were confident that engagement with the different KEYS indicators could lead to improved conditions. Robb, especially, also noted that she believed that faculty members could "learn" that they had the power to make changes. She hoped that the sense of ownership afforded to teachers by the KEYS model would push them into goal setting and planning for improvements in the classroom.

When I first met Jill Freeman on one of my early visits to Wallace, she was on campus to work with teachers on strategies for addressing California's accountability mandates. She was quite enthusiastic about what was happening at this site, noting it seemed to her that faculty had begun to assume ownership of a reform process. Her concern, borne out of observations of a large number of sites, was that change—under any conditions—is difficult. She was especially aware of the potential for teacher empowerment to become derailed when a flood of mandates from the state and districts threaten to control practice. Her goal in working with teachers at Wallace was to help them "see that KEYS can put them in a *great* [original emphasis] position to respond to the other challenges they are facing."

Freeman, Robb, and Arnold identified other concerns they had about the ongoing implementation of KEYS. As discussed earlier, all—and especially Robb and Arnold—were worried that teachers would become discouraged if their plans did not quickly lead to some visible desired results. Robb and Arnold also worried about their lack of training to "see this implementation through." Both, in separate conversations and later in a shared interview, stated that the KEYS training had been "great about getting us fired up and selling KEYS to the faculty." They noted, though, in Arnold's words,

"After the beginning, we felt sort of on our own." Robb said that she had had other training in areas such as "group facilitation, goal setting, and developing action plans" and reported that she "tapped into this knowledge" to help facilitate the process at Wallace. Both begged me to get the word back to the state association that persons at KEYS sites needed lots of training. Freeman agreed with them and suggested that each regional association should consider budgeting for a person on staff whose primary or only responsibility was to work with schools engaged in KEYS and other association-sponsored reform efforts.

A final issue of special concern to Arnold and Robb related to a possible change in Robb's status. During my visit in April 1999, Robb confided that she had been asked to consider accepting an appointment to complete the term of an association director. This opportunity was attractive to her, and she planned to pursue it if a formal offer was, in fact, extended. She was worried, though, about who would shepherd KEYS. Her hope—again shared in confidence—was that another teacher would take a leadership role, but she noted that this individual "is more of a worker bee than a leader." Arnold expressed even greater trepidation about the progress of KEYS if Robb was not on campus. He confided, "Anna has been the driving force behind KEYS and that's really been critical. It's especially important because she's a teacher and this has got to come from the teachers. I believe we can do this even if she's not here, but it will be hard. This school hasn't had much experience with change. It's going to take awhile to develop leadership, and we may not have the time."

Arnold then articulated a thought that had been implicit in the words of Robb and Freeman and that, in fact, mirrored my own thoughts about the progress of KEYS at this site. He noted that all reform efforts that lasted more than a few weeks tended to go through phases—excitement and activity was often followed by a leveling off of energy. At this phase, reforms often stalled. If they survived this, they frequently took off in new and deeper directions. Arnold suggested that Wallace might be entering the leveling off phase and that stalling was a distinct possibility. He was concerned that Robb's leave of absence—even if it only lasted for one year—would make sustaining change harder. His comment, "Next year will test our mettle. It's our 'fish or cut bait' year" reflected not only his opinion. It also captured my own view as I moved into the second year of this case study.

KEYS Implementation at Wallace: Year Two

During the summer of 1999, Robb and Arnold had the opportunity to attend an NEA-sponsored training for teachers and administrators in schools using KEYS as a reform tool. This training, developed by the University of Maryland and NEA, was delivered at the University of Washington in Seattle and sponsored by the Washington Educational Association.

Robb later noted that this training had been "excellent," and she spoke with great enthusiasm about the opportunity to "network" with other KEYS schools. She mentioned, with some regret, that Arnold, although he attended the training, did not participate in every session because he had responsibilities related to a graduate course he was taking. Robb was especially concerned about Arnold's spotty participation because she was, indeed, going to accept the appointment to a director position for the next year. She realized that he would need to be especially attentive to the progress of KEYS and worried that he had missed important information and inspiration.

On one level, Robb was concerned for good reason, for her leave of absence left a leadership void at Wallace. This void had affected the KEYS project most directly by removing one of the driving forces behind it. The situation was further complicated by the presence of a new assistant principal at Wallace. This individual had not participated in the initiation and early implementation of KEYS and, thus, lacked a strong commitment to honoring the processes of faculty work on the indicators. She also had a number of tasks assigned to her and was searching for a way to enlist faculty and staff in accomplishing these.

The biggest impact of the changes in leadership on KEYS related to the use of professional development days for work by the KEYS committees. One of Robb's primary strategies for facilitating work on KEYS had been providing faculty with time to work together on their chosen indicators. She accomplished this by persuading the site-based management team to allocate several of the professional development days that were built into the academic calendar to KEYS work. During the 1998–99 year, there had been some competition for the use of these days. Robb, however, had managed to work with others on the leadership team to create a calendar that allocated some time (and some days) to other activities but that also protected a good portion of time for work with KEYS. She then, strategically, planned activities for these days well in advance and announced her plans to others in the school community in a variety of ways. This had the effect of making KEYS a very central part of the agenda at Wallace.

During the 1999–2000 year, there was no individual on-site with a strong commitment to KEYS. Arnold, to be sure, was committed on one level, but he was also committed to a style of democratic leadership that responded to the voices of those on the leadership team. The new assistant principal exerted a great deal of leadership on the team's thinking and, in essence, shifted the emphasis of the professional development days. This pushed KEYS work to short after-school meetings when faculty were tired and much less engaged in the hard thinking and planning required by intensive change efforts.

Interestingly, in spite of a lack of quality time, work on the KEYS initiatives continued. This was partly due to Robb's persistence in keeping these activities on the minds of teachers and administrators. Although she was on leave from the site, she was still on staff at Wallace. She maintained a tele- phone line with voice mail and checked it several times a day. She also was able to arrange her schedule so that she could be on-site for a few days dur- ing the year. Furthermore, during her years at Wallace, she had developed close personal relationships with many teachers and earned the respect of even more. Both formally and informally, Robb stayed in close contact with many on the staff and managed to talk often about KEYS. The continuing work on the KEYS initiatives was also linked to teachers' enthusiasm for the process. In a conversation near the end of the academic year, Robb noted that several teachers had been vocal in complaining about the lack of time to work on their projects and many others had, at least, expressed a concern about this issue and indicated interest in a greater focus on the work that had begun the previous year.

Yet another reason for continued interest in and commitment to KEYS relates to successes that had occurred as a result of the work during the 1998–99 year. One small, but not insignificant, part of the plan developed by the committee attempting to promote "non-threatening communica- tion" between teachers and administrators and among teachers was the development of an in-house newsletter. As described earlier, a member of the committee who developed this plan began this newsletter during the 1998–99 academic year. This teacher, in her first year at Wallace in 1998, continued to create and distribute this newsletter into the 1999–2000 aca- demic year. Not only did this provide a vehicle for faculty to get to know one another, it also became a symbol of a real and useful product that had come for teachers working together to try to address two KEYS indicators. Its presence served as a reminder that change was possible and that educa- tors could play a role in creating better conditions at a site.

A second success—in manner of speaking—came as a result of the work of the committee addressing the issue of adequate space. As discussed ear- lier, Robb and Arnold had concerns because this group was so focused on pressing for a new high school. In their view, the odds of their being able to convince the school board to put a bond for a new school on the ballot were slim, and the likelihood that two-thirds of the voters in this fairly conser- vative community would support such an initiative were even slimmer.[5] To their surprise (and to mine as well), this group began to implement their plan to raise community and school board awareness of the overcrowded conditions at Wallace. This involved a media campaign highlighting the need for a new school and extensive lobbying of school board members. This effort, coupled with efforts from other quarters, did result in the plac- ing of a bond initiative on the ballot during the spring of 2000. Although the initiative did not pass, the percentage of votes was most definitely per- ceived as a "victory" for proponents of a new school. In California and in this region, initiatives that mean additional taxes rarely win the support of the "super majority" required by state law. Typically, when they win the approval of at least 55 percent, they have a good chance of passing on subsequent ballots. Certainly, the KEYS committee was heartened by the results of their efforts. Others also were encouraged to think that they could mobilize and promote conditions that would improve conditions for teaching and learning.

These successes, coupled with a strong press from Robb, and the fact that faculty had "bought into" KEYS and their appreciation of the control it gave to them, kept KEYS going during its second year at Wallace High School. This year, however, was not one where KEYS was a central and defining feature of the culture. At the end of the year, reflecting on lessons she had learned and on plans for the next year, Robb shared two important observations with me. The first relates to the importance of drawing all stakeholders into the reform process early and often. Robb noted that she and Arnold had concentrated on teachers during the 1998–99 year and had not done a really thorough job of involving parents, the school Decision-Making Team, and other administrators and staff. She acknowledged that any reform needed a strong and robust base of support to buffer it against shifts in personnel or changes in state or district guidelines. Robb also stated that the experience of being off-site and watching KEYS related work be relegated to a position of less importance made her realize that this kind of reform requires strong and committed support from the larger administrative team. She noted that the principal's commitment is vital but also remarked that there needed to be wider support from those in leadership positions. Because she is still a member of the leadership team herself, she planned to have open and serious discussions with this group to ask them for a reaffirmation of their willingness to "do what it takes" to keep KEYS going. Such a commitment, especially if it were issued in some sort of public arena, would do much, in her view, to sustain and reignite faculty energy.

LESSONS FROM THE WALLACE STORY

The story of KEYS at Wallace High School is one of a group of teachers and administrators attempting to find their way through a reform process. Worthy of note is the fact that teachers in this normally change-averse school embraced the ideas and processes advocated by KEYS and have stuck with them for two years. Also impressive is the fact that KEYS seems to have pervaded the culture to the extent that teachers appear to have internalized the central premises undergirding this reform. Also noteworthy is the fact that the second year of implementation has witnessed a slowdown of work and energy. Some of the lessons from the story of KEYS at Wallace High School relate to the hard task of initiating and sustaining reform in any school. Other lessons are more specifically linked to the nature of this data-driven, teacher-managed reform. In this section, I focus on the latter. As I sought to tease these lessons out of this case, I looked to two resources to assist me. The first of these was research on school change and, especially, on change in secondary schools. The second resource was Anna Robb. Throughout this process she served as a valuable partner in sense-making, helping me to understand the events at Wallace and the meanings behind them.

The lessons about KEYS implementation concern four facets of this reform: its focus on teaching and learning, its nature as a teacher-managed reform, its dependence on data, and its sponsorship by the teachers association. I elaborate on each next.

KEYS as Reform Focusing on the Conditions of Teaching and Learning

One of the premises underlying KEYS is that "as much as fifty percent of student achievement can be linked directly to the organizational structure of schools and how that structure hinders or fosters quality decision making" (*KEYS Training Manual*, 1996, pp. 1–3). Building on this premise, KEYS is designed to help schools assess those dimensions of their structure and culture most likely to influence student teaching and learning and to guide their planning for improvement. At Wallace, faculty have focused on a few structural issues but have not yet really pursued changes in teaching. Their experience supports a point made by Elmore, Peterson, and McCarthy (1996), and Murphy and Beck (1995). All of these scholars, while acknowledging that structure can support or hinder powerful teaching and learning, note that changing structure rarely leads directly to improvements in the core technology of the school. The members of the KEYS committees at Wallace—especially during the first year of implementation—focused enthusiastically on changing certain structures. They consistently overlooked, however, opportunities to work on curriculum, pedagogy, and assessment. Louis and Miles (1990), in their analysis of two high schools that successfully transformed themselves, note that one of these schools began with a focus "almost exclusively on superficial improvements in facilities and school climate, then moved to programs" (p. 207) that focused more directly on issues related to learning and student development. Their work suggests that Wallace may be in a position to move toward serious work on curriculum and instruction. However, the work of the other scholars cited earlier in this paragraph suggests that this move will not necessarily be an easy or natural one and will probably require focused attention.

KEYS as a Teacher-Managed Reform

Not surprisingly, KEYS, as a reform tool developed by the largest teacher association in the world, is focused on enlisting, equipping, and inspiring teachers to take a lead in creating good conditions for teaching. This focus is, however, not merely a political one, for the reform is built upon research that asserts that "participants [i.e., teachers] must . . . have a meaningful and responsible role in accomplishing the school's objectives" (Verdugo, Uribe, Schneider, Henderson, & Greenberg, 1996, p. 88). This feature of KEYS was cited by many of the teachers at Wallace as being a central reason they were willing to embrace this reform. As noted earlier, at least six persons directly stated that they were drawn to KEYS because it gave teachers "a choice." And many others implied that this was an important feature for a group of high school teachers who tended to resist having programs and plans imposed on them.

The fact that teachers essentially controlled the progress of KEYS at Wallace made it potentially a powerful vehicle for change. It also meant, however, that there were certain vulnerabilities attached to this effort. One of the vulnerabilities can be seen when we look at the decline in activity after Robb's leave of absence. As a champion of this reform and a member of the leadership team at the school, she had managed to position KEYS in a central place through allocating a number of professional development days to work on the various indicators. When she was no longer there on a regular basis, others in a leadership role controlled the use of these days. Many teachers had an interest in continuing more focused work on KEYS, but they were not in the formal decision-making roles to ensure that quality time would be allocated to this work. A large body of research (e.g., Berman & McLaughlin, 1977; Hall, Hord, & Griffin, 1980; Leithwood & Montgomery, 1982, 1986) suggests that reform is more likely if the principal is an active proponent for it. Other research (e.g., Comer, 1996; Epstein & Dauber, 1991) stresses that reform is further strengthened if parents are active participants. KEYS at Wallace has a much greater chance of succeeding and of resulting in enhanced student learning if the administrative team (both the principal and assistant principals) are strong in their support and if parents—especially those on the site decision-making team—are also enthusiastic about and supportive of this work.

KEYS as a Data-Dependent Reform

One of the primary features of KEYS is its dependence on data to guide school improvement efforts. Indeed, the *KEYS Training Manual* (National Education Association, 1996) asserts that the collection and representation of data about site conditions is a hallmark of this reform: "This is the significance of KEYS. It gives us a benchmark. It gives us data upon which to make decisions, decisions that can enhance the quality of our schools" (pp. 2–5). Certainly few would contest that change efforts need to be built on good data. A question about KEYS relates to the robustness of the data. As noted earlier, one of the concerns expressed by several individuals at Wallace related to the structure of the questions. Parents and students who took the survey both noted that they were not able to answer some of the questions because they addressed issues outside their sphere of knowledge or experience. Some stated that they skipped these questions. Others, according to Robb, said that they "made a 'best guess.'" It is certainly possible that some of the data generated by the KEYS survey misrepresented the situation at Wallace because some of the respondents guessed at answers. This is one potential weakness in this reform. Another relates to dependence on only one source of data. Most thoughtful researchers note that surveys—especially if they only elicit the view of a small number of respondents—provide limited insight into a phenomenon (Rossi, Wright, & Anderson, 1985). Schools using the KEYS instrument as a tool for data collection might find it helpful to complement the results of this survey with other sources of information about their institutions.

KEYS as an Association-Sponsored Reform

The developers of KEYS designed this reform to be delivered through existing association structures (National Education Association, 1996). On one level, this plan makes a great deal of sense. It has a certain efficiency to it and it certainly allows for the possibility that state and regional UniServ directors will be sensitive to state contexts. Certainly Jill Freeman was able to support KEYS at Wallace by helping teachers and administrators see the ways that work with this reform could help them address various state mandates and requirements. She was a strong supporter of KEYS and helped Robb and Arnold especially during the early days of adoption and implementation. Freeman and Robb, however, both suggested that the current structures in the California Teachers Association were not sufficient to support a reform like KEYS. A huge volume of work in California meant that CTA staff had an incredible workload. KEYS for them was an add-on, one many were committed to but forced to relegate to a secondary position. Coupled with this reality was the fact that leaders of the reform at Wallace were grappling with the complexities and hard work of reform and longing for more training and support. Robb specifically commented on the need for help with leading the process once KEYS was underway. "We got lots of help in selling KEYS to the school. Then we sort of felt on our own." Central to her recommendations to NEA and the state association was the establishment of a position or positions specifically devoted to supporting schools using KEYS as a reform.

CONCLUDING THOUGHTS

KEYS was adopted by teachers and administrators at Wallace High School with high hopes and great enthusiasm. Two years later, the hopes continued although they had been adjusted a bit, and some of the enthusiasm had dimmed. Louis and Miles (1990) suggest that this is not an unusual state for a high school tackling a major reform. Their findings and framework imply, however, that certain things probably need to occur if Wallace is to weather this lull and proceed with KEYS with a new enthusiasm. Evolutionary, shared planning, successful navigation through problems, and the strategic and wise use of resources were characteristics of high schools that transformed themselves in Louis and Miles' investigation. Attention to these and a renewed commitment to KEYS by site and district leadership hold great promise for getting Wallace back on track in the pathway to reform.

NOTES

1. Proposition 227 essentially ended bilingual instruction in California schools, mandating that English Language Learners be provided with one year of intense instruction in English before being moved into an English-only classroom. Proposition 8 called for mandatory and permanent class size reduction in all California schools.

2. This figure reflects a 26.2 percent increase in the number of school-age children between 1989 and 1999. An additional 7 percent increase is expected between 2000 and 2010 (California Teachers Association, 2000a, p. 1).

3. According to Robb, several of the students and parents expressed frustration with some questions on the survey. They felt that a number of queries had been designed specifically for teachers and that they, as students or parents, were not in a position to answer them with accuracy. Specifically, they noted that they did not have the information or experience to answer questions about the principal's communication with teachers and about his/her visibility in hallways during the school day.

4. In 1999, the California Legislature passed four bills with great significance for schools. The one exerting the most pressure on teachers and administrators at Wallace was the Public Schools Accountability Act (described earlier in this paper).

5. California Law requires a "super-majority" of 66 percent for any initiative that will raise taxes.

REFERENCES

Berman, P., & McLaughlin, M. (1977). *Federal programs supporting educational change: Vol. VIII. Implementing and sustaining innovations.* Santa Monica, CA: Rand Corporation.

California Department of Education. (2002). *Key Elements of Senate Bill IX (Chapter 3 of 1999).* Available: http://www.cde.ca.gov/psaa/

California Teachers Association. (2000a). *CTA facts sheet.* Available: http://www.cta.org/who_we_are/index.html

California Teachers Association. (2000b). *CTA's Blueprint for Educational Excellence.* Burlingame, CA: Author.

Cantlon, D., Rushcamp, S., & Freeman, D. (1991). The interplay between state and district guidelines for curriculum reform in elementary schools. In S. H. Fuhrman & B. Malen (Eds.), *The politics of curriculum and testing* (pp. 63–80). Bristol, PA: Falmer.

Comer, J. (1996). *Rallying the whole village: The Comer process for reforming education.* New York: Teachers College Press.

Elmore, R., Peterson, P., & McCarthy, S. (1996). *Restructuring in the classroom: Teaching, learning, and school organization.* San Francisco: Jossey-Bass.

Epstein, J. L., & Dauber, S. L. (1991). School programs and teacher practices of parent involvement in inner-city elementary and middle schools. *Elementary School Journal, 91*(3), 289–305.

Glass, F. (1989). A history of the California Federation of Teachers. In F. Glass (Ed.), *A history of the California Federation of Teachers: 1919–1989* (pp. 4–43). San Francisco, CA: California Federation of Teachers.

Hall, G. E., Hord, S., & Griffin, T. (1980, April). *Implementation at the school building level: The development and analysis of nine mini-case studies.* Paper presented at the annual meeting of the American Educational Research Association, Boston, MA.

Leithwood, K., & Montgomery, D. (1982). The role of the elementary school principal in program improvement: A review. *Review of Educational Research, 52*(3), 309–339.

Leithwood, K., & Montgomery, D. (1986). *The principal profile.* Toronto: Ontario Institute of Education Press.

Louis, K .S., & Miles, M. (1990). *Improving the urban high school: What works and why.* New York: Teachers College Press.

Murphy, J., & Beck, L. G. (1995). *School-based management as school reform.* Thousand Oaks, CA: Corwin.

National Education Association. (1996). *KEYS training manual.* Washington, DC: Author.

Porter, A. C., Archbald, D. A., & Tyree, A. K. (1991). Reforming the curriculum: Will empowerment policies replace control? In S. H. Fuhrman & B. Malen (Eds.), *The politics of curriculum and testing* (pp. 11–36). Bristol, PA: Falmer.

Rossi, P. H., Wright, J. D., & Anderson, A. B. (1985). *Handbook of survey research.* San Diego, CA: Academic Press.

Verdugo, R. R., Uribe, O., Schneider, J. M., Henderson, R. D., & Greenberg, N. M. (1996). Statistical quality control, quality schools, and the NEA: Advocating for quality. *Contemporary Education, 67*(2), 88–93.

6

Finding Meaning in the Mirror: Self-Reflective Improvement in Two Washington State Schools

Bradley S. Portin and Michael S. Knapp

The intense interest in reflective practice across a decade and more (e.g., Hatton & Smith, 1995; Schon, 1983) along with more recent attention paid to data-driven approaches to schooling, coincides with an explosion of activity by reformers offering various models of school-based reform. It is not surprising, then, that a number of such models, including the National Education Association's KEYS Initiative, place great emphasis on a process of self-reflection, built around data concerning the school's organizational health and functioning.

Self-reflective strategies demand a lot of a school and make assumptions about the capacity of the school staff to move beyond their current way of doing business to one that represents, to them and others, an improvement, a renewal. In effect, self-reflective improvement strategies hold up a mirror to the school and invite the staff to examine themselves. The process of doing so begs several questions. What do they see in the mirror? What influences what they see? How do the images in the mirror come to suggest new possibilities for the school, as well as encouraging action to realize these possibilities? How do school staff come to understand the act of looking in the mirror? Answering these questions will help to develop a better understanding of the potential of these strategies and the conditions under which they are most likely to serve a school.

Local implementation of the KEYS initiative in Washington State provides an opportunity to extend our understanding of these matters. The Washington initiative, undertaken in parallel with those in other states described in this volume, invited schools across the state to participate in the KEYS process, commencing with a self-assessment of the school on the thirty-five Keys to Excellence (Schneider, Verdugo, Uribe, & Greenberg, 1993). A number of Washington schools took up the invitation, and their experiences offer an initial way to explore the potential and dynamics of self-reflective improvement strategies.

This chapter considers the experiences of two such schools, a rural high school and a state institutional school for young offenders, each operating within distinct yet parallel institutional contexts. In the chapter, we contrast the way the school staffs encountered the KEYS Initiative, made sense of its potential to help them address pressing reform tasks facing the school, and used it in their attempts to engage in school renewal. The contrast highlights critical differences in the readiness of the two schools to make use of KEYS, and in the role of various contextual forces in shaping their understanding and actions.

UNDERSTANDING THE WASHINGTON CASES

Conceptually, three sets of ideas help us to understand the response of these schools to the KEYS Initiative. The first concerns the character of reflective school improvement processes in general, and the KEYS Initiative in particular. The second addresses organizational sense-making in the face of ambiguity, and the third, the connections between a school's improvement processes and the external environments in which the school is nested.

Reflective, Data-Driven Strategies for School Renewal

As described in greater detail in the introductory chapter to this volume, self-reflective school renewal strategies have a particular character that invokes particular issues and dynamics. First, the strategy places great emphasis on the school-driven process of school renewal, leaving the content of renewal efforts to be determined by the participants. Second, the process is set in motion and guided by systematically collected data about the school, in these instances, responses by participants to the KEYS survey instruments. The direction for renewal efforts and the school's organized efforts to pursue these directions emerge from deliberation about the data. Subsequent progress toward renewal goals are documented by future data collection, including repeated administrations of the KEYS instrument. Third, the process is facilitated and supported by state and local union staff, along with any other experts that the school or district choose to involve. Fourth, the process is intentionally open ended, leaving the school with complete flexibility to adapt and amend their renewal effort in accord with local preferences and conditions, along with emerging events.

This kind of approach to school renewal contrasts sharply with many popular school-based reform approaches that often prescribe renewal goals and content, along with models of school governance and programmatic organization. While such approaches have many virtues and may be appropriate to many school renewal situations, they do not necessarily nurture the capacity of the school to understand its own functioning and to imagine alternative courses of action that are specifically tailored to the school's strengths and weaknesses.

Organizational Sense-Making and School Improvement

The core activity of data-driven strategies such as KEYS is guided reflection on the nature of the school staff's work, the school program, and the outcomes of this program. Systematically collected data, such as the information yielded by the KEYS surveys, act as a prompt to reflection, and the understanding of such a picture leads to planning for school renewal and action steps. But what do the data mean? The information afforded through a self-study process is likely to be fundamentally ambiguous in most respects, as are many things about organizational life. Because ambiguity is one of the fundamental preconditions for sense-making in organizations, as spelled out by Weick (1995) and others, we would expect that a variety of sense-making dynamics might play out.

First of all, the collection and presentation of data on the school's functioning represents an "occasion for sense-making" (Starbuck & Milliken, 1988), a set of "incongruous events" that "violate" or "interrupt" participants' perceptual frameworks. Second, the sense that participants make of this ambiguity rests heavily on preexisting frames of reference—premises, traditions, theories of action, and stories about the organization (Weick, 1995). However, these frames of reference are not immutable; rather, they evolve over time as organizational participants develop new vocabulary for understanding their work and the setting in which they work. Sense-making, as an ongoing, active, and social process, is thus open to the development of new meanings, both in response to ideas (e.g., a reform prompt, information from a survey) or actions (a new way of teaching, a different kind of collaborative meeting experience).

Sense-making in schools that are engaged in school improvement activities is likely to focus initially on the actions, ideas, or events that drive improvement. In order for a school to attempt some kind of schoolwide renewal, something violates widely held perceptual frameworks—that is, prompts collective attention, dissatisfaction, desire for change, and willingness to consider departing from business as usual. For example, a leadership transition, new educational legislation, pressure by community advocates, and other such contingencies may set in motion the collective search for meanings, at the same time opening the way for meaning-makers, individuals who take the lead in giving meaning to events.

Contexts for School Renewal

The school's environment—which simultaneously intrudes on the working lives of people in the school and is "enacted" by them (Weick, 1995)—plays a central role in the making of meaning and subsequent action. Inescapably, the struggle to make sense of ambiguous conditions within the school takes place in an environment that both permeates the practice of the school and constrains or prompts its efforts to undertake renewal activity. Work on the contexts of teaching practice has characterized the environment as composed of multiple, nested contexts that inform and guide what educators in classrooms do (McLaughlin & Talbert, 1993). By extension, the school as a whole operates within, and responds to, a similar set of contexts.

Three contexts—organizational, professional, and historical—are especially pertinent to the unfolding story of self-reflective renewal in a given school. First of all, as public educational institutions, schools are fundamentally dependent on a local and state environment. This includes the particular community, district jurisdiction, and state within which the school sits. From these sources come participants (e.g., students, parents, new staff), resources (e.g., funding, materials, intellectual resources), and a sense of direction (e.g., local and state standards, requirements, and expectations of schools). Taken together, state government and school districts create a web of policies, often calling for reform of local practice, always sending multiple, frequently contradictory messages to the schools. School staff who are bent on understanding their own school's trajectory and imagining alternative courses of action for it cannot escape the framework for action that this broad organizational context sets up. Nor can they ignore the various demands that emanate from this environment or the resources it may or may not afford.

Related to this organizational situation is a professional context that defines norms of good practice and seeks to influence the conditions of educators' work. The local and state teachers' association figures prominently in this context, as can other professional associations (e.g., those concerned with subject disciplines) and organizations that offer professional development support to schools and teachers. Efforts to renew the school (in the case of KEYS), set in motion and supported by an initiative coming from a prominent professional association, are likely to be responsive to this professional context. The trajectory of school renewal is therefore likely to reflect the commitments and capacities of this local and state professional infrastructure.

A third important context is rooted in the school's history with reform activity. Engagement with self-reflective renewal is unlikely to be the first time anyone in the school ever participated in school reform activities.

Because reform is a perennial concern, the school's history of reform activity, carried forward in institutional memories and possibly in structural or cultural changes, as well, is an important backdrop to the renewal concerns of the present. This historical context provides a frame of reference within which participants interpret events thereby affecting the way they imagine possibilities, anticipate barriers, or bring relevant experience to the current situation. The school's reform history may be a source of optimism or pessimism regarding the potential of a self-renewal effort to bear fruit.

THE WASHINGTON STATE CASE STUDIES

To explore the dynamics of school response to the KEYS Initiative, we developed case studies of two small high schools, each in an isolated rural setting within Washington State, across a three-year period of time. The sites were selected purposively to represent contrasting patterns of response, under somewhat comparable conditions (despite differences in the two schools' institutional mandates). We begin with synopses of each case story.

Kirkby High School: From a "Gleam in the Eye" to "One More Thing"

Kirkby High school (pseudonym), a rural high school (grades 9–12) with 354 students, is part of a three-school district located on an island approximately forty miles from the Seattle metropolitan area. The school is organized along a traditional departmental model with a six-period day. Four-period block scheduling occurs on Wednesday and Thursday. The staff consists of one administrator, twenty teachers, eleven instructional support and auxiliary staff, and three secretaries. The school has an 8 percent minority population and a dropout rate of less than 5 percent.

Staff at Kirkby began their involvement with KEYS in September 1997. Their initial connection to the initiative arose through links with their local teachers' association staff, who recommended that it might be a useful tool to undertake some of the development work that they had in mind. At the initial training in 1997, the school sent two teachers who were accompanied by the principal and two teachers from a middle school, which adjoins Kirkby High School. Staff from both schools expressed interest in KEYS and used the training to prepare plans for sharing what they learned at the workshop with their colleagues, thus preparing for administration of the KEYS instrument.

The main events shaping early implementation of KEYS were the anticipated change of principals (in the year following the initial training workshop), planning for an accreditation review of the school (to take place soon after the arrival of the new principal), a district-wide program of strategic planning and extensive curriculum realignment to match the new state *Essential Academic Learning Requirements,* and ongoing culture building in the school following the reorganization of the middle and high schools as separate programs and staffs (from an earlier consolidated secondary program). A number of secondary issues were guiding the thinking of school staff including program changes to address the loss of students to *Running Start* (an early entrance program for students to take courses in the local community colleges), as well as extensive efforts to realign the district curriculum (K–12) through monthly district-directed staff in-service days.

The KEYS survey was administered to the Kirkby teachers and educational support personnel in the spring of 1998. The survey data were returned, after some delay, to the school design team in August 1998. The survey administration process, and all aspects of KEYS implementation, was guided by two teachers who were acting as the school's KEYS design team. When the data were returned, the school was in the midst of principal transition. The departing principal had delegated responsibility for the KEYS process to the two teachers who attended the state workshop. The incoming principal was interested in the process, but a variety of district-directed and accreditation responsibilities were of more immediate concern to him. The KEYS data were prepared and presented by coordinators from the state teachers' association. In addition to summary data, the association personnel reorganized the data into the five thematic areas of KEYS and made resources available for implementation and further planning.

At this initial data review meeting, several issues arose. The first concerned who would be responsible for pressing the KEYS process forward. It was not clear who besides the two teachers would be available and interested to share this responsibility. Second, the overlap between KEYS and other projects—specifically, the school accreditation review and the superintendent's strategic planning efforts—came up. In both cases, KEYS was seen as a possible adjunct to these efforts but also appeared to be an add-on to the already existing projects. Third, the nature of the data themselves, which appeared to evaluate the quality of the school, raised questions about whether the community would focus on the school's weaknesses.

All told, the responses to continuing the KEYS process were best articulated by one member of the design team who voiced concern on behalf of colleagues that it would be viewed as yet "one more thing." In the end, the KEYS data were put aside (and were never even shown to the whole school staff) and efforts were prioritized toward working on the district aims of curricular realignment, strategic planning, and the school's accreditation review.

Essex School: "How Will This Help Us Do Our Work?"

The second case study site is a unique school that operates on the site of a state medium- to maximum-security correctional facility for young offenders. Located in a rural area forty miles from Seattle, the Essex School (pseudonym) is operated dually by the State Juvenile Rehabilitation Administration and the local school district. Correctional staff provide security and see to the health and welfare of the students during the period of their sentence. The school's educational programs are run by educational staff who are employees of the local school district. The 28 teachers provide instruction to approximately 230 juvenile offenders (ages 10–18) under state custody in classes of approximately 11 students each. The students come from largely low-income backgrounds and many have multiple learning problems. The racial and ethnic mix, as reported by the state (Office of Juvenile Justice, 1998), for the entire population of sentenced juveniles is 53 percent non-Hispanic white, 19 percent African American, 15 percent Hispanic, 7 percent Native American, 5 percent Asian, 2 percent not reported.

Besides the obvious, the school's student population is highly transient. They are enrolled in the school for only the period of their sentence, which means that there is almost daily change in who is in the school. This presents unique challenges for how the teachers conceive of learning opportunities and instructional priorities for their students. In addition, the students return to the residential facility of the institution at the end of the school day, not to their homes. As a result, the school's contact with the parents is limited and their custodial interaction is with the correctional staff who supervise the living situation of these students.

While the unique character of this school may appear to make it not comparable to Kirkby High School, there are actually many parallels, and the contrasts help to bring into sharper focus the conditions that may influence the implementation of self-reflective improvement strategies. Essex School is run in a manner that resembles other small, isolated secondary schools. School staff respond to the same set of state educational reforms and are working with similar pressures for meeting the learning needs of their students. Staff engage in instructional planning, participate in staff development, and try to meet external accountability pressures in much the same way as their counterparts in high schools serving the general population. The specific problems addressed may differ, but the process of addressing those problems, including consideration of a process such as KEYS, appears more alike than different.

As with Kirkby High School, this school sent a team of two teachers to the initial KEYS facilitator training in September 1997. As with other teams at this training, the Essex team used the training to plan for implementation of KEYS in their school. The school administrators were actively involved in the KEYS process (though not present at the training workshop) but gave primary responsibility for oversight of the KEYS process to the two teacher leaders who participated in the initial training. The process, however, quickly expanded to involve other teachers and the school's administrators.

The initial administration of the KEYS surveys took place in roughly the same time frame as at Kirkby—midway through the 1997–98 school year. Although initially startled by the KEYS results (which tended to look negative), Essex staff examined the data and were able to offer an explanation for each of the patterns found in the responses. Drawing on the KEYS data (and prior experience with a teacher/school needs assessment), the staff deliberated the needs of their unique population and identified four goals for the school. The KEYS data were organized around these goals and every staff member participated in planning related to at least one of the four goals.

In relatively short order, all participants in the process started treating the data as something that could be useful to them. The main concern of the staff appeared to be how to make the resources available to them work to realize the aims they set for their students. As they proceeded, the KEYS process became an organizing rubric for ongoing improvement work, some of which had started before this process came along. The process worked its way into their language for identifying improvement related activity: teacher professional development committees, for example, were called "KEYS Committees." KEYS, thus, came to be seen as a way to focus improvement activities that the school had been wrestling with for several years, including plans to align the academic program with the state learning requirements. Staff appreciate the fact that KEYS offers them a staff development experience that is "ongoing rather than one-shot," as one staff member put it.

Essex School has also made extensive use of the state teachers' association (WEA) support staff. Association personnel were involved in preparing the data and helping plan for its presentation to the staff. They have also been to the school and consulted by telephone on numerous other occasions to assist with ongoing planning and interpretation of the KEYS data.

UNDERSTANDING THE TWO SCHOOLS' EXPERIENCES WITH KEYS

As these case synopses indicate, the two schools had strikingly different experiences with the KEYS process. The parallels and contrasts between them reveal how, under certain circumstances, KEYS can work to serve the needs of a school engaged in site-based self-reflective renewal. Comparative analysis of the two cases suggests that the prospect for self-reflective improvement process to take hold in the school lies in the interaction among the reform tasks before the school staff, the role of meaning-makers, and the internal and external sources of meaning, especially those residing in historical, organizational, and professional contexts.

Reform Tasks Before the Two Schools

While these two schools faced different reform tasks, there are many parallels in the way the staff in each situation understood the work that lay before them. Both were trying to respond to a demanding set of state learning standards and prepare students to perform well on assessments associated with these standards. Both had set in motion a variety of improvement initiatives, some linked to the state reforms, others not. Both faced uncertainties about managing their student populations.

To be sure, the specifics of the reform tasks facing each school differed, as did the details of the local context in which the school operated. Kirkby High School had to undergo a leadership transition as the new principal came in partway through the KEYS process, and the school faced an imminent requirement for accreditation review soon after the principal arrived. At the time, the school was recovering from a somewhat upsetting restructuring process in which the school's grade 9–12 staff had separated from those responsible for grades 6 through 8. These conditions added to a growing concern over enrollment decline as high school juniors and seniors looked to community colleges for challenging learning experiences. Simultaneously, the district was organizing a serious strategic planning effort with its own set of priorities (e.g., "educating for knowledge and character") and had established processes for realizing those priorities. In a small school staff these developments meant that individuals inclined to participate in reform activities were pulled in many directions at once.

In the case of Essex School, leadership transition was not an immediate issue, nor was the school's accreditation status. However, the task of meeting state learning standards and standards from the State Department of Corrections loomed large and raised anew perennial tensions between education and punishment. Part of this situation, and contributing to the tension, was the ongoing need to manage a relationship between the school and the institutional *cottage* system, in which children were housed at night—cottage correctional staff, for example, sometimes imposed punishments on inmates who misbehaved (e.g., with a 24-hour lock-down) which interfered with their participation in school. Managing this relationship was linked to the continuing uncertainty of serving a transient population and trying to create meaningful and challenging learning experiences for students whose length of stay in the school varied tremendously. The school staff were not short of ideas about how to approach these various tasks, yet here, as in Kirkby, everyone's plate was full, and there were questions about how staff would be able to "do it all."

Making Sense of KEYS in the Context of Reform Tasks

Confronted by these multiple tasks, the staff of the two schools encountered the KEYS process. As an unfamiliar and relatively unstructured process, KEYS posed a new contingency to the educators in each setting— one that could be construed as a useful resource, a welcome support, or an unwelcome complication in their already busy lives. The sense made of this contingency and what it might enable staff to do contrasted sharply. At Kirkby High School, KEYS came to be viewed as "one more thing," while in Essex School, it became seen as a way to realize their reform goals. These divergent outcomes came about through an intricate interplay among the availability of resources, the exercise of leadership by principals and key staff, their prior experience with self-study, and their perceptions of risk.

Availability of Necessary Resources

In one sense, both schools had access to a similar set of external resources (chiefly, the expertise of facilitators from the state teachers' association), but as the KEYS story unfolded, differing levels of internal resource (chiefly, time and attention dedicated to KEYS related activities) were made available. Essex School allocated these resources throughout the process and, in conjunction with external expertise, made full use of these resources. The Essex design team was readily responsive to offers from the WEA staff, who came to the school on several occasions to facilitate planning sessions. Time was set aside in whole school meetings and for subgroups to define and carry out KEYS related improvement activities. At Kirkby High School, by contrast, staff never took advantage of the expert help offered by the state association, and time was never set aside (beyond several design team meetings) to engage the whole school staff in KEYS related thinking and work. The workload thus never spread from the few individuals who formed the nucleus of KEYS activity in the school.

Principal Leadership

Not surprisingly, the principal played a key role in determining how external and internal resources would be used and setting a tone that guided their use. At Kirkby, the exiting principal (who presided over the first year of KEYS) had assumed a hands-off stance; the new principal had other tasks to attend to, wasn't versed in KEYS, and was aware that the district train was on the move in another direction. Furthermore, he came fresh from the experience of guiding a high school through an accreditation process and had a proven model for managing accreditation reviews in his repertoire. While not opposed to KEYS, he did not champion it either. The principal of Essex School, on the other hand, saw in KEYS an opportunity for consolidating a number of the school's improvement efforts. Accordingly, she orchestrated external and internal resources to support work by staff stimulated by the KEYS process.

Teacher Leadership

The principal was not the only person in the school who could, or did, carry the banner on behalf of the KEYS process. While initially excited by the prospect of working on KEYS implementation, the two teachers at Kirkby High School entrusted with KEYS implementation were heavily loaded with other tasks. Their responsibilities escalated at the time of the new principal's arrival, as one of these teachers took on responsibility for organizing an honors curriculum, while the other prepared for retirement. Teacher leaders at Essex School who became involved with KEYS were not so encumbered by other responsibilities, or put another way, saw in KEYS a vehicle for energizing themselves professionally at a senior stage of their careers.

Participants' Experience with Self-Study

Participants in the two schools brought a different experience base to the encounter with KEYS. While no one in either school had specific knowledge of KEYS beyond what they gleaned from the state's introductory workshops, staff at Essex School had participated in a broad-ranging needs assessment survey, with the support of the district during the transition period to a new principal several years before KEYS came along. This experience appeared to provide the new principal and staff a level of comfort with data, which was displayed in various forms of charting, and strategic use of the KEYS results as they moved through the KEYS-stimulated improvement process. Staff at Kirkby High School, on the other hand, had nothing comparable in their repertoires.

Perceptions of Risk

Perhaps because of their earlier experience with school-based surveys, their more insulated situation, or their cohesiveness as a staff, teachers in Essex School saw little potential harm in undertaking the KEYS survey, pouring over its possible meanings and fashioning action plans based on their interpretations of what they saw. Where they saw opportunity, their counterparts in Kirkby High School saw potential dangers. In the fishbowl of a small rural community, perceptions of the school suggested by the KEYS survey, whether or not they were justifiable, seemed to the design team members to be a liability. They even doubted that their colleagues in the school would feel comfortable with the picture of the school that the KEYS data instruments yielded, and they perceived further internal risks in bringing the results to the full faculty. Even with the availability of competent outside help, and assurances that initial negative reactions could be turned to the school's advantage, the participants in Kirkby were not ready to move forward.

These intertwined conditions and forces contributed to varying states of institutional readiness in the two schools. Clearly, Essex was more ready, institutionally, to take on the challenges and uncertainties of a self-reflective improvement process than Kirkby. But the readiness of the two schools for these challenges and uncertainties resided not only within the school—that is, in the experience base, perceptions, and leadership exercised by school-based participants—but also in the relationship between the school and key features of its context.

How Context Shapes Sense-making

The sense-making by staff in the two schools occurred within contexts that shaped the meanings they made of KEYS and the reform challenges they faced. Thus, the interplay of forces and conditions noted earlier derived, in part, from features of the environments in which the schools sat and from the relationship of the school to those environments. To some extent, these features were the same for both schools, and so they do not help much in accounting for the differences in school response to KEYS. Factors such as state reform initiatives, the state's implementation of KEYS, and the resources made available by the state teachers' association exerted a comparable influence in the two cases. But in other ways the configuration of environments in which each school was nested was unique and played a unique role in the sense-making we have been describing. Four nested contexts were pivotal.

District Context

In each case, the school districts to which the schools were connected colored the sense of possibility or constraint afforded by the KEYS process. The relatively tight coupling between district and school in the first case meant that school staff were more likely to take seriously what was going on at district level. The small size of the district (three school buildings all located in close proximity to one another) and the proximity of the superintendent meant that district officials could exercise a fairly directive role in school-based reform efforts. As it was, the coming of KEYS coincided with a district-led strategic planning process that spelled out procedures for constructive school improvement plans. This fact meant that staff felt more constrained as they sought to understand the implications of self-study data for the improvement of the school. The connection to a host district was far looser in the case of Essex School and was limited to administrative matters and teacher compensation. The school's institutional connections to the Department of Corrections provided another form of connection, yet still the school staff had considerable autonomy to construct and operate its academic program (and hence, its improvement efforts) as it saw fit.

Local Community Contexts

Another set of influences on the way KEYS was interpreted lay in the relationship of the school to its local community. As noted with regard to the first case, the local community's scrutiny of the school and the power to influence school priorities and resource base (e.g., through levy and bond elections)—whether imagined or real—contributed to the perception of serious risk in exposing the school's self-study profile to public view. In a community in which parents, business leaders, local press, and the retirement community keep a watchful eye on all that happens in the school, the

KEYS design team decided not to administer the parent survey instrument and to keep the results of the teacher survey under wraps. The relevant community for Essex School—the residential staff of the institution (acting in loco parentis) for the residents—took much less interest in the affairs of the school and exerted little or no influence over the resource base or directions of the school. The tensions between the cottage staff's approach to the resident students and the school's approach were very real but did little to affect perceptions of risks or benefit from self-reflection.

Local History of Reform and Organizational Change

In both sites, events in the recent past had influenced school staffs' perceptions of, and approaches to, change; as a consequence, these events colored the way KEYS was perceived. In both cases, the events of the recent past had not been easy. For Kirkby, a painful reorganization of the school occurred when a new middle school was built and the district split up the old 6–12 configuration into a middle school and high school. Colleagues long working side by side were split into the two new staffs. Although housed in contiguous facilities and sharing the same staff room and administrative wing, the move created a sense of loss that still resided below the surface. In this instance, the school leaders and staff were less ready for further change. KEYS thus came along at a time when the school staff and leaders were seeking ways to calm the waters and focus on what was going well, rather than making dramatic new changes.

Staff in Essex School had experienced a comparable event prior to KEYS—in this instance, a turbulent change of principals at a time when staff morale was low and the school facility was in poor condition. By embracing a comprehensive audit process (union-sponsored) and doggedly pursuing equipment and maintenance improvements in the school, school leaders and staff moved to a point at which they felt confident in their ability to accomplish things and ready for new challenges. The coming of KEYS represented one such challenge, or else a vehicle for tackling new challenges.

Local Union Context

Both sites had strong local teachers' association links. In the case of Kirkby High School, one member of the design team had been a past union president and another member of the staff was the current president. Within a small community and district, the union relationships appeared cordial. In some sense, the cordial working relationships between the district and local teachers' association seemed to develop a sense of autonomy in the school—a lack of need for resource assistance from either the Uni-Serv or state association office. At the Essex School, teachers expressed a perception that their union contract was another protection in a school environment where the personal risks can be high. They readily accepted the assistance from the state office for the KEYS activities they undertook.

LEARNING FROM THE TWO CASES

The contrasts between these two schools tell us some things about the potential of self-reflective improvement strategies in schools and about schools' readiness to make good use of such strategies. In short, this kind of strategy appears to offer schools a highly adaptable, though complex, way of approaching the challenges schools face. Rather than giving school staffs a specific answer to their problems (as many more structured school improvement processes do) the KEYS process engages school staff in the difficult work of evolving a locally appropriate set of answers to their problems. Through the KEYS data, their plans have the advantage of being rooted in a clear picture of the current operations of the school. In doing so, the flexibility and content-free character of strategies such as KEYS asks much of the staff, and not all are equally ready to take advantage of the opportunity. That readiness seems to lie in the interplay among the tasks before the school, the contexts in which school staff find themselves, and the sense-making they engage in at the intersection between school tasks and contexts.

The two case stories offer a striking contrast in the way school staff sized up and took advantage of the occasion and resources offered by the KEYS Initiative, and in that contrast lie images of the potential of this kind of improvement strategy. Despite clear differences between them, the two schools are comparable in many ways. Both schools were small, isolated secondary schools with staffs who knew each other well and had worked at the school for relatively long periods of time. Staff from both schools were exposed to KEYS in the same way and at the same time. They exhibited similar enthusiasm initially, returned to the school with similar ideas about the ways KEYS might provide an organizing device for reform activities already underway, and received similar offers of support from capable state facilitators. Both schools were confronted with mounting external pressure to adapt their programs to the demands of state standards-based reforms. Both schools had a full agenda of improvement goals and activities under consideration at the time, not including what the new state reforms were calling for.

Why the difference in the way the schools responded to KEYS? What does it say about the KEYS process, in particular, and about reflective, data-driven school improvement, in general? We find explanations in three sources: (1) in the ambiguities and associated tensions that attend self-reflection guided by data; (2) in the interaction among several kinds of meaning-makers (individuals and groups who extract insight and images of possibility from the ambiguity); and (3) in the school's institutional readiness for reflective school improvement.

Ambiguities and Tensions in the Self-Reflective Renewal Process

We look first to the core event and activities of a reflective, data-driven school-based reform process—the deliberate attempt to assemble data that characterizes the school's nature, accomplishments, and shortcomings, as a prompt for further reflection on the school's activities. We are at once struck by how fundamentally ambiguous this information is and how unclear its implications are for the actions of the school staff or the school's constituencies. These events take place in an organizational setting already characterized by enduring ambiguities.

Consider the nature of the KEYS data summary provided to a school after administration of the instrument. When a school completes the KEYS survey, NEA scores the survey and returns a report to the school that indicates its performance on the thirty-five "Indicators of a Quality School" that are central to the KEYS initiative. The report is in the form of quantitative descriptive data (and accompanying graphical representations) on a 1 to 4 scale for each of the thirty-five indicators.

The first question school staff encounter is: what do these data mean? At the extremes of each scale, the descriptive meaning may be somewhat clear (i.e., we do or don't do that around here), but the same is not true for most values on the scale, which fall between the extremes. Whatever the descriptive meaning of scale values, their interpretation is anything but straightforward. What do the data tell the school staff about how they do things or why things are this way? What does the value imply about what might be done differently? To compound matters, data produced by a process such as KEYS may appear to be value-laden. Educators are steeped in an environment where quantitative measures are used both as indicators of performance and as a basis on which school success is evaluated. In Washington State, as the statewide school reform legislation is implemented, teachers and administrators are keenly aware of the impact of test scores, particularly aggregated scores published as an indicator of an individual school's effectiveness.

The tension may also reflect anticipation, as much as the ambiguity of the data itself. At Kirkby High School, for example, design team members reported a high level of "tension in the room" when the survey was administered. An interpretation by at least one of the design team members was that the very wording of the questions—asking about their perceptions of school quality indicators—unsettled their view of themselves. In other words, responding to the questions startled their tacit assumptions about their school. Responding to questions about goal commitment, communication, collaboration, professional learning, and teaching practice, among others, may have shaken the embedded beliefs of some about the quality of their school.

The staff in the two Washington case study schools responded to the KEYS data in a similar manner: they were unsure of what these data meant and in some ways they were anxious about the use and interpretation of the data, especially at Kirkby. In both instances, school staffs were initially confused, perhaps put off, by what they saw in the results. In both instances, they needed help to read the data (and got that help from WEA staff).

To be sure, the leaders of the design teams in each school had been trained by teachers' association staff to interpret these quantitative data and identify themes of strength and areas of growth for the school in planning for school improvement. Even so, what mean scores, response ranges, and take-off points indicate are not clear initially to school staff or anyone else, for that matter. However, the brief orientation offered at the beginning of the KEYS process was not enough to offset the staff's propensity to see the survey summary as a report card on the school, an assertion about whether the school was good (i.e., above the take-off point) or bad (below the take-off point).

These dichotomous interpretations, compounded by prior experience with performance indicators, appear to have thrust teachers in these schools into a zone of uncertainty, both when administering the survey and in examining the initial results. So the question for each school staff became one of resolving the ambiguity and reducing the tension associated with it. Leaders in Kirkby High School took what they viewed as the safest course of action—to stop looking further at the data, keep the data from being circulated to others in the school or school community, and turn attention to other pressing matters. Leaders in Essex School strategized about how the data could be examined productively with the whole school staff, and how it could be linked to the ongoing process of addressing improvement goals in the building. Both courses of action dealt with both the ambiguity and the tension associated with it.

The Role of Meaning-Makers

Ambiguous, tension-filled events in organizational life beg to be interpreted, to be assigned meanings that are acceptable to the school staff and others involved. The KEYS process thus sets the stage for individuals to assign meaning to the data on behalf of their colleagues. In these cases, two sets of individuals, the teachers association staff and school building leaders (both administrators and teachers), stepped forward. The joint effect of their efforts was to enable the school to move—or refrain from moving—from the point of data interpretation to action.

Teachers Association Staff

For both schools, staff from the state teachers association office played the role of interpreter and facilitator. These individuals brought back the survey results to a small leadership group in each school, offered alternative formats for displaying the data, discussed possible meanings for the data, and offered strategies for presenting the data to the school staffs. Further, the state association offered other facilitators with special skill in action planning as further assistance (one school took them up on this offer, the other didn't) and provided overt and subtle pressure to see the data as a stimulus to further action by the school. They did so in a way that was generally reassuring and validating.

The experience of these schools seems to highlight the catalytic role that outside interpreters may play, at least when these are skilled at their interpretive work and sufficiently trusted to be listened to. Given its established relationship with the schools in question and the fact that it had qualified staff on board, the state teachers association in Washington State was in a good position to play this external interpretive role. Put another way, internal interpreters are not enough. There are several reasons why this may be so. For one thing, few school staff have much expertise in working with quantitative survey data, and anyone with such experience who also speaks the language of schools is in a position to fill this need. Furthermore, it may be that the school leaders and staff are too embedded in the culture of the school—and, therefore, its tacit assumptions about itself—to provide an objective frame from which to examine the survey findings.

In this instance, it is also important to note what meanings association facilitators found in the data. They approached their task within a set of assumptions about good schooling and the improvement of schools that highlights certain goals and deemphasizes others. Their attention was singularly focused on the use of data to surface programmatic issues and possibilities for each school building, possible topics for further professional development, and new action steps school staff could take on their own to make a better learning experience for children. They did not approach the data as indicators of teachers' satisfaction with working conditions, pay, or other issues that form a more traditional union agenda.

Building Leaders

While association facilitators were clearly helpful to both schools, they approached each building in a similar way, and so their efforts at meaning-making do not explain the difference between the two schools' response to KEYS. School building leaders, including principals and teacher leaders close to the KEYS process, were also central to the meaning-making process and they arrived at clearly different meanings. At Kirkby High School, the primary forces were two teacher leaders who proceeded to explore the possibilities of involvement with KEYS with the consent of a principal who played a hands-off, but supportive, role. Soon after the KEYS survey results were returned to the school this principal moved to a different school, setting in motion the process of leadership turnover and its attendant uncertainties. Somehow, in the inevitable resorting of priorities that takes place with a new leader at the helm, KEYS did not emerge as an identifiable process or rubric for organizing reform efforts. The new principal, for one, had a great deal to undertake and didn't find KEYS (to the extent that he understood it) to be a helpful organizer for thinking or action.

In contrast, the administrators (principal and assistant principal) and the teacher leaders in Essex School who were primarily responsible for the KEYS process offered continuous, uninterrupted support for the process to continue. In different ways, these people saw in KEYS the potential to address important matters on the school's agenda as a well as a useful organizing rubric for ongoing improvement activities.

Institutional Readiness for Reflective School Renewal

The making of meaning by individuals or groups presumes a ready audience among the rest of the school staff and a convergence of conditions that predispose the audience to accept these meanings. Put somewhat more interactively, the school staff and other players jointly construct images of what a process like KEYS means about their work and implies for their future. The patterns of meaning-making and associated conditions in these two cases suggest that schools vary in their institutional readiness for a reflective, deliberative process like KEYS.

Readiness for reflective school renewal thus resides at the intersection of factors that are internal to the school and those that originate in the school's historical, organizational, and professional contexts. Internal and external factors interact as staff consider the prospect of engaging in self-reflection, or as they take part in the process itself. In this interaction lie powerful forces shaping the meanings found in KEYS or other similar process, and, hence, its potential to be useful to the school. The net effect is to predispose both the meaning-makers and the professional community of which they are a part to see in such a process possibilities or limitations, benefits or risks.

What school leaders or staff see when they look in the mirror of the KEYS process is mediated by the manner in which they perceive the tasks before them, the contextual contributors to their task, institutional history, leadership density, and experience with data. The readiness of schools to find useful meanings in the mirror thus rests on a series of internal and external conditions that school staffs and others would do well to appraise before engaging in such a process. At least the following appear to be key dimensions of readiness:

- A cadre of teacher leaders in the school who have time, capacity, and inclination to assume responsibility for a self-reflective process and the planning and action that come from it
- A principal who is supportive and involved at some level
- Sufficient building-level autonomy and/or district support to engage in a self-reflective improvement process, as a way to realize district priorities

- Available resources for supporting this process from within the school or district (e.g., the allocation of time to collective staff work associated with reflection and improvement) and from the external environment (e.g., expertise in the teachers' association infrastructure or other support structures)

- A history of reform experience in the school that encourages staff to consider new challenges

- Some familiarity with self-study data, or ways to gain this familiarity

The presence of these conditions seems to predispose schools to make more of the opportunity that a KEYS-like process affords. Their absence may limit the likelihood that such a process will bear fruit.

CLOSING COMMENTS ON WHAT WE HAVE YET TO LEARN

This analysis shows how a self-reflective process can provide an organizing rubric for ongoing renewal efforts by a school staff and also helps to sketch the dimensions of a school's readiness to make good use of this process. Yet it leaves unexplored several important aspects of the encounter with a KEYS-like process. First, we have not studied the act of meaning-making itself. To do so, we would have had to observe in finer detail the thinking of the central actors in each case story and tried to identify the turning points in thought and action that led each school's story in one direction or another. Understanding the fine detail of meaning-making is important because at some level, the convergence of elements we have studied only suggests a likelihood that actors will move one way or another. It doesn't help us know how well the active problem solver construes events at the point of determining whether the cup is half full or half empty.

Second, our analysis tells us relatively little about the *content of deliberation* and the *sources* of this content—that is, how a content-free process such as KEYS invites new content into the discussion beyond the initial profile of the school. In the cases we studied, the content appeared to come from the most natural source: preexisting improvement activity of various kinds, which either was subsumed within the KEYS process or overwhelmed it before it could get started. The cases are silent, however, about the possibility that other sources of ideas about improvement, perhaps richer than what was already underway, might be tapped. One can well imagine schools that look in the mirror, see pretty much what they are already doing, and go nowhere fast.

Third, we do not know how much the different meanings the actors found in the KEYS process guided action, as contrasted with simply offering a convenient rhetoric to describe events that were largely driven by other forces. In the case of the Essex School, for example, would the school staff have done more or less the same things had KEYS not showed up? Did this improvement process qualitatively change how the staff went about addressing its needs? We simply can't say.

Fourth, the two cases we explored do not exhaust the range of school and district conditions under which KEYS might be implemented. In one sense, its adaptability should make it fit in a wide variety of local circumstances. Yet, at the same time, the conditions of institutional readiness we have identified would seem to preclude or discourage many schools from using KEYS to full advantage. For example, many schools across the land now lack the autonomy, district support, or leadership qualities that seem associated with the success of a self-reflective process such as the one we have studied. The possibilities we have identified beg to be tested in a larger range of school settings.

These considerations deserve further exploration as more schools consider engaging in self-reflective improvement. The ultimate test of this kind of strategy lies in its power to stimulate new thinking by school staff, under a variety of conditions, about the possibilities for their program, which supports subsequent action to make these possibilities realities. The strategy appears to have some power to do so, under the right kind of conditions. Learning more about its heuristic power and range of application would serve schools well.

REFERENCES

Hatton, N., & Smith, D. (1995). Reflection in teacher education: Towards definition and implementation. *Teaching-and-Teacher-Education, 11*(1), 33–49.

McLaughlin, M. W., & Talbert, J. E. (1993). *Contexts that matter for teaching and learning: Strategic opportunities for meeting the nation's goals.* Stanford, CA: Stanford University: Center for Research on the Context of Secondary School Teaching.

Office of Juvenile Justice. (1998). *Governor's juvenile justice advisory committee 1998 juvenile justice report.* Olympia, WA: Author.

Schneider, J. M., Verdugo, R. R., Uribe, O., Jr., & Greenberg, N. M. (1993). Statistical quality control and school quality. *Contemporary Education, 64*(2), 84–87.

Schon, D. (1983). *The reflective practitioner: How professionals think in action.* New York: Basic Books.

Starbuck, W. H., & Milliken, F. J. (1988). Executive filters: What they notice and how they make sense. In D. C. Hambrick (Ed.), *The executive effect: Concepts and methods for studying top managers* (pp. 35–65). Greenwich, CT: JAI Press.

Weick, K. E. (1995). *Sensemaking in organizations.* Thousand Oaks, CA: Sage.

7

Walter Rumsey Elementary School: Buried Beneath the Churn

Mark A. Smylie

This chapter presents the case of KEYS at Walter Rumsey Elementary School, a K–5 school located in a suburban district outside Chicago, Illinois. Rumsey was one of the first schools in the state to participate in KEYS. When it took on the NEA initiative in spring 1995, Rumsey was experiencing dramatic changes in its student population. The faculty and administration were uncertain and anxious about the future. Some had begun to question the adequacy of the school's curricular and instructional programs and its staffing to meet the changing needs of the school's changing student population. Rifts were developing among groups of teachers and in some quarters, the relationship between teachers and the school's principal was strained. The school was having some difficulty developing a new participatory leadership and decision-making team. Rumsey's administration and local teachers association saw KEYS as a way to help the school understand and address these challenges. The faculty completed the KEYS survey and the data were returned to the school and presented to the faculty. But the findings were never engaged and KEYS vanished from the school without a trace.

At Rumsey, KEYS fell victim to a convergence, a churn of internal and external factors that undermined its implementation and led to its failure. In order to understand the initiative's failure at Rumsey, it is important to understand the organizational context into which KEYS was introduced and to examine external factors that affected KEYS at the school. By design, KEYS depends on a long, loose-linked system of supports that extends from the NEA and the state association to the school level. In this case, external elements of this support system were not well developed. Coupled with strains and tensions inside the school, weaknesses in this support system contributed to KEYS' failure at Rumsey.

Even though it was a failure, the story of KEYS at Rumsey is worth telling. The story is instructive because it points to several structural and logistical issues with KEYS that might compromise its implementation and effectiveness at the school level. The story is also instructive because it identifies stress points and potential areas of breakdown in a system of supports that is crucial for KEYS' success. Finally, this story is instructive because it draws attention to the critical role that local context and the organizational capacity of schools play in the implementation of innovation generally and KEYS implementation in particular. There is some irony in this story. On one hand, Rumsey was a perfect candidate for the NEA initiative. It faced important organizational challenges that KEYS is designed to illuminate and lead staff to action. On the other hand, the very organizational strains that made Rumsey a strong candidate for the initiative contributed substantially to KEYS' undoing.

This chapter begins with a description and analysis of the story of KEYS at Rumsey, followed by a discussion of implications raised by this case. The chapter ends with a postscript that updates briefly KEYS activity in Illinois after Rumsey ceased to participate in KEYS and points to ongoing issues surrounding the support and implementation of KEYS in this state.

RUMSEY ELEMENTARY SCHOOL

Rumsey Elementary School is located in Illinois District 555, a community consolidated school district located in the northwest suburban corridor of metropolitan Chicago. District 555 consists of ten elementary schools and three junior high schools. It enrolls students in pre-kindergarten and kindergarten programs through the 8th grade. The district employs about 725 people, including about 470 certified personnel. During the past ten years, the size of the district's teaching faculty has grown steadily from about 360 full time equivalent (FTE) teachers in 1991–92 to 410 FTE teachers in 1998–99. Growing numbers of teachers in the district hold graduate degrees. Between 1991 and 1998, the proportion of teachers with master's degrees rose from 59 to 68 percent. While the faculty has become somewhat more racially and ethnically diverse, it remains about 90 percent white. The average years of teaching experience among the district's faculty is about sixteen years.

COMMUNITY CONTEXT

District 555 serves portions of four contiguous townships and covers twenty-four square miles of rapidly growing, highly developed industrial, commercial, and residential areas. The commercial and industrial base of the district is remarkably diverse with several multi-acre office and industrial parks. The district is home to corporate offices of Fortune 500 companies and high-tech research firms. A large number of light and heavy manufacturing companies, warehouses, and distribution centers are located there. District 555 also includes a substantial number of hotels, corporate meeting facilities, hospitals, and community colleges.

During the past thirty years, the general population of the area has grown rapidly. In some neighborhoods, the population is expected to rise by almost 20 percent during the next fifteen years. At the same time that it has grown, the general population has become more racially, ethnically, and socio-economically diverse. As might be expected from the diversity of its commercial and industrial base, the area's workforce has diversified and is distributed somewhat evenly among professional and managerial jobs; sales jobs; and service, production, and laborer jobs. The area supports a wide range of housing, from low- to moderate-priced single-family and multi-family dwellings, to rental properties, to estate homes. In some parts of District 555, more than 30 percent of the population lives in rental property.

Rumsey Elementary School serves a primarily residential community in the north central part of the school district. The community has a wide variety of housing, including a substantial number of low- to moderately-priced single- and multi-family homes and rental properties. This residential community is surrounded by commercial strips and on one side is one of the largest industrial and warehouse complexes in the area. Unlike other school attendance areas in the school district, Rumsey's community has experienced substantial in-migration of low-income Latino families seeking work in the area. According to school officials, this in-migration has promoted white flight from the community and from the school.

THE "CHURN"

In the years leading up to Rumsey's participation in KEYS, the school experienced accelerating change in its student population and growing instability in its leadership and staff. As shown in Table 7.1, Rumsey's student enrollment shifted from being majority white to predominantly Latino. Between 1991 and 1992 and 1995 and 1996, the year Rumsey completed the KEYS survey, the white proportion of Rumsey's enrollment fell from about 54 percent to 36 percent. During the same period, the Latino proportion of Rumsey's enrollment rose from 30 percent to 52 percent. By the

1996–97 school year, the year Rumsey had expected to begin school improvement planning using KEYS data, the Latino proportion of Rumsey's enrollment rose to 55 percent. Concurrently, the proportion of limited-English-proficient students increased from 24 percent to 53 percent and the proportion of low-income students rose from 15 percent to 49 percent. Annual student mobility rates fluctuated dramatically during this period, rising from 30 percent in 1992 to 1993 to 51 percent in 1994 to 1995 to 29 percent in 1996 to 1997. These mobility rates may explain the instability in Rumsey's total enrollment. As shown in Table 7.1, total enrollment rose from 432 to 461 students between 1991 and 1992 and 1992 and 1993 and then fell by 20 percent to 367 students in 1993 to 1994. Enrollment began to recover the next school year, rising to about 400 students in both 1995 to 1996 and 1996 to 1997.

As shown in Table 7.1, these demographic changes at Rumsey were substantially greater than demographic changes in District 555 as a whole. The changes at Rumsey were unique among schools in the district. According to the district administration and local teacher association officials, no other school in the district was experiencing such dramatic demographic changes.

At the same time, Rumsey's students' performance on state-mandated standardized tests seemed to indicate that the school was able to sustain reasonably high levels of student achievement, albeit at or somewhat below district average. In some subjects, it appeared that achievement was improving. Annual schoolwide average student performance indicators on the Illinois Goal Assessment Program (IGAP) tests are presented in Table 7.2, which shows the proportions of students who met or exceeded state goals on these tests. In 3rd grade reading, for example, the school scored below the district average until 1995–96 when the reading scores began to exceed that average. The same pattern of improvement is apparent for 3rd grade math and writing, although the school scored below the district average in 4th grade science and social studies as often as it met or exceeded this average.

These performance indicators seem higher than expected for a school experiencing such dramatic demographic changes. It is important to note that as Rumsey's performance on IGAP tests held their own and even improved, the proportion of students taking these tests declined from 71 to 59 percent (see Table 7.2). Illinois law permits local exemption of bilingual and special education students from state testing. This decline mirrors in large part the increase in the proportion of limited-English-proficient students enrolled at Rumsey. On the surface, these data suggest that Rumsey was doing relatively well academically; however, these data probably underestimate schoolwide achievement and mask declines that might have been associated with the substantial increases in low-income and limited-English-proficient students at the school.

In addition to the dramatic demographic changes in its student population, Rumsey was beginning to experience a number of organizational

TABLE 7.1   School and District Demographic Characteristics, 1991–1996

	Enrollment	% White	% African American	% Latino	% Asian American	% Limited English Proficient	% Low Income	Mobility Rate
School								
1991–92	432	53.5	5.3	30.3	10.9	24.3	14.6	NA
1992–93	461	50.3	4.8	35.4	9.3	26.2	17.4	30.3
1993–94	367	43.6	7.4	41.7	7.4	26.7	31.3	37.4
1994–95	385	35.1	9.1	49.9	6.0	42.1	30.4	51.0
1995–96	409	36.2	8.6	51.6	3.7	44.3	46.7	44.8
1996–97	393	33.6	7.1	55.2	4.1	52.7	48.9	29.1
District								
1991–92	5,770	74.8	2.3	11.3	11.5	8.0	4.7	NA
1992–93	5,878	73.6	2.8	12.1	11.3	8.0	5.8	15.3
1993–94	6,156	70.6	3.5	13.9	11.7	9.6	7.3	19.0
1994–95	6,276	67.6	4.0	15.8	12.4	13.4	15.4	22.1
1995–96	6,354	66.5	3.7	17.0	12.6	16.5	17.1	22.9
1996–97	6,495	66.6	3.5	17.2	12.5	17.8	19.4	19.4

Note: These data are from the Illinois State Board of Education School Report Cards, as compiled by Ed.Dat, Inc. The Illinois State Board of Education defines these demographic characteristics as follows. Enrollment is for last day of September. Percent low income includes students from families receiving public aid and/or are eligible for the federal free or reduced-priced lunch program. Percent limited-English-proficient students are students eligible for bilingual education. The mobility rate is an indicator of enrollment turnover and is the sum of students transferring out and in of the district and school divided by the average daily attendance. NA = data not available.

TABLE 7.2   School and District-Level Percentages of 3rd and 4th Grade Students Who Met or Exceeded Goals on the Illinois Goal Assessment Program Tests, 1993–1997

	Average % of students tested	3rd Grade			4th Grade	
		Reading	Math	Writing	Science	Social Studies
School						
1992–93	71	71	89	90	90	92
1993–94	76	64	93	100	97	76
1994–95	60	84	98	97	89	90
1995–96	60	93	100	100	98	93
1996–97	59	94	100	95	88	80
District						
1992–93	88	88	98	95	96	94
1993–94	86	89	98	98	97	92
1994–95	83	91	98	98	96	96
1995–96	81	91	98	98	98	96
1996–97	80	89	99	97	96	93

Note: These data are from the Illinois State Board of Education School Report Cards, as compiled by Ed.Dat, Inc. Tests are administered in the spring of each school year. Percentage of students tested is an approximate average across 3rd and 4th grade and across different sections of the test. State law permits exemption of bilingual and special education from testing. Third grade students are administered tests in reading, mathematics, and writing. Fourth grade students are administered tests in science and social studies.

stresses. In 1994, District 555 hired Dr. Wagner Dodge as Rumsey's new principal. Dodge was described as a "child-centered principal." At the same time, he was described as lacking vision and creativity. Several informants were critical of his "people skills" and characterized him as a heavy-handed administrator who was inclined to "consolidate power." Soon after Dodge became principal, the superintendent began to encourage all schools in the district to develop more participatory leadership and decision-making processes. Given the characteristics of Dodge's leadership, it is not surprising that Rumsey had difficulty developing its participatory school leadership team. It is also not surprising that some staff began to perceive a developing "culture of distrust" at the school. Several informants described the growth of a "political division between the faculty and the principal." They also pointed to divisions developing between the school's regular classroom teachers and its bilingual teachers. According to Billie Hellman, the school's assistant principal, increased attention by the district and by the community to standardized test scores "put added pressure on the school."

There is little doubt that the rapidly changing demographic characteristics of Rumsey's students contributed to these organizational stresses. There was a growing sense among district and school administrators and among some teachers of the need for new curricular and instructional programs, increased attention to bilingual education, and reexamination of staffing needs at the school. According to Hellman, a number of teachers had difficulty understanding the implications of the demographic changes that were occurring at Rumsey. Some were "in denial." They were proud of the instructional program at the school and saw no problem with it. Others were "stuck" in their thinking. Hellman spoke of teachers who wondered "why the kids aren't the way they are supposed to be." As demographic changes at Rumsey accelerated, uncertainty and anxiety increased among the faculty, not just with respect to how to think about and work with a new student population but also with respect to staff organization and job security. "There was lots of uncertainty and clinging to the past," Hellman said, "and, a sense that teachers really didn't know what to do." Organizational psychologist Karl Weick (1993) calls this "vu deja" where a person feels "I've never been here before, I have no idea where I am, and I have no idea who can help me" (pp. 633–634). Predictably, teacher turnover at Rumsey had begun to increase.

In summary, Rumsey had become a school undergoing rapid change and coming under increased organizational stress. Hellman described Rumsey as "a school running scared." Rod Norum, the university consultant who came to work with Rumsey, characterized the school as "mired in rapid change." The student population, the school's leadership, and the faculty all were in a "state of churn." It was into this context that KEYS was introduced.

KEYS COMES TO ILLINOIS

In 1995, Illinois became one of the first states to become involved with KEYS. The state teachers association appointed Robert Jansson its state KEYS coordinator. Jansson was an IEA regional representative to Chicago suburban school systems. That year, Jansson and two other association staff members, Henry Hersey and Helen Lewis, received KEYS training from NEA.

KEYS was first introduced to Illinois school systems in autumn 1995 through the Network for School Improvement (NSI), a confederation of several dozen Chicago suburban school districts. Jansson formed the Network in the late 1980s with several area superintendents and local association presidents to support member districts in efforts to improve their schools. NSI provided professional development opportunities for district leadership. It was a conduit through which new ideas, research findings, and innovative programs could be brought to these systems. It was a forum to promote exchange and collaboration among school districts and to link districts with external expertise and technical assistance. Finally, it was a means to encourage collaboration between school administrative leadership and leadership of local teacher associations in working for school improvement.

From the beginning, Jansson and his state association colleagues saw KEYS as a "potentially useful diagnostic tool" that schools could use for self-assessment. They offered it to schools as "one of many" self-study instruments. Participation in KEYS was completely voluntary. Districts and schools were encouraged to assess KEYS' usefulness, and according to Jansson, "use it only as they perceived it to be helpful."

Jansson and his colleagues did not consider KEYS as a program of school improvement. For KEYS to work well as a diagnostic tool at the school level, it had to be connected to a program for school improvement. It had to be given a context, an infrastructure, to support the interpretation and use of KEYS data for planning and decision making. Thus, KEYS was presented to Network member districts as part of a thirty-hour leadership development program that emphasized participatory leadership and decision making, two important areas of KEYS indicators. Jansson and his colleagues believed that this leadership development program would provide the vehicle needed for KEYS to be used effectively. In their view, linking KEYS with this leadership development program had several advantages. Districts participating in the Network for School Improvement were familiar and generally happy with this program. Associating KEYS with this program might help schools accept and use KEYS. In addition, tying KEYS to this program might help develop a school's capacity for leadership that was necessary for effective improvement planning and implementation.

KEYS AT RUMSEY

KEYS was introduced to District 555 through the Network's leadership development program. It was presented as an opportunity for schools to gather useful information about themselves, identify strengths and weaknesses, and suggest directions for improvement. Rumsey was one of the district's schools participating in the leadership development program. Robert Jansson considered Rumsey a good candidate for KEYS. He saw KEYS as a resource that might provide Rumsey a comprehensive, data-based diagnosis of the challenges it faced. Jansson reasoned that because it could provide a broad base of internally generated information and because its components had been validated externally, KEYS might be more readily accepted by Rumsey's faculty and administration. The superintendent concurred and encouraged Rumsey to participate. Leadership of the local teachers association also expressed commitment and hope for KEYS.

Rumsey's administration saw KEYS as an opportunity for getting information to "understand what's going on in this changing school." According to Billie Hellman, Rumsey's assistant principal, the administration "hoped that KEYS would reveal options for moving forward and addressing changes." Rumsey had been an NEA Learning Lab School. The administration hoped that KEYS would provide a similarly positive experience for the school. Rumsey's principal, Wagner Dodge, introduced KEYS to his faculty as an opportunity and as a resource. The faculty agreed to participate and some teachers were quite enthusiastic about it. Hellman observed, however, that serious doubt existed among some members of the faculty as to whether KEYS would be much help at all.

In spring 1995, Rumsey's faculty completed the KEYS survey. The following autumn, the local teachers association sponsored a KEYS "kick-off" at Rumsey. According to the district's UniServ director, Earlene Cooley, "everyone was there," including the building administration, the faculty, and leadership from the local association. The local association passed out KEYS tee-shirts. There was a KEYS cake. This event was meant to generate excitement and set the stage for a subsequent meeting where Rumsey's survey findings would be presented to and discussed by the faculty.

Rumsey's data became available from NEA early in the fall, but this meeting did not take place until January 1996, some five months after the kick-off. Cooley explained the delay, "It was hard to coordinate everybody's schedules." The January meeting was attended by the school administration and leadership team; the faculty; the UniServ director; and a KEYS trainer, Henry Hersey, from the state teachers association. Hersey presented the school's results, which revealed several problem areas in leadership, open communication and problem solving, and teachers' working relationships. A follow-up meeting was scheduled before this meeting adjourned. Shortly thereafter, Dodge cancelled that follow-up meeting. In the spring, Cooley asked Dodge when this follow-up meeting might be rescheduled. According to Cooley, Dodge replied that it was too late in the year to hold the meeting and that it would have to wait until the next school year.

During the following summer, Cooley met with an NEA representative to discuss how to get KEYS on track when school reopened in the fall. Their joint conclusion was that KEYS had little support from the principal, and for that reason they should "let it go." As a result, no follow-up meeting occurred. According to Hellman, "The results were never engaged and KEYS died before it ever got off the ground."

One year later, the superintendent brought Rod Norum into the district and offered his consulting services to all of the district's schools. Norum had been working with Jansson to incorporate KEYS into the Network's leadership development program. Rumsey asked for Norum's assistance. Norum reported that when he arrived at Rumsey "there was no trace of KEYS." During the course of a school year, he heard no one speak of KEYS. Indeed, two years after KEYS was introduced at Rumsey, Cooley observed that "KEYS is nowhere in this district."

WHAT HAPPENED TO KEYS AT RUMSEY?

It is easy to place full responsibility for the failure of KEYS at Rumsey on Wagner Dodge. Clearly, Dodge played a crucial role in KEYS' demise. Several informants speculated that Dodge stopped the process because he personalized the survey results. Offered one informant, "He thought the data were all about him." Another informant suggested that Dodge had come to think of KEYS not as a tool for self-assessment and improvement but as a potential weapon against him. This concern may have been heightened by the local teachers association's initial enthusiasm about KEYS and the developing tension between Dodge and members of his faculty. Others who were interviewed for this study thought that Dodge was not threatened by the findings so much as he really didn't know what to make of them or know what to do with them. One informant suggested that making sense of the data and moving from data to action might have been made more complicated for Dodge because "he did not have a very clear sense of where the school should be going" or "what the school should be doing to address the changes it was experiencing."

Whatever the explanation for his actions, the reasons for KEYS' lack of success are more complicated than Dodge's failure to move the process forward. The informants interviewed for this study revealed that KEYS faced a convergence of factors that seriously challenged its success. These factors fall into three categories: (1) structural and logistical problems with KEYS; (2) lack of external support and imperative; and (3) weaknesses in Rumsey's capacity to use KEYS effectively.

Structural and Logistical Problems

KEYS faced several structural and logistical problems. The first problem was timing. As the earlier description of events at Rumsey show, the KEYS surveys were administered in spring 1995, but the data were not returned to the school until the next fall. The KEYS data were not presented to the faculty until January 1996, some eight months after the survey was completed. Then, there was no follow-up. Several informants observed that early enthusiasm for KEYS dissipated during this period. Henry Hersey, the state association KEYS trainer who presented Rumsey's data to the faculty, observed, "This was deadly. A lot of initial momentum was lost."

A second problem had to do with the way in which KEYS data were presented to schools. The problem lay with the data displays. Both Hersey and Norum observed that the data were not delivered in a useful format and this lead to problems reading and understanding the data. Hersey explained it this way: "The graphs can be overwhelming. It's difficult to get people to understand them. They place a heavy burden on local leadership from the UniServ director to explain them. If local folks can't do that, you've got trouble." (The role of the UniServ director will be examined later.) In this case, Hersey presented the data to Rumsey's faculty. Even though he was among those receiving KEYS training from NEA and among the best prepared association staff members to work with schools on KEYS, several informants indicated that Hersey's presentation to Rumsey's faculty did not go particularly well. Norum recounted that a number of teachers came away from the meeting confused about the data and what they meant.

This points to another structural problem. KEYS is not designed to suggest what schools should do to improve, but rather to identify areas of strength and weakness and thereby possible targets for improvement efforts. The KEYS survey does not provide answers or a *guide to action*. As Hellman observed, "Data are data. The crucial question is `what do you do with them?'" According to Norum, "Rumsey didn't know what to do with the data." The KEYS process depends on technical support from UniServ directors and state trainers not only to help schools understand their data but also to engage school personnel with the data and get "to action." Where that support is strong, KEYS is more likely to succeed; where it is weak, problems are likely to occur. As indicated earlier and as discussed in more detail subsequently, this support system at Rumsey had weaknesses that may have led some teachers and the school's administration to question KEYS' value and usefulness.

Finally, KEYS faced an important problem of relevance. Several informants identified a "misalignment" and "lack of coherence" between KEYS indicators and Rumsey's most immediate and pressing problems. Several KEYS indicators were relevant to organizational stresses at Rumsey. Cooley observed that most teachers thought that the KEYS findings "got right" Rumsey's organizational problems. Nevertheless, Norum pointed out, "The KEYS data didn't deal with the most important problems at Rumsey at the time." As Hellman observed, "One problem was that KEYS didn't connect to learners, to our local [curricular and instructional] problems and needs. KEYS did not help this faculty think differently about the future of working with a different student population." It is not unreasonable to think that KEYS might have been given low priority if it addressed matters that some would see as not problematic (e.g., Dodge's view of his own leadership) but neglected issues that most thought were problematic (e.g., how to meet the curricular and instructional challenges posed by a rapidly changing student population). This issue of relevance contributed to some teachers' initial skepticism about whether KEYS would help Rumsey. It related directly to one informant's observation that dropping KEYS was "no great loss" for the school.

Lack of External Support and Imperative

As noted earlier, KEYS success depends on a long and somewhat loose-linked system of supports that extends from NEA, to the state association, to the UniServ director, to the local association, to the school district, and finally to the individual school. Where that system of support is strong, KEYS is more likely to succeed at the local level. Where that system is weak, KEYS will likely run into trouble. According to Robert Jansson, "The district lacked both internal and external support for KEYS," and this contributed to its failure at Rumsey.

Several weaknesses in this support system are evident in this case. First, the district superintendent realized that Rumsey was experiencing problems. He recognized that Rumsey was having difficulty adjusting to its demographic changes and developing teamwork and participative leadership. He thought that KEYS might prove a useful resource for Rumsey and lent his support to KEYS implementation there. Most of the people interviewed for this study observed, however, that the superintendent did little more to support KEYS than "make the introduction." There was "no sense that the superintendent worked actively to support KEYS at Rumsey." Norum recalled that at the time Rumsey "needed a lot of attention [from central office] but didn't get it." Even though the district and Rumsey were among the first in the state to participate in KEYS, there was little support or imperative "from the top" to make KEYS succeed. In this context, there was not only no expectation or support from the central office for KEYS to succeed at Rumsey; there was no accountability to the central office for failing to move the initiative forward.

Second, there were weaknesses in support and imperative from the state teachers association and regional school improvement network. Hersey reported that the state association liked KEYS and expressed commitment to it. At the same time, Hersey had "no substantive support" from the association. Hersey, who bore primary responsibility for getting Rumsey started in KEYS, observed that the association did not give KEYS a very high profile. It did not "buy-in" to KEYS as much as Hersey thought was necessary to provide adequate support. Part of the problem was that the association staff already had "lots on their plates" when they brought KEYS to Illinois. KEYS was "an add-on." As a result, Hersey and other association staffers found it difficult to give KEYS the priority and attention they thought it deserved.

Another issue concerned the regional school improvement network and the packaging of KEYS within its leadership development program. Rumsey was one of the first schools in Illinois to participate in KEYS, and Jansson wanted to see it work. Packaging KEYS within this leadership development program created a potential benefit and a potential problem. While the leadership development program may have provided a necessary context and delivery mechanism for KEYS, its being subsumed within this program created the potential for it to be "forgotten" or "lost" within this broader context. The leadership program could have functioned effectively without KEYS, and it has in other schools and school districts. Furthermore, KEYS was presented to schools and districts as "one of many" diagnostic tools that schools might use voluntarily. All this probably compromised developing a sense of priority or imperative for KEYS "from the top" on the association side.

Third, the local teachers association seemed committed to KEYS, worked actively to give the initiative a good start at Rumsey, and did most of the initial work to get KEYS underway. At the same time, the local association failed to involve the district's UniServ director until the January 1996 presentation of KEYS data to Rumsey's faculty. The UniServ director is the primary link between the school and the state association. In addition, the UniServ director is, or is supposed to be, the primary source of assistance to help schools interpret their KEYS data and put those data "into play" through planning and implementing school improvement activities. Across all aspects of their work, UniServ dirctors' ability to get close to a district and school is influenced by the relationship between the director and the local association president. In this case, the UniServ director and the local association president had had "an off-and-on-again relationship." According to Jansson, "Cooley was not used well in the district by the association president." She had been "kept in limited capacity" by the association president during bargaining some years earlier. Both Jansson and Norum observed "tension" and "strain" between the association president and the UniServ director at the time KEYS was introduced to the district and to Rumsey. Jansson observed that Cooley "never quite hit it off with the superintendent, either." These dynamics might have contributed to Cooley's late involvement in KEYS at Rumsey and may have compromised the support she could have given the process.

But even if she was involved earlier, Cooley acknowledged that she was not prepared adequately to support KEYS at Rumsey. She never received formal KEYS training. She said that she learned KEYS "on the job" from watching Hersey work at Rumsey. It is doubtful, given other obstacles at the school, that Cooley could have provided the substantive and procedural assistance required to help Rumsey continue with KEYS.

Weaknesses in School Capacity

As discussed throughout this case, Rumsey was experiencing organizational problems that made it a good candidate for KEYS. At the same time, these problems revealed weaknesses in the school's capacity to use the initiative effectively, which contributed to KEYS' undoing.

One crucial weakness in Rumsey's capacity to use KEYS effectively was leadership. Cooley and Norum identified lack of strong school leadership as one of the most important factors that led to KEYS' failure. Both cited Dodge's tendency to consolidate power, his difficulty working collaboratively with teachers, and the growing tension between Dodge and a number of teachers on his faculty. Both agreed that Dodge was well intended but simply failed to give KEYS the priority that was needed to make it work. There were also weaknesses in teacher leadership. Norum observed that while Rumsey's fledgling school leadership team was hard-working and well meaning, "it couldn't stick to a subject and had trouble making decisions." He further described the team as "flighty and distracted." In general, then, Rumsey lacked a critical mass of leadership "on the inside" that could have advocated for KEYS, given it priority, and worked strategically to "make it happen."

Another weakness in school capacity concerned lack of a productive mind-set concerning the use of data for self-assessment and school improvement. While a number of teachers agreed with Rumsey's KEYS results, Hellman observed that few people at the school "saw the value of using data" for informing work and making specific decisions. Indeed, Hellman pointed to a tendency toward "data aversion" at Rumsey. Some teachers resisted the use of data for decision making. In Hellman's view, this resistance was grounded in a lack of understanding of how data might be helpful to planning and decision as well as in a concern that data might threaten them and be used against them.

This observation points to a third important weakness in Rumsey's capacity to implement KEYS effectively. Under most circumstances, engaging in public self-assessment is risky business. It has the potential to expose problems and weaknesses that can be painful and potentially risky to individuals and groups. A strong sense of social trust is needed among all participants to identify problems, explore alternative solutions, and risk failure along the way to success. Social trust concerns confidence in the reliability and integrity of individuals and social relations (see Smylie & Hart, 1999). According to the late sociologist James Coleman (1988), social trust is the cornerstone of reciprocal action, mutual assistance and accountability, and collective activity. Sociologists Anthony Bryk and Barbara Schneider (1996) associate social trust with the predisposition toward cooperation and confidence that individuals have in one another, in leadership, and in the group as a whole. They argue that social trust is necessary to create a context of predictability, stability, assurance, and "safe ground" that can support genuine public conversation and critique, examination of taken-for-granted assumptions, and risk-taking when individuals and the organization are confronted with the need to make change (see also Evans, 1996).

At Rumsey, this sense of social trust may not have been strong enough to support KEYS, at least for very long. At the time that KEYS was introduced, there was a growing sense of distrust in the school. Political divisions were developing between the principal and some groups of teachers. Tension was growing between regular classroom teachers and bilingual teachers. There was a growing sense of uncertainty within the faculty about what the changing demographics of the school might mean for their jobs.

Any of these conditions might have weakened the social trust necessary for KEYS to succeed at Rumsey. Many of the informants interviewed for this study suggested that a "fear of findings" existed among some teachers. It was certainly possible, thought Norum, for "some conspiracy-minded teachers to have seen KEYS as an evaluative weapon rather than as a tool for school improvement." This perspective could reasonably have been held by teachers who viewed the principal as heavy handed and resistant to sharing power. At the same time, Dodge may have been affected by a sense of distrust. While Hellman reported that Dodge did not really see KEYS as a threat, both Cooley and Hersey thought otherwise. They reasoned that Dodge would have been aware of growing tension with some members of his faculty. And, along with his faculty, he would have experienced the uncertainty associated with the rapid changes taking place at Rumsey. He would certainly have realized that he bore primary responsibility for the success of his school and bad KEYS data might reflect poorly on him. Cooley and Hersey also observed that Dodge would have realized that, even though it was introduced through the regional school improvement network—a collaborative organization—KEYS was a union-driven initiative and was strongly supported by the local teachers association. At a time of high stress for his school and growing tension within his faculty, it was certainly reasonable for him to think that bad findings could be used against him by his own teachers or the local association.

SUMMARY AND IMPLICATIONS

While Dodge may have played an instrumental role in KEYS failure at Rumsey, KEYS faced a convergence of factors that compromised its success. Several structural and logistical problems undermined the initiative at Rumsey, including bad timing, difficult-to-understand presentation of data, and apparent irrelevance of KEYS indicators to some of the school's most important problems and needs. The long-linked system of supports needed for KEYS to succeed had crucial weaknesses that hurt the initiative's implementation in the school. KEYS did not receive strong external support or imperative from the central office, the UniServ director, the regional school improvement board, or the state teachers association. Finally, Rumsey lacked important organizational capacities to support KEYS internally. School leadership was weak overall. The school was not prepared to understand and appreciate the value of data in self-assessment, planning, and decision making. Levels of social trust at Rumsey may have been inadequate to diminish the risks associated with self-assessment and improvement. Rod Norum summed up this case well when he described the school as "mired in rapid change." "Probably nothing would have worked at Rumsey," he concluded. "KEYS got buried under the churn."

Rumsey's story raises several important implications for KEYS implementation and effectiveness. First, this case points to the importance of preparing schools adequately to participate in the KEYS process. It cannot be assumed that if a school expresses interest in participation that it is ready for this kind of initiative or that it has the internal organizational capacity to support it. This applies to the disposition the school holds concerning the use and value of data, school-level administrative and teacher leadership, and social trust. This case highlights the importance of associating KEYS with a vehicle that can support its implementation through the development of school capacity, particularly leadership.

Second, the KEYS process, including its indicators, must be perceived as useful and relevant to local school needs and interests.

Third, the KEYS process must pay particular attention to timing and to maintaining momentum. Seymour Sarason (1972) observed that a crucial issue in implementing innovations is not only the adequacy of financial resources, but also the availability of time and energy to support change. Equally important is his observation that sustaining the active participation of teachers is fundamental to change (Sarason, 1996). Sustaining attention to a particular initiative is difficult given complex, changing contexts of schooling. As the Rumsey case illustrates, the longer it takes to get from completing the survey to presenting the data, and to engaging the school with its data in school improvement planning, the greater the likelihood that initial enthusiasm will diminish and that important issues will emerge that will draw attention away from KEYS.

Finally, this case points to the importance of developing a strong, coordinated system of external political and technical support for KEYS. As the case of Rumsey illustrates, this system is as strong as its weakest link. The whole system needs to be developed to function properly and to provide the support necessary for KEYS to succeed at the local level.

POSTSCRIPT

This case focused on one of the first schools in Illinois to participate in the KEYS process. Since the initiative was introduced in Illinois in 1995, more than two dozen schools in nine school districts have completed KEYS surveys. Several of these schools have used their KEYS data in school improvement planning. One school has readministered the KEYS survey to assess its progress. Most of the schools now active in KEYS entered the process in 1998 and 1999, when the regional School Improvement Network began to give KEYS a more prominent place in its leadership development program. A new training manual, revised by Rod Norum, contains a specific recommendation for schools to use KEYS. While the initiative has made substantial progress in Illinois in recent years, a number of the issues revealed in the Rumsey case are still present and remain to be addressed.

According to Henry Hersey, KEYS has still not attained a very high profile in Illinois. There has been little effort to promote more widespread participation in the initiative. The primary way that schools and school districts learn about it is through the regional network and summer leadership training. Beyond that, observed Hersey, "it's serendipity." Hersey reported that there is not as much "buy-in" from the state association as there was when KEYS first came to Illinois. The association continues to express support for KEYS and wants to promote it, but has not developed a sense of priority or imperative for KEYS. Hersey also indicated that no one within the association's top leadership has assumed personal responsibility for KEYS. Instead, KEYS has been left to Jansson, Hersey, and his fellow trainers. And, it is not clear to Hersey where KEYS sits with respect to the association's programs and priorities.

The overall system of supports for KEYS implementation has developed little during the past few years. In February 1997, two state association trainers provided KEYS training to twenty UniServ directors. Little follow-up support has been provided to these UniServ directors after their initial training. Since this session, no more KEYS training has been provided for UniServ directors or association staff. KEYS trainers are of the strong opinion that more training is needed. In addition, when KEYS first came to Illinois, neither NEA nor the state association involved staff from the instruction and professional development divisions of the state association. According to one association trainer, these staff members were offended that they were not involved from the beginning. As a result they have given KEYS little support. This trainer argued that their lack of involvement became a crucial "missing piece" of the system to support KEYS implementation at the local level. Little has been done to incorporate these staff members. Finally, little has been done to "make more room" for KEYS in the work roles of association trainers and UniServ directors. Said one KEYS trainer, "KEYS still comes on top of lots of other work. It's hard to give KEYS the attention, the priority it deserves."

The fact that other schools in Illinois have taken on KEYS and have apparently made greater use of it than Rumsey suggests that the continuing issues in the state and regional support infrastructure have not doomed the initiative. Nonetheless, these issues pose a challenge for the future of KEYS in Illinois, and raise questions about whether this kind of self-reflective improvement process will achieve its full potential in the state.

REFERENCES

Bryk, A. S., & Schneider, B. (1996, June). *Social trust: A moral resource for school improvement*. Chicago: University of Chicago.

Coleman, J. S. (1988). Social capital in the creation of human capital. *American Journal of Sociology, 94*, S95-S120.

Evans, R. (1996). *The human side of change: Reform, resistance, and the real-life problems of innovation.* San Francisco: Jossey-Bass.

Sarason, S. B. (1972). *The culture of the school and the problem of change* (2nd ed.). Boston: Allyn & Bacon.

————. (1996). *Revisiting "The culture of the school and the problem of change."* New York: Teachers College Press.

Smylie, M. A., & Hart, A. W. (1999). School leadership for teacher learning and change: A human and social capital development perspective. In J. Murphy & K. S. Louis (Eds.), *Handbook of research on educational administration,* 2nd ed. (pp. 421–441). San Francisco: Jossey-Bass.

Weick, Karl E. (1993). The collapse of sensemaking in organizations: The Mann Gulch disaster. *Administrative Science Quarterly, 38,* 628–652.

8

The KEYS Case Study in Mississippi: A Failed "Graft" of One School Reform onto Another

Charles Teddlie

Multiple school reform initiatives that compete for the attention of schools or districts are a common challenge. The school portrayed in this chapter represents one way that schools may choose among many alternatives and what might happen when multiple initiatives are merged. In this case, an appropriate metaphor is that of a failed *graft* of one school reform (KEYS) onto an existing school reform (*Onward to Excellence*, or OTE). Hamilton Consolidated Elementary School, the pseudonym for this case study site, had been involved in the OTE school improvement initiative before KEYS was introduced, and the school committee that was responsible for the combined reform activity was subsequently renamed the OTE/KEYS committee.

The Mississippi KEYS case study may be called a "cautionary tale" because the "grafted reform" has failed to achieve many of its goals, as will be described throughout this case study. There are multiple reasons for this failure, including the following:

1. The "grafting" of KEYS onto OTE was largely unsuccessful because there was inadequate external and internal support for either initiative.
2. The faculty at Hamilton Consolidated Elementary School was not adequately prepared for undertaking a school improvement process, primarily due to the local educational and social culture.
3. The OTE/KEYS committee developed a list of goals too numerous to accomplish successfully.

4. There was inadequate support for the OTE/KEYS Initiative from the teachers' association, from the local UniServ representative to the state office.

5. There was inadequate support for the OTE/KEYS Initiative from all levels of the Mississippi educational bureaucracy, from the principal to the local education agency to the state educational agency.

6. The KEYS delivery system for Hamilton was too loosely coupled to work; that is, the reform activities were never adequately tied to human and material resources outside the school that could have enhanced their chance for success.

This chapter will detail the development of the OTE/KEYS school improvement initiative. Most of the chapter will consider reasons for the program's failures. On the other hand, there were some successful aspects of the initiative: the empowerment of a small group of teachers in a school in which faculty governance had historically been nonexistent; the successful development of a school improvement plan by the faculty; and the successful accomplishment of some of the goals of the plan. These positive results of the OTE/KEYS Initiative will also be analyzed.

CONTEXT AND HISTORY OF THE HAMILTON CONSOLIDATED ELEMENTARY SCHOOL CASE STUDY

Hamilton Consolidated Elementary School is a large, urban, middle-class school in the "deep South," an area of the United States that is considered to be the most typically "southern" and the most conservative. The faculty is large (thirty-four regular education teachers plus more than forty other staff) and is segregated to a great degree by grade level. Since there are only four grades, some have as many as nine or ten teachers, which constitutes a rather large subgroup of the entire faculty. The faculty was stable, with an average tenure at Hamilton of over nine years.

During the course of the case study (1996–2000), the student body was primarily middle-class, with over 60 percent white students, 33 percent African American students, and 5 percent other ethnic groups. Class sizes were near the state maximum of 27:1 for elementary schools.

Achievement was average to below average on the state administered norm-referenced tests. For example, in the fall 1997 administration of the Iowa Test of Basic Skills (ITBS), the Grade 2 NCE Total Battery score was at the 42nd percentile, while the Grade 3 NCE Total Battery score was at the 53rd percentile. Additionally, the district within which Hamilton resides (Hamilton County School District) habitually ranks "3" on a five-point state accreditation scale, indicating average performance from a population area with certain economic advantages.

Given the middle-SES student profile of the school, one might have expected somewhat higher achievement scores at Hamilton. Nevertheless, since the scores are about average, there has been no cause for alarm among the majority of the teachers and parents associated with the school. Stoll and Fink (1997) have referred to institutions such as Hamilton as "cruising schools."

As for school leadership, there were two principals during the Hamilton case study, neither of which was enthusiastic about the OTE/KEYS Initiative. The first principal, Ms. McEnroe (all names are pseudonyms), refused to disseminate the results of the KEYS survey to the faculty. The second principal, Ms. Ruttles, seemed more sympathetic to the OTE/KEYS goals initially, but never actively supported their accomplishment. The district superintendent was popularly elected and seemed acutely aware of the importance of district political forces.

The Mississippi Association of Educators is one of the weaker state affiliates of the NEA as there is no collective bargaining in Mississippi. To further complicate matters, there was a split between the professional staff (led initially by the Executive Secretary) and the traditional MAE organization. The Executive Secretary bypassed the MAE in setting up the KEYS project at Hamilton, by calling, instead, on industry collaboration for help. This behavior "turned off" the MAE with the result that there was no UniServ involvement at the school during the entirety of the case study.

As for the community, Hamilton is located in a greater metropolitan area of over 200,000 that is growing due to recent business expansion. That expansion has led to an increase in economic activity, population growth, and social problems. Mississippi ranks near the bottom of the states on many educational and socioeconomic indicators.

A history of the OTE/KEYS Initiative at Hamilton must begin with a description of how OTE became a commonplace school reform in the late 1980s and into the 1990s. In 1982, the state legislature passed the Mississippi Education Reform Act, which included a provision requiring that local school districts ensure that their students achieve at high levels (Mullins, 1992). Therefore, this legislative act made local school districts primarily responsible for educational reform in the state rather that the state itself or the individual schools.

Staff members at the Hamilton County School District were the first to identify OTE as a process for implementing improvement in their schools. Initial training for Hamilton County School District staff occurred from 1984 to 1987. Following the lead of the Hamilton County School District, several school districts throughout the state eventually adopted the OTE process. In 1992, the Mississippi Department of Education (MDE) adopted OTE as a generic method for improving the achievement of its lower performing schools. At that time, the MDE also began providing training by OTE cadre members to staff members from interested districts (Kushman & Yap, 1997).

Hamilton became involved in the OTE process in 1993–94. While the state provided the basic OTE training, the local district was responsible for overseeing the reform initiative. The OTE process fosters site-based management and decision making. There is a ten-step process led by a school team composed of teachers and other school community members. The ten steps in the OTE process are getting started, learning about research, making profiles, goal setting, checking use of practice, making prescriptions, making an implementation plan, implementation, monitoring, and renewal (Blum, 1997).

The generic training on OTE for Hamilton staff members occurred in 1994–95. An OTE committee was formed and this group developed a survey to assess the faculty's perceptions regarding the respect that students felt toward one another. An OTE Prescription Document was developed in 1995–96 based partially on the results from this respect survey. The survey results revealed that 36 percent of the faculty members believed that students did not respect one another. The principal (Ms. McEnroe) and others (faculty members, central office staff) were not pleased with the respect survey and the OTE goals that were established from it.

It was around this time that Executive Secretary Andrew Smith from the MAE began promoting KEYS as a process for school assessment in the state. In May 1995, NEA and MAE made a KEYS presentation to the educational power brokers in the state (e.g., the state superintendent, the executive director of the school board, legislative leaders, members of business and industry). NEA and the MAE felt that they needed to seek permission from the educational establishment to bring the KEYS process to the state, due to local culture issues.

Following this introduction to the local educational establishment, KEYS training occurred in Jackson in the summers of 1995 and 1996. Two Hamilton staff members received KEYS training in the summer of 1996, and in April 1997 Smith and the OTE committee administered the KEYS survey to the Hamilton faculty. The KEYS survey became a substitute for the questioned OTE respect survey.

Representatives from the NEA participated in KEYS training in Mississippi. Interviews with these staff members indicated that MAE representatives were not present at one training session, and that UniServ representatives were not present at another training session. Over time it became apparent that there was a schism between the professional staff (represented by the MAE Executive Secretary) and the traditional MAE organization. As indicated previously, Smith bypassed the MAE in setting up the KEYS project at Hamilton, calling instead on industry collaboration (e.g., Mississippi Power and Light) for help.

The situation was further complicated when Smith failed to provide technical assistance to the Hamilton staff other than reporting and interpreting the survey findings. One NEA staff member stated: "Smith did not walk the Hamilton people through the KEYS process." Smith held the opinion that the KEYS Initiative at Hamilton should "sink or swim" on its own.

KEYS survey results were given to the OTE/KEYS committee in July 1997. (At about this point, the OTE committee was renamed the OTE/KEYS committee.) Only about 60 percent of the faculty/staff responded to the KEYS survey. The results were worse than the OTE/KEYS committee and the principal (Ms. McEnroe) had anticipated. Results from the survey indicated that fifteen KEYS indicators were significantly below the take-off point, while the remaining twenty were below the take-off point.

Some of the lowest rated KEYS indicators were in the following areas: (1) parents and school employees are committed to long-range, continuous improvement; (2) central and building administrators are committed to long-range, continuous improvement; (3) teachers, education support personnel, parents, school building administrators, students, school board members, district administrators, and civic groups are all involved in improving education; (4) everyone seeks to identify barriers to learning; (5) there is two-way, non-threatening communication between the school staff and district administrators; (6) academic programs are assessed; and (7) there is ongoing, consistent staff development in the areas of decision making, problem solving, leadership, and communication. These responses indicated that there were problems at the beginning of the OTE/KEYS Initiative in such basic areas as readiness of faculty and staff to be involved in meaningful school change, communication with district level staff, utilization of available assessment information, and staff development.

Ms. McEnroe delayed giving the KEYS survey feedback to the faculty through the end of her tenure at Hamilton, which occurred in October 1997 when she resigned to take another job. In November 1997, Ms. Ruttles (the second principal) assumed office and immediately arranged to have feedback on the KEYS survey given to the entire faculty. She then solicited faculty input regarding how to solve problems uncovered by the survey. The OTE/KEYS committee collected these faculty responses and began the development of the school improvement plan. In December 1997, the OTE/KEYS committee gave their initial set of goals to the school's Title I committee, which endorsed the goals, with some suggested changes.

In January 1998, the OTE/KEYS committee revised the goals, retrofitting them to the OTE objectives. The faculty was asked to assist in prioritizing the OTE/KEYS goals. In April 1998, Ms. Ruttles and the OTE/KEYS committee presented the prioritized school goals to the district superintendent. He rejected one outright (#20, smaller student-teacher ratio), but agreed in principle to support the others. Table 8.1 contains the twenty-two goals of the OTE/KEYS plan.

In March 1998, Smith resigned as executive secretary of the MAE. His successor had no knowledge of the KEYS process. UniServ representatives never worked on the OTE/KEYS Initiative during the course of the case study.

TABLE 8.1 OTE/KEYS School Improvement Goals

	School-level goals
KEYS strand	**Hamilton OTE/KEYS goals**
Communication and problem solving	1. Excuse should be requested from the parents when signing children in late or early. 2. Encourage positive attitudes.
Assessment for teaching and learning	3. Out-of-pocket expenses to implement hands-on learning should be eliminated. 4. Revise resource classes. 5. Encourage use of different approaches to learning styles.
Personal and professional learning	6. More training on ADD, AHD, alcohol, and drug babies. 7. Staff development should be related to classroom situations. 8. Have meetings on problem solving, decision making, team building through other programs.
Resources to support teaching and learning	9. Freer access to copy machines. 10. Information on adopt-a-school program needs updating. 11. Need storage shed with shelves to store learning supplies.
	District-Level Goals
Shared understanding and commitment to high goals	12. Administrators and school board members should spend a day with teachers in order to acquaint themselves with the realities of today's teaching. 13. Parent-teacher conferences in order to receive child's report card. 14. Administrators and school board members should meet one or two times annually with school personnel.
Communication and problem solving	15. More teacher input in hiring of personnel. 16. More planning time—perhaps dismissing early one afternoon per week. 17. Improve and update reading requirements for 1st and 2nd grades. 18. Require an exit test for each grade.
Personal and professional learning	19. Professional days should be given to attend workshops.
Resources to support teaching and learning	20. Smaller student-teacher ratio. 21. More behavior modification classes are needed. 22. Student supply lists should be extended.

During the summer of 1998, the OTE/KEYS committee met to develop specific plans for the first year implementation (1998–99) of their program. The PATS (Positive Attitude Toward School) points concept was developed during these meetings as a method for reinforcing students and teachers. Teachers were given PATS points for participation on committees; this was seen as a method to get recalcitrant teachers involved in the OTE/KEYS process.

Ms. Loughlin, a key informant for the case study and a member of MAE, participated on both the OTE and the OTE/KEYS committees. She described the current school improvement process as "OTE with a KEYS overlay. They are using the KEYS goals to do OTE." In an interview conducted during 1998–99, Ms. Loughlin concluded: "The OTE/KEYS process has worked for us. Without it, we wouldn't have gotten this far. The survey established some directions for us to follow. We didn't follow the KEYS steps per se; instead, we interpret KEYS in a way relevant to Hamilton. We have adapted KEYS to our local conditions here at Hamilton. On the other hand, we need more of an emphasis on academic topics, more on classroom specific teaching strategies than is supplied by KEYS."

In June 1999, I distributed an evaluation survey to members of the OTE/KEYS committee and other faculty members to assess faculty perception of the progress that has been made in accomplishing the OTE/KEYS goals. This survey listed the twenty-two OTE/KEYS goals, with instructions to respondents to rate the progress that had been made on each one. No further survey data was collected to assess progress during the second year of implementation; an update from Ms. Loughlin in mid-year of 1999–2000 indicated that the OTE/KEYS committee had not met yet, and that the school's principal and lead teacher were making most decisions.

A new era of school accountability was about to begin in Mississippi, according to information disseminated through the MDE website. Through Senate Bill 2156, Laws of 1999, the state legislature developed a school-based accountability system that holds individual schools accountable for student performance. The new focus of accountability on the school building level, rather than the district level, is more in line with accountability plans throughout the United States, such as in Kentucky, Louisiana, and Texas (Teddlie, Kochan, & Taylor, 2000). It is not clear what effect this new school accountability program will have on the OTE/KEYS Initiative at Hamilton. Typically, each new wave of reform subsumes the previous ones (e.g., Cuban, 1990).

CONCEPTUAL UNDERPINNINGS FOR THE CASE STUDY

The Mississippi case study was developed within a framework which placed the KEYS Initiative within several contexts: the union (NEA) context, which was layered at the national, state, and local levels; the state and district educational agency contexts; and the community and school contexts. Throughout this chapter, I argue that there was inadequate support for the OTE/KEYS Initiative at Hamilton at all of these context levels. Furthermore, I argue that support from several of the levels adjacent to an educational reform is necessary for that reform to optimally succeed.

Other conceptual underpinnings included the *cruising school* (Stoll & Fink, 1997), *readiness for change* (Fullan, 1993), and *loose coupling* (Murphy, 1992). Hamilton exemplified several of the cultural norms of what Stoll and Fink (1997, pp. 194–197) call the cruising school. These characteristics include the following:

- Contentment—"If it ain't broke don't fix it."
- Avoidance of commitment—"Let's send it to a committee."
- Goal diffusion—"We do our own thing but we do it well."
- Perpetuating total top-down leadership—"It's your job, not mine."
- Conformity—"Don't rock the boat."
- Blaming others—"They're pushing new ideas down our throats."
- Denial—"The research and data are biased."

During my observations at Hamilton, I frequently heard comments from the staff that exemplified several of these cultural norms, including contentment and conformity. The presence of the OTE/KEYS committee led to the emergence of the following cultural norms:

- Avoidance of commitment—"Let's send it to the OTE/KEYS committee."
- Goal diffusion—The OTE/KEYS plan had twenty-two goals, which were far too many to enact.
- Perpetuating total top-down leadership—The faculty, in general, wanted either the principal or the OTE/KEYS committee to deal with school improvement at Hamilton.
- Blaming others—The OTE/KEYS committee was seen by some faculty members as "pushing ideas down their throats."
- Denial—Ms. McEnroe believed that the results of the KEYS survey were biased.

Hamilton is a good example of a school with a faculty that was not ready for change. Very few teachers had the capacity to take ownership of the OTE/KEYS Initiative, or any other school improvement plan. Much of the reason for this is cultural: schools by their very nature are conservative institutions, and elementary schools in the southern United States are among the most conservative in the country. Fullan (1993) described the fundamental conservative nature of the educational system as follows:

"We have an educational system which is fundamentally conservative. The way that teachers are trained, the way that schools are organized, the way the educational hierarchy operates, and the way that education is treated by political decision-makers results in a system that is more likely to maintain the status quo than to change." (Fullan, 1993, p. 3)

Hamilton Consolidated Elementary School had many factors that led to the maintenance of the status quo. Located in the deep South, teachers in Mississippi are, in general, more conservative than those in other parts of the country. Teacher unions have had difficulties getting started in some states in this region, and teachers tend to accept a top-down management style more readily than do teachers in other areas of the country. Therefore, faculty readiness for successfully accomplishing a school improvement initiative at Hamilton was relatively low.

The South has the highest percentage of female teachers in the United States, and they are paid at the lowest regional rate (Newman, 1989). Hamilton is an elementary school with a totally female teaching faculty. There are also only a handful of African-American teachers at the school, and there was no African American teacher on the OTE/KEYS committee when it was first constituted. The OTE/KEYS committee was composed of the teachers who were the most committed to change in the school. Despite this, I noticed that the members of the committee often referred to the principal during their meetings. These references concerned issues such as whether or not she would be supportive of certain initiatives. There was a pervasive sense of a top-down leadership pattern in the school.

With regard to "loose or tight coupling," Murphy (1992) summarized differential linkages in effective and ineffective schools by noting: "One of the most powerful and enduring lessons from all the research on effective schools is that the better schools are more tightly linked—structurally, symbolically, and culturally—than the less effective ones. They operate more as an organic whole and less as a loose collection of disparate subsystems" (1992, p. 96).

There was evidence of loose coupling at Hamilton. Each of the four grade levels (K–3) operated somewhat independently of the others. The OTE/KEYS committee was supposed to represent the entire school, yet there was grumbling about the committee "pushing things down our throats." The principal and the OTE/KEYS committee appeared to work independently of one another, with the principal often "reacting" to the committee's work.

Perhaps the best example of loose coupling comes from the relationship between Hamilton and the various levels of the NEA (local, state, national). The NEA KEYS delivery system for Hamilton was so loosely coupled that it could not work: the reform activities inside the school were never adequately tied to the MAE or NEA human and material resources outside the school that could perhaps have made them succeed.

THE STORYLINE AT HAMILTON CONSOLIDATED ELEMENTARY SCHOOL

Several possible storyline themes (the initial capacity of a school for change, the alignment of KEYS with school needs, power of association support) will be discussed throughout the following section as they relate to six broad areas: (1) the influence of the district and state contexts on the outcomes at Hamilton; (2) the processes of KEYS implementation at the state and local levels; (3) how KEYS influenced the school improvement process at Hamilton; (4) the effect of KEYS on the organizational health of Hamilton; (5) the effect of KEYS on the core technology and teaching at Hamilton; and (6) the effect of KEYS on student outcomes.

The Influence of the District and State Contexts on the Outcomes at Hamilton

Fink (2000, p. 7) recently concluded from the results of several studies (e.g., Hallinger & Murphy, 1986; Teddlie & Stringfield, 1993) that: "The research evidence is fairly clear that schools can be understood only in their context."

Similarly, the evidence from the case studies is clear that the implementation of KEYS initiatives can be understood only in their own district and state contexts. The Mississippi case study is a prime example of the importance of context, as might be expected from a state that has produced several authors (e.g., Eudora Welty, William Faulkner) who have defined what a *sense of place* means in American literature (Wilson, 1989).

Unfortunately, as the previous sections on the context and history of this case study made clear, almost all the contextual factors negatively affected the OTE/KEYS Initiative in Mississippi. To recapitulate, the negative context factors included the following: (1) Mississippi is located in the southern United States, a region known for its conservatism and mistrust of change; (2) the Hamilton teachers were a very stable faculty, and such faculties are often entrenched in the status quo of life in the school as it has always been; (3) neither of the Hamilton principals were interested in making significant changes at the school; (4) the district office was headed by an elected superintendent, who had a "don't rock the boat" mentality; (5) there is a mistrust of unions in the deep South, which was apparent at both the school and district levels; and (6) the·MAE executive secretary who initiated the KEYS project provided little support to the initiative and effectively cut out UniServ participation.

In order for the OTE/KEYS Initiative to succeed, it needed union or school system support, but no one external to the school (the district superintendent, the MDE, the MAE executive secretaries, the UniServ representatives, the national NEA) wanted to get involved in the effort. Additionally, the OTE/KEYS committee, composed of the teachers most willing to advocate for change, had little experience or training in making school improvement work. This inexperience can be readily seen in the school improvement plan that they wrote, which was flawed in several respects. The initial capacity at Hamilton for change was low, and the local culture dictated against the development of that capacity.

As noted throughout, the local and state union were of little help. The Executive Secretary took several actions that effectively reduced the role of the regional UniServ representatives; additionally, there were three different representatives during the course of the case study. In fact, the only context or historical factor in favor of the OTE/KEYS Initiative was the existence of the semi-failed OTE initiative, which was the responsibility of the district by law. As long as the district was responsible for the OTE/KEYS initiative, it would be kept alive.

The Processes of KEYS Implementation at the State and Local Levels

According to Ms. Loughlin, KEYS was promoted first as an assessment tool, and then as a way to generate school improvement at Hamilton. The OTE/KEYS Initiative did have at least four positive consequences. It provided:

1. a detailed and realistic assessment of faculty attitudes toward the initiation of a change effort at Hamilton.

2. the OTE/KEYS committee the opportunity to exercise faculty governance by developing a school improvement plan and then attempting to implement it.

3. the Hamilton faculty an opportunity to prioritize the goals in the OTE/KEYS plan and to be involved in a school improvement initiative.

4. the teachers a small boost in self-efficacy, since a handful of the twenty-two goals were at least partially accomplished during the first two years of implementation.

One of the major difficulties in implementation of the OTE/KEYS Initiative was the fact that many faculty members did not buy into the plan. As Ms. Loughlin described it: "A lot of the teachers aren't involved because this is just a job to them. They don't volunteer—they put in their day and that's it. The PATS points are to encourage those who don't do much extra to get involved." This lack of a "buy in" by many of the teachers at Hamilton underscores why special strategies for school improvement, such as

Accelerated Schools and *Success for All,* require that a large percentage of the faculty be supportive of their programs before they are started.

With regard to other themes: (1) the OTE/KEYS Initiative was aligned with the school needs as determined through the KEYS survey; (2) there was consistency between KEYS and the existing school reform agenda (OTE) that was forged through the work of the OTE/KEYS committee; (3) there was consistency between KEYS and the larger reform environment of the state, although the new state initiative in school accountability may cause discordance soon; and (4) the OTE/KEYS process definitely made the Hamilton faculty more aware of data-based change.

On the other hand, the OTE/KEYS Initiative was only marginally successful in fostering the building of organizational capacity, due to the cultural norms described throughout this chapter. Additionally, the metaphor of KEYS as a *linker* to multiple reforms (booster rocket) had definite limitations in the Hamilton context, a case more appropriately referred to as a semi-failed graft of two educational reforms.

How KEYS Affected the School Improvement Process at Hamilton

The faculty response to the KEYS survey determined the particulars of the OTE/KEYS process. The improvement plan was based on faculty responses to the KEYS survey, which were overlaid onto the OTE goals. There were several flaws with the promulgation of the OTE/KEYS goals: (1) there were too many goals; (2) five of the twenty-two goals dealt with administrative issues that were irrelevant to the school improvement plan (see goals 3, 9, 10, 11, 22 in Table 8.1); and (3) few of the goals dealt with the learning core of the school (Fullan, 1993). With regard to the last point, the KEYS survey itself did not address many of the components of the school's learning core, especially as it relates to instructional practices.

After the goals were disseminated to the faculty, the OTE/KEYS committee tried various methods to see that they were accomplished. These methods, such as the use of PATS points, have been described throughout this chapter.

The success of the first year implementation (1998–99) of these goals was assessed, and the results of this assessment will be discussed in the remainder of this section. The OTE/KEYS goals, with the exception of the five administrative goals noted earlier, are related to topics discussed under the final three section subheadings: (1) organizational health related to eight goals (goals 1, 2, 8, 12, 14, 15, 16, 19 [see Appendix B]); (2) core technology/teaching related to seven goals (goals 4, 5, 6, 7, 13, 20, 21); and (3) student outcomes related to two goals (goals 17, 18).

Table 8.2 contains the results from the summer 1999 survey regarding progress made in accomplishing the OTE/KEYS goals. Members of the OTE/KEYS committee and other faculty members completed these responses.

TABLE 8.2 Results from Summer 1999 Survey Regarding Progress Made in Accomplishing Goals

OTE/KEYS committee goal	Mean
1. Excuse should be requested from the parents when signing children in late or early	2.00
2. Encourage positive attitudes.	3.44
3. Out-of-pocket expenses to implement hands-on learning should be eliminated.	2.78
4. Revise resource classes.	3.44
5. Encourage use of different approaches to learning styles.	3.56
6. More training on ADD, AHD, alcohol, and drug babies.	1.67
7. Staff development should be related to classroom situations.	2.56
8. Have meetings on problem solving, decision making, team building through other programs.	2.67
9. Freer access to copy machines.	3.33
10. Information on adopt-a-school program needs updating.	1.44
11. Need storage shed with shelves to store learning supplies.	1.00
12. Administrators and school board members should spend a day with teachers in order to acquaint themselves with the realities of today's teaching.	1.00
13. Parent-teacher conferences in order to receive child's report card.	1.22
14. Administrators and school board members should meet one or two times annually with school personnel.	1.11
15. More teacher input in hiring of personnel (school interview committee).	4.11
16. More planning time—perhaps dismissing early one afternoon per week.	2.67
17. Improve and update reading requirements for 1st and 2nd grades.	4.22
18. Require an exit test for each grade.	3.22
19. Professional days should be given to attend workshops (even if teacher pays).	3.44
20. Smaller student-teacher ratio.	1.78
21. More behavior modification classes are needed.	1.89
22. Student supply lists should be extended.	2.00
Average across all Goals	2.48

Note. A rating of "1" indicates "made no progress," a rating of "2" indicates "little progress," a rating of "3" indicates "made some progress," a rating of "4" indicates "made notable progress," and a rating of "5" indicates "made great progress." Nine faculty members completed this survey. I also completed the survey, based on the interviews and observations that I made during 1998–99. My response pattern is similar to that of the faculty members. The distribution of my responses is as follows:

1. Made no progress at all—7 goals
2. Made little progress—5 goals
3. Made some progress—3 goals
4. Made notable progress—4 goals
5. Made great progress—2 goals
6. Not enough information to make a determination—1 goal

Response options ranged from 1.0 (made no progress) to 5.0 (made great progress). The overall mean score across all twenty-two goals was 2.48, which is midway between "made little progress" (2.0) and "made some progress" (3.0). The average rating was only 2.11 for the five goals described earlier that deal with administrative issues irrelevant to the school improvement plan. This means that little progress was made on these goals.

The Effect of the KEYS Process on the Organizational Health of Hamilton

The average rating for the eight goals (goals 1, 2, 8, 12, 14, 15, 16, 19) associated with the organizational health of Hamilton was 2.56, which is midway between "made some progress" and "made little progress." The most progress was made on three goals: goal 2, encourage positive attitudes, average rating of 3.44; goal 15, more teacher input in hiring of personnel, average rating of 4.11; and goal 19, professional days should be given to attend workshops, average rating of 3.44.

With regard to goal 2 (encourage positive attitudes), data gathered during 1998–99 indicated that the OTE/KEYS committee thought progress was being made due to the PATS (positive attitude toward school) points. Students and teachers received these points for positive behavior at the school. Other examples of success related to this goal include the fact that PTA attendance was up, teachers were attending more meetings after school, and students were getting better report cards.

Ms. Loughlin added the following comment about PATS points in an interview conducted in the fall semester 1999: "This was positive until about March of last year. Then, assistant teachers (and some teachers) started complaining about having to work the PATS store and run the movie for the students. Some teachers gave their students points they did not earn in order to get the students to go to the movie and out of the room."

With regard to goal 15 (more teacher input in hiring of personnel), interviews indicated that the OTE/KEYS committee talked about it in 1998–99, but didn't go through with it. The committee was empowered by the principal to come up with a policy but didn't have time to complete the work. Ms. Loughlin added the following in an interview conducted in the fall semester 1999: "Ms. Ruttles selected a team of teachers to interview and hire personnel this past summer (1999). The teachers have had a positive reaction to this. There has been much less complaining about the selection of new teachers."

In regard to goal 19 (professional days should be given to attend workshops), the principal agreed so long as workshops were on the "approved list."

The lowest scores in the organizational health area came with regard to administrators spending a day with teachers in order to "acquaint themselves with the realities of today's teaching" (goal 12) or meeting one or two times annually with school personnel (goal 14). The administrators and board members simply did not do this, even though they knew it was a priority at Hamilton. Some members of the OTE/KEYS committee made excuses for the board members, stating that they all worked a regular job in addition to their board duties.

Fink (2000) discussed the importance of district office support of school improvement: "Evidence suggests that more effective schools are located in districts where supportive interactions occur between schools and central office staff . . . schools unsupported by larger networks find school improvement exceedingly difficult" (p. 39).

The attempt by the Hamilton OTE/KEYS committee to develop a closer working relationship with the district central office was a valid way to increase the initiative's chances of success. Unfortunately, this attempt was rebuffed.

The Effect of the KEYS Process on the Core Technology and Teaching at Hamilton

The average rating for the seven goals (goals 4, 5, 6, 7, 13, 20, 21) associated with the core technology and teaching at Hamilton was 2.48, which is midway between "made some progress" and "made little progress." The most progress was made on two of these goals: (1) goal 4, revise resource classes, average rating of 3.44; and (2) goal 5, encourage use of different approaches to learning styles, average rating of 3.56.

With regard to goal 4 (revise resource classes), interviews during 1998–99 indicated that the OTE/KEYS committee thought progress had been made, but that there were still some problems. Time for resource was increased in the 2nd and 3rd grades, but there were still problems with regular and Title I teachers working together.

With regard to goal 5 (encourage use of different approaches to learning styles), data gathered during 1998–99 indicated that Hamilton had an in-service on "Different Reading Styles." The OTE/KEYS committee felt that they had come a long way, but still had a lot of work to do. The OTE/KEYS committee also indicated that there were several retirements coming up in the next couple of years, and new teachers were "more amenable to change."

The district superintendent had indicated that goal 20 (smaller student-teacher ratio) could not be accomplished. This changed somewhat in 1999–2000, according to Ms. Loughlin: "There is a smaller student-teacher ratio this year with the federal funds that President Clinton gave schools. The Superintendent is trying. Kindergarten has about 20 students in each class, while first grade has about 23. We are also hoping to hire another second grade teacher."

The Effect of KEYS on Student Outcomes

Only two goals related to student outcomes (goals 17, 18). Both of these goals received fairly high ratings (4.22 and 3.22 respectively). Goal 17 (improve and update reading requirements for 1st and 2nd grades) was accomplished at the district level with Hamilton's input and support. Some of the teachers were having second thoughts in 1998–99 because the new policy did not allow for the "slow learner."

Goal 18 (require an exit test for each grade) was not accomplished, and the average score for this goal (3.22) indicates that the teachers were not sure if they still wanted these exit exams.

IMPLICATIONS FOR REFORM AND SCHOOL IMPROVEMENT

There appear to be three major areas in the generic KEYS process about which implications can be drawn from the Mississippi OTE/KEYS case study: the importance of context factors to the success of KEYS; the effect that the merging (grafting) of school reforms can have on the success of KEYS; and the effect of the lack of institutional support on the success of KEYS.

A litany of contextual factors limited the impact of the OTE/KEYS Initiative in Mississippi: (1) the deep South is known for its conservatism and mistrust of change, including antipathy toward union activity; (2) the Hamilton faculty appeared to be entrenched in the status quo of school life as it had always been; (3) leadership for the change process at the principal level was lacking; (4) the district office did not want to be involved; and (5) the MAE executive secretary behaved in a manner that effectively cut out UniServ participation.

A context analysis (Teddlie & Stringfield, 1993) performed before investing in a KEYS school improvement initiative might have revealed these limitations. Part of that analysis could be the administration of the KEYS survey as a screening tool to determine if the school is ready for a school improvement program, or if some remedial staff development is needed before the initiative is undertaken. Another context analysis screening tool could be a faculty poll to determine the level of support for a KEYS school improvement initiative, similar to the polls employed by strategies such as *Accelerated Schools* and *Success for All*.

The Mississippi case study was also an example of the adaptation (or grafting) of KEYS onto an ongoing school improvement initiative (OTE), which had been failing, thus resulting in a hybrid school improvement effort (OTE/KEYS). While in the interaction with other school improvement initiatives KEYS may function as a booster rocket, the KEYS assessment process in Mississippi was incapable of lifting the semi-failed OTE initiative off the launching pad.

It may be that the NEA, or the local state affiliate, needs to assess the existing school improvement initiatives closely and avoid those cases where the reform is already fizzling. This could be part of the context analysis discussed earlier in this section.

The virtual lack of external support for the OTE/KEYS Initiative from two general external support structures: the union structure, layered at, state, and local levels; and the state and district educational agency structures were influential in this case. The OTE/KEYS Initiative needed some external support to succeed, but that support was not forthcoming from any of the major external players: the district superintendent, the local school board, the MDE, UniServ, the MAE executive secretary, and so forth.

When the NEA took KEYS into Mississippi, it wanted KEYS to help rebuild the organization, but the process didn't work. The KEYS survey process did open a space for possible school improvement. However, entry into that space by reformers was blocked substantially due to lack of support from the educational system and the union.

REFERENCES

Blum, R. E. (1997). *Development of Onward to Excellence training and technical capacity.* Portland, OR: Northwest Regional Educational Lab.

Cuban, L. (1990). Reforming again, again, and again. *Educational Researcher, 19,* 3–13.

Fink, D. (2000). *Good schools/real schools: Why school reform doesn't last.* New York: Teachers College Press.

Fullan, M. (1993). *Change forces: Probing the depths of educational reform.* London: Falmer.

Hallinger, P., & Murphy, J. (1986). The social context of effective schools. *American Journal of Education, 94,* 328–355.

Kushman, J. W., & Yap, K. (1997). *Mississippi Onward to Excellence impact study.* Portland, OR: Northwest Regional Educational Lab.

Mullins, A. P. (1992). *Building consensus: A history of the passage of the Mississippi Education Reform Act of 1982.* Jackson, Mississippi: Mississippi Humanities Council.

Murphy, J. (1992). School effectiveness and school restructuring: Contributions to educational improvement. *School Effectiveness and School Improvement, 3*(2), 90–109.

Newman, J. W. (1989). Teachers. In C. R. Wilson & W. Ferris (Eds.), *Encyclopedia of southern culture,* pp. 265–266. Chapel Hill, NC: The UNC Press.

Stoll, L., & Fink, D. (1997). The cruising school: The unidentified ineffective school. In L. Stoll & K. Myers (Eds.), *No quick fixes: Perspectives on schools in difficulty,* pp. 189–206. London: Falmer.

Teddlie, C., & Reynolds, D. (2000). *The international handbook of school effectiveness research.* London: Falmer.

Teddlie, C., & Stringfield, S. (1993). *Schools make a difference: Lessons learned from a 10-year study of school effects.* New York: Teachers College Press.

Teddlie, C., Kochan, S., & Taylor, D. (2000, April). *ABC+: Variations on a context-sensitive model for school performance measurement and school improvement.* Paper presented at the annual meeting of the American Educational Research Association, New Orleans, LA.

Wilson, C. R. (1989). Place, Sense of. In C. R. Wilson & W. Ferris (Eds.), *Encyclopedia of southern culture,* pp. 1137-1138. Chapel Hill, NC: The UNC Press.

9

Florida and the KEYS

Kathryn M. Borman

CONTEXT FOR THE CASE

The State of Florida as a context for the KEYS Initiative changed over the three-year period that KEYS remained on the state affiliate's agenda. During this time the state became a gradually more hostile environment for teacher-led reforms of any kind. When the initiative was introduced in 1997, the NEA enrolled the largest number of teachers in the state (as it does today). In addition, its network of UniServ directors routinely assumed authority in carrying out programs such as KEYS designed to undertake change at the level of the school and school district. School districts in Florida are quite large in geographical size, corresponding in jurisdiction with counties in the state and resulting in intra-district diversity both in population and in urbanicity. However, the very fact that districts are highly centralized and often contain large numbers of schools can mean that initiatives introduced at the UniServ level can enjoy substantial impact. There was every reason to believe that schools in the central part of the state including both Orange (Orlando) County and Osceola County, its neighbor to the west, would be particularly hospitable sites for the implementation of KEYS. Lee Littlefield, the UniServ director, had been one of the most enthusiastic participants in the NEA's KEYS training workshops.

What went wrong? Several things—some outside the control of NEA and others within its charge to correct or modify. The State's Democratic Governor Lawton Chiles completed his last term in 1997, dying unexpectedly before turning over the Governor's Mansion to his successor, Jeb Bush. Governor Bush's agenda for education in the state has been freighted with a number of policies that can be construed as unfriendly to both NEA's agenda, including KEYS, as well as to public education in grades K–12 generally. Particularly troublesome are policies framing the so-called *A+ Plan*. This plan calls for the annual grading of Florida schools based upon student scores on the state's high stakes test, the Florida Comprehensive Assessment Test (FCAT). The *A+ Plan* currently does not seek to assist schools assigned low grades by providing staff development or other needed resources but, instead, targets such schools for reconstitution. In addition, vouchers are provided for students whose schools remain at "D" and "F" levels for two years. Policy projected for 2002 calls for teacher assessments based on students' scores such that teachers whose students do not demonstrate a year's growth as measured by the FCAT will have 5 percent of their salaries withheld. Policies of this kind are extremely antagonistic to the best interests of teachers—creating climates in schools antithetical to the establishment and maintenance of collegial ties, a critical component in carrying out reforms such as KEYS at the school level.

In the face of the state's hostile approach to policy making affecting the public schools, NEA continued to implement a complex agenda including a plan to merge with the American Federation of Teachers. Although the national membership at this writing had not as yet voted to accept the plan, the FTP-NEA affiliate in Florida led the charge in creating a jointly managed organization. During a recent telephone conversation, Karen Olivares, the FTP-NEA Manager of Instructional Professional Development and Organizational Development, talked about how her role in coordinating the KEYS Initiative had changed over the four-year period of its implementation. When I asked her if she still coordinated KEYS, she said:

Well, KEYS is something that does get . . . shepherded is probably a better definition—from our division at FTP-NEA. And when we started the project, which is now . . . four years ago or so, we had more hands-on involvement in the earlier stages. It's pretty much taken on a limited life of its own where it's being worked with. But that role will probably expand again when the two organizations merge, and we have FEA United locals; FEA United locals will be interested in using this instrument.

During the course of this same conversation, Karen, while enthusiastic about the intent of KEYS, assessed the implementation of the KEYS Initiative in largely negative terms, noting that in her view NEA had been "extremely naive" in its view of carrying out reform at the local level and urging the consideration of what she referred to as "a different model" of reform:

If a local association really wants to embrace this and have many schools that are willing to do this, they're going to have to find some way to create a joint partnership with the district and put a teacher on release that the association can then train and support. Then you have one teacher either full-time or part-time guiding this process. Because Lee [Littlefield], for all his talents and all of his commitment to this, he still has probably 2,000 direct members he's responsible for and all the other stuff he's supposed to be doing. So I think that we've been really naive about what it would take to have something like this really happen, and happen at a high level of effectiveness, and at some quantum level, helping a whole district change.

Olivares' comments on reform emphasize the importance of coordination and maintenance of the reform agenda at the local school level supported by at least one teacher who is responsible for championing the reform. However, Olivares herself was distracted from the KEYS reform agenda by her involvement in both guiding the merger of the state affiliate with the AFT and challenging Governor Bush's educational agenda for the state.

CONCEPTUAL UNDERPINNINGS

A set of interrelated concepts provides a roadmap for understanding why the KEYS Initiative failed to take off in Florida. Fred Hess has used the term *policy churn* (Hess, 1991) to describe the landscape of educational reforms currently confronting schools and school districts. School reform initiatives come from many sources and with unremitting urgency in an era when high stakes tests drive accountability at many levels. As a result, schools and school districts are expected to be receptive to programs and plans that accelerate student achievement, build teacher learning communities, and strengthen school capacity (Sykes & Darling-Hammond, 1999). On the negative side, the resulting disorderly mix of policies, particularly in large states or school districts, creates an atmosphere of policy churn with the frequent end result of much activity with few long-term results.

Within such an atmosphere, the KEYS Initiative made good sense. Informed by lessons learned from effective schools research, the KEYS conceptual framework as articulated by Jeff Schneider, Ron Henderson, Don Rollie, and others from NEA focused at the school level and provided school staff, parents, and others who completed the survey an opportunity to assess the school's strengths and weaknesses. In places such as Memphis, where KEYS was implemented with clearly successful results, the instrument became a tool to guide subsequent efforts at change, providing a compass in the fog of policy churn. In other places such as Osceola and Orange Counties in Florida, the outcome was less fortuitous.

In Florida where KEYS was stillborn, policy churn overwhelmed the state affiliate in Tallahassee as well as the state's teachers and school-based administrators who were faced with accountability policies that forced them to focus on strategies to improve student test scores. Schools and teachers concentrated on how best to provide teaching and learning experiences that that might best result in marked improvements in student performance on the FCAT. This is not to say that there was a lack of appreciation for what the KEYS might accomplish. Manager of Instructional Professional Development and Organizational Development Karen Olivares told me that she believed "that there's real merit to this tool. I don't think . . . we have enough capacity to use this tool effectively. By capacity, I mean time, money, time [laughs]. And also when you look at what's on the landscape for local associations, and what they're fighting on a daily basis, this is not real high on their list of things to do." Despite her negative appraisal of both the difficulty in finding resources in the form of time and money and the problem of convincing local affiliates to place KEYS on their agendas, Olivares remained hopeful that things might change in the coming months and was also convinced that KEYS was a promising strategy to employ in undertaking whole school reform.

RESEARCH ISSUES: CARRYING OUT THE STUDY

The case study undertaken in Florida was aimed at chronicling the story of implementation of the KEYS Initiative from its introduction into the state to its adoption at the school level using one school as a focal point. Work on the project was undertaken from the fall of 1997 until the summer of the year 2000.[1] When our work in the state was getting underway, the KEYS Initiative had just been introduced strategically in several counties and their corresponding districts. These districts were seen as likely to commit themselves to the demands of the system of assessment and reform required in addressing KEYS school change strategies. Several middle schools in Osceola and Orange Counties were suggested to us by national NEA officers as possible sites for our research. We selected Stonewall Jackson Middle School in Orlando because it seemed to have a number of characteristics including its large percentages of Latino students, dedicated teaching staff, and well-established track record of school-based reforms lead by teachers in the school to warrant our interest. Other schools were considered and rejected, but later visited if only to undertake interviews with school-based teaching and administrative staff and others to determine the process that had been followed in other attempts at implementation. We also interviewed Lee Littlefield, Karen Olivares, and others whose perspectives on the implementation of the KEYS process seemed important to take into account.

In addition to interviewing school-based administrators and teachers, we also carried out observations in the school selected for closest scrutiny, Stonewall Jackson Middle School. These observations occurred in classrooms and hallways and also involved informal interactions with both teachers and students. Finally, we began our study and also concluded it with interviews conducted with the UniServ director working in the region and with state-level NEA personnel. Along the way we had helpful informal conversations with national-level NEA officers who provided their insight into events in Florida that we observed. We also interviewed a principal at another middle school in the same UniServ area as our focal middle school. This interview was undertaken in order to compare our focal school with another that had also taken on the KEYS reforms.

KEYS AT STONEWALL JACKSON MIDDLE SCHOOL AND IN FLORIDA

Stonewall Jackson Middle School in Orange County is a large, sunlit, airy school just north of downtown Orlando. This school reflects the runaway growth of the Orlando area with a student population of 1,300 in grades 6, 7, and 8. At the time of its construction in 1965, the school was expected to house fewer than 900 students. While the school building itself is large, and built around a courtyard arrangement, many students and their teachers are housed in twenty-three portable individual classroom structures. The student population is 44 percent Hispanic, primarily first and second generation Puerto Rican, Dominican, and Honduran students; 40 percent white; 13 percent African American; and 3 percent Asian compared to student populations in the rest of the county with 13 percent African American and 18 percent Hispanic, primarily Puerto Rican. The school is located near a highway that links the city with the airport in a neighborhood of three-story apartment buildings, neat but also exuding shabbiness and transience.

Teachers at Stonewall Jackson historically have displayed considerable interest in educational reform generally and curricular reform specifically. For example, the school program, put in place largely through teacher-led initiative, includes a dual language program across all grades in Spanish and English and an aerospace program that cuts across math and science curriculum and includes courses such as meteorology aimed at directing students toward Florida's Space Coast industries. The school practices teaming and other strategies aimed at improving teaching and learning at the middle school level, all of which require considerable amounts of teacher time in carrying them forward. A teacher in the dual language program, Mr. Cosme, himself a native Puerto Rican, when asked to characterize his work environment observed:

In the classroom level, it is very important, the most important is that we help people that are new in the nation. Aside from the academic, people who are scared, their parents, they don't have jobs or they have two jobs, the kids don't have enough clothes, shoes. . . . We help. I have even found students from my home town here. . . . The environment is very good. Let me tell you this, I was a teacher many years in Puerto Rico. And there is no difference between my classroom and my students here and in Puerto Rico. No difference. Same environment, same slang expression, like in my hometown.

Throughout his interview, Mr. Cosme underscored both his confidence in the school administration and his pride in the work that he and his colleagues accomplish through their teaching. At another point in the interview Mr. Cosme discussed the two overarching goals of the dual language program. The first is to prevent students from dropping out. As Mr. Cosme sees it, "some students are waiting until they reach age 16 to throw away the books, say bad words to the teacher and go to the streets to sell drugs." The second goal is to move students into high-achieving academic careers. Attaining the second goal requires that the bilingual program be sold to the rest of the faculty, preparing them to receive "mainstreamed" students whom Mr. Cosme characterized as "top of the line people":

So our main objective is to sell the bilingual program to the rest of the faculty, tell them it's a special program . . . someday our people [Hispanics] will walk into the classroom, . . . [the teachers need to] give them a warm welcome and not a 'What are you doing here? Don't you have a program downstairs?' . . . We send top of the line people and they are successful there, they can compete. They compete with the gringos, with the Anglos, no problem. As a matter of fact, the teachers, they say, 'That kid you sent me—good worker, good discipline, if you have more of those, send them to my room.' That's what the teachers say.

Indeed, the only improvement that this teacher proposed for his program and the school generally was to provide more planning time: "So when do we meet? We meet before school, after school, but we have no common planning period. The administration tries hard, but it is impossible due to the different grade levels, subject areas. . . . Do you see that teacher I saw in the hall? Did you see that teacher that called me [laughs]. Those [e.g., brief hallway conversations] are my meetings."

In the fall of 1997, as we began our observations and interviews for the school year, we observed a teaching staff ready to take on the KEYS Initiative. It was clear that teachers were burdened with a student body too large for the facility and with too little planning time in common with other teachers on their teams. Nonetheless, given the strong dedication to their students, widely held respect for building administrators and teacher colleagues alike, and the established track record in initiating successful innovations at the school and classroom level, there was every reason to believe that the teaching staff at Stonewall would successfully address the KEYS project. Two years later in the fall of 1999, the principal and assistant principal Tim Smith, a driving force in supporting the initiative, were no longer at Stonewall and the teachers whom we interviewed were reluctant to have us audiotape their interview. The teacher leaders at Stonewall were keenly aware of the pressures that they and their colleagues faced in the current state political climate and preferred to not have their positions made public.

On October 30, 1997, a memorandum addressed to Florida KEYS consultants was sent by Karen Olivares from the state office of NEA in Tallahassee. It was addressed to Florida Keys consultants and was an information update on the status of the initiative. At that time, forty staff members had been trained in using the KEYS instrument and were prepared to assist school sites. Pointers were provided to guide schools in using survey data. First, Karen pointed out that results would be presented to each school in line with five themes or clusters of information from the surveys.[2] The next step would follow once analyzed survey data were received from NEA, signaling that it was time to "really get into the work of school improvement." Schools would review the results with the assistance of the local or FTP staff, establish a plan of action, consult the interactive start-up guide and involve the school improvement team, and finally, set aside time. The memo concluded with a request for a status report to be submitted the following month.

One year later, in the fall of 1998, it was difficult to tell where the initiative stood at the local school level. It is clear that schools in Florida's Orange and Osceola Counties, including Stonewall Jackson, had not moved along the continuum of school improvements steps Karen outlined in her memo. While the KEYS Initiative in 1998 was not entirely off the stove, it had certainly been placed on a back burner. Tim Smith, still the optimistic and energetic assistant principal, did not dismiss out of hand the possibility that faculty and staff might become re-engaged:

Tim: I believe there is merit to the program, but it has shut down since the time of our discussion of survey results last spring. Currently among the teachers, there is some talk about reviving KEYS, but not much. The teacher leadership got very discouraged when the faculty turned on them. The leaders don't want to repeat the experience!

Kathy: What was the nature of the problem?

Tim: The data were not readable and comprehensible to the staff. I think that NEA needs to rethink the implementation of the survey. It would have been very helpful to have had a researcher who could have come to present the data, someone who could have said 'Here are some red flags.' The range was so small—I mean what does a 3.0 on a 4.0 scale really mean? The problem was really about the statistics and how to interpret them.

Kathy: It sounds like it would have been helpful to examine comparable cases?

Tim: Actually, that is what some of the teachers said. If you are in the business world, you would want to compare yourself to other companies. As it was, it almost became guesswork trying to figure out what the scales meant and what we should do to address the various areas of concern. You know, I think the 35 key factors are good . . . but the survey . . . some of the questions were difficult to interpret. One concerned how parents viewed the school . . . what perspective should you take in interpreting the question . . . the parents' or the school staff's? You come to the point of what is the return on the effort and have to ask: 'Is this a worthwhile pursuit?'

Kathy: So, there was a lot of frustration?

Tim: Well, yes. It seems to me there is some good . . . there really is lots of potential in the KEYS.

Tim's words were echoed in Karen Olivares' take on the status at that time of the initiative in Florida overall. Without the commitment and direct involvement at the school level of an NEA UniServ director or other staff member, it seems unlikely that any school can remain focused on the steps necessary to address the KEYS reforms:

Karen: In general the initiative [KEYS] has such merit—the reality is that at no level in the association [NEA], no one has put in the resources it needs. For this to take hold, someone is needed at the local school. [It cannot be] . . . an add-on. If anything can be learned by the association, it is that.

Kathy: I am looking at your memo date October 30, 1997, and I see that there are a large number of schools taking part in the KEYS that are located in either Orange or Osceola County.

Karen: It was done on purpose—sites in Osceola and Orange—when the project first began four years ago, the sites were spread across the state. So we made a strategic change—by having local and district staff engaged, this would overcome roadblocks. But, look, if I am a classroom teacher, there is preparing for the FCAT, KEYS, for all of the local, district, state, and now national initiatives on my plate. I plan to contact Lee Littlefield next week to see what is going on.

We concluded our conversation and promised to stay in touch. However, the next time we spoke was over a year later in the spring of 2000. By this time the state's emphasis on testing and accountability under Governor Jeb Bush had utterly transformed Florida's public education landscape and KEYS was virtually dead in the water.

THREE CONTRASTING EXAMPLES

Not willing to concede that Stonewall Jackson might be the best or even the only example of KEYS reform efforts in Florida, I determined to chronicle the experience of at least one other school undertaking reforms using the KEYS survey. The first school we contacted at the suggestion of NEA staff was Horizon Middle School in Osceola County, just west of Orlando. The principal, Penny Noyer, worked closely with both her school advisory committee (SAC) and her staff to gain their support for a "research-based" approach to evaluating the school's progress. Unlike Stonewall Jackson, Horizon was only four years old and also eager to establish a process for tracking the school's accomplishments and needs. According to Penny Noyer:

We're only four years old. So we had parents, teachers, and students take the survey. And we looked to see if we were all on the same page or did anyone feel there was a need. And . . . our three groups were very close together in our perception of the school. It was a pretty positive perception. Communication was an area we felt we needed to work on. And so we've done that through staff development, with parent conferencing. We've done that through forming these committees that . . . these sub-committees that will work on things like school uniforms, incentive program for kids, for attendance, and incentive programs of recognition. That's how we've used it. If we've needed staff development [this] came out through the KEYS.

Penny Noyer's use of the KEYS process allowed her school to use the instrument as a public relations tool, winning support of parents and community members through the SAC for school reforms and policy changes. She also used KEYS as a method for organizational development and to bolster institutional self-confidence. Given its status as a relatively new school, Horizon as an organization was prepared and eager to confront information about itself. KEYS was adopted as the process for understanding organizational progress because it was perceived by the principal and other important opinion makers to be a legitimate, research-based tool that provided a means to understand data-based achievements and pathways to change.

Once the self-evaluation had been completed, all agreed that the findings indicated that the school should consider hiring another staff member to assist in staff development on site at the school, an unusual and expensive cost for an individual public school to take on. Findings from the KEYS self-evaluation process were given further legitimacy because they overlapped with recent findings reached by the southern association's accreditation review of the school. Penny also noted that starting a school de novo just a few years earlier had ensured a measure of solidarity among the teachers in the school. In her words: "Because we got to hire our whole staff, we have people that are philosophically closer together than a school typically is except once or twice over a period of 20 years." Having a staff on board whose values and teaching philosophies are closely aligned, in addition to having made the initial hiring decisions herself, Penny was fortunate to be serving as principal during a period when the school was uniquely poised to take on change in accord with KEYS' assessment results.

In reflecting on her successful utilization of KEYS, Penny believed that several factors contributed to the favorable outcome:

I think you'd need a commitment from your staff first. And a commitment to provide . . . staff development. One of the biggest changes that came from our KEYS Initiative, I think, is this year we're adding a curriculum resource teacher. And I think it's because that committee felt we needed our own in-service person on staff. So, I guess, you know, before you asked me about financial impact . . . that's about $45,000 financial impact, to add a staff development person.

In the case of Horizon Middle School, KEYS became a tool for assessing the school's progress to date. Because the results of the assessment mirrored those of the accreditation body as well as the felt needs of faculty and others, the next steps were relatively easy to undertake once funding was secured. Nonetheless, carrying out whole school reform using the KEYS process is never easy or without costs of one kind or another. In addition to financial resources required to hire new personnel as in the Horizon case, the always-scarce resource of teachers' time is required to assess, plan, and carry out reform.

The second contrasting case, Walker Middle School, like Horizon saw the advantage to using the KEYS process to have a tool that provided "objective" data both teachers and parents could use to guide the school's improvement efforts. In undertaking the implementation of the KEYS process at Walker Middle School, two teachers had been instrumental in providing leadership. One of them, Nilsa Garcia, saw the KEYS process as the only path for schools to take in altering their day-to-day work because it is grounded in a teacher-led course of change:

Interviewer: What appealed to you about participating in this project?

Nilsa: Anything that would improve the student's achievement I always participate in. It was something that we could use in the classroom, so I didn't hesitate even though it was my summer time.

Interviewer: What opportunities did you see as a participant or what vision did you see for the school?

Nilsa: I thought with the improvement plan [derived from the KEYS survey analysis], we would have some information that we could actually use instead of just meeting with parents and wonder what are we are going to work on this year . . . we would know from the data . . . what we were going to do each year, and it's ongoing, and there's 35 indicators, and they're not all high. We would decide which of the two [areas of weakness] we would work with, and we would always have something to work on as an improvement.

Nilsa and her teacher colleagues saw the KEYS instrument as a tool to provide data-driven school reform over the long haul. At Walker, the student population was approximately a third Latino, primarily Puerto Rican American children and a number from other Caribbean nations. Nilsa was fluent in Spanish and made a point of translating the KEYS survey into Spanish so that it became accessible to a larger number of parents. In addition, the survey was administered to all participants at the same time. A brief meeting at the school was held, refreshments were served, and all attending cleared their calendars to take the time to complete the survey. Nilsa and her colleagues did their best to ensure the participation of as many different interest groups as possible:

Nilsa: The whole school [participated] including part of the parents. The whole faculty including the custodians, the cafeteria people [many of whom] couldn't understand it . . . and they were like this doesn't apply to me. But you need to include everyone because of [the nature of] this project. In education, no matter if he is in the line making the lunch or buying the lunch, if something is gonna happen you have to know how to deal with those kids. You need to know certain things.

Interviewer: How much time did it take to get all of those surveys done?

Nilsa: We made a meeting for the faculty and it took the staff 45 to 50 minutes to an hour and some of the staff members with some of the terminology because you [could] go either way—they [the items in the KEYS survey] were so similar—they were picky—and that was a time we had help from the FTP-NEA office just in case. They did it, didn't complain that much—still they were saying for some people it was too difficult. One-hour commitment from the whole school to be there—you were not allowed to have a doctor's appointment, you have to be there!

In a third school, an elementary school in Orange County, problems arose both from the ambiguity of the items and the school's internal political infighting as well as from the competing demands of the unsettled policy environment in the district. One of the teacher-leaders at Oak Elementary School said:

The more I am with KEYS, I realize it is the *only thing* that would ever change this place. If we had a new pivotal person, that might help; if we had a few changes in teachers, that might help. Those are just a few things that I see could make school better without KEYS. But with KEYS—the KEYS system—I have been with education long enough to know that you can't have someone from the county office tell you what you need to do. You can't have a consultant come in and tell you what you need to do. You need to work together from your own school site and plan what you feel is best for your school site. And I have *always* said that and the minute I saw KEYS it was . . . an affirmation of what I really, really believe. And what most of my friends that I respect very much believe. I have lots of discussions with my friends at other schools and they think that KEYS would be an incredible asset to their schools and they keep saying, 'How can you make this happen if those people aren't with you?' And I say, 'I don't know, they *are* with me some times and some times they are not,' and that's the point that they keep coming back to me with.

Despite this teacher's ringing endorsement of KEYS, the initiative has enjoyed only relatively limited success at her school. This she ascribes to both internal and external pressures including large scale turnover in faculty, competing claims on teachers' time, and the relentless pressure to focus on students' readiness to perform well on the state's high stakes test, the FCAT. Nonetheless, teachers were successful in using KEYS results (interpreted with the assistance of Lee Littlefield who attended the meeting at which results were discussed) to change the school's staff development policy from a "one size fits all" approach to one that takes into account the wide variation in teachers' classroom experience and length of time on the job.

CONCLUSION

What generalizations can be drawn from the Florida case? Several can be extrapolated at both the macro (state and county or district levels) and micro levels—the level of the school. At the state level, policy churn—the formation and implementation of a series of state education policy initiatives as well as the association's own initiatives (including both KEYS and the proposed merger of the NEA with the AFT)—prevented serious and focused attention to the KEYS process. While state-level NEA officers, as well as their counterparts at the UniServ level, valued the initiative, both sets of individuals were frustrated by the association's naïveté—in the words of one of these officers. This naïveté sprang, she thought, from the association's difficulty both in framing the process used by schools to identify their needs and in devising strategies at the school level to address them. Schools were left to founder in the wake of KEYS survey results, paralyzed by a lack of information and tools to interpret the meaning of survey results in light of framing school-level changes.

By contrast, Horizon school was able to take up an agenda for change as a result of a set of favorable circumstances. First, the school's recent accreditation review had pointed to the same problems and needs as those identified through the KEYS process, giving the survey results heightened validity. Second, the principal was herself a strong advocate of data-driven accountability and reform. In addition, the school is located in Osceola County, a district that is more experimental in its approach to school design—it is the district that worked with Disney interests to build a highly innovative school as part of Disney's Celebration community development project (Borman, Glickman, & Haag, 2000).

Of particular interest, in conclusion, are assumptions made by participants about the possible meanings of the data in self-study and how they believe these meanings will affect their involvement in the KEYS project, their commitment to other programs and initiatives, and the overall organizational health of the school. Some data about the school as presented in the KEYS survey data analysis are inherently ambiguous and, therefore, pose a fundamental challenge to educators who generally have little practice at interpreting or using formal data of any kind. Interpretations are heavily colored by salient events in the school's local and state context. In schools where Lee Littlefield, the UniServ director, provided assistance in interpreting school survey findings, the outcome frequently led to the creation of a teacher-led agenda for change based on survey results. In the case of one of the schools, Walker Middle School, KEYS data became an important tool for informing parents and getting their support for change.

In all of the cases considered in this chapter, those players at the local school level who were active in the KEYS process, particularly the teachers and usually the principal, mentioned a number of obstacles in common: (1) insufficient time to meet, plan, and carry out identified reforms; (2) issues related to the school's ability to marshal the political will and enthusiasm among teaching staff to sustain the KEYS process; and (3) competing claims resulting from ongoing policy churn in the district and the state, notably the emphasis placed on FCAT scores.

These, in addition to the frequently mentioned criticism of the instrument itself, namely its ambiguity, and the difficulty school staff members and others had in interpreting (and living with) the results were often enough by themselves to prevent further action at the school level.

NOTES

1. I acknowledge the participation in data collection and analysis of Allyson Haag as well as the helpful advice of Joe Murphy, Don Rollie, Jeff Schneider, Ron Henderson, Mark Smiley, and other KEYS case study researchers.

2. The themes included shared understanding and commitment to high goals; open communication and collaborative problem solving; continuous assessment for teaching and learning; personal and professional learning; and resources to support teaching and learning.

REFERENCES

Borman, K., Glickman, E., & Haag, A. (2000). Celebration: Disney designs a school. In K. Riley & K. Louis (Eds.), *Schools and school reform*. London: Falmer.

Hess, G. A. (1991). *School restructuring: Chicago style*. Newbury Park, CA: Corwin Press.

Sykes, G., & Darling-Hammond, L. (Eds.). (1999). *Teaching as a learning profession: Handbook of policy and practice*. San Francisco, CA: Jossey-Bass.

10

Implementing School Reform in a High-Stakes Testing Policy Environment: The Case of an Urban Elementary School

Pedro Reyes

The work of school restructuring is difficult. School principals and teachers must deal with different, and sometimes contradictory, policy environments as they engage in restructuring their schools. Thus, it is important to describe the policy environments surrounding the school reform process at Bates Elementary. First, I present the national context, followed by the state policy environment. Then, I describe the school context. This is followed by the lessons learned in this school. The account that follows includes three years of fieldwork and intensive training by the local National Education Association (NEA) and teachers at reforming schools.

THE NATIONAL POLICY ENVIRONMENT

The 1983 report, *A Nation at Risk: The Imperative for Educational Reform* (National Commission on Excellence in Education), provided the initial impetus to reform or restructure public education in the United States. The report invoked national attention to education by accentuating that "unthinking, unilateral educational disarmament" threatened our national prosperity, security, civility, and our livelihood as a democratic society. Educators unaware of the "rising tide of mediocrity" were confronted suddenly with alarming evidence of eminent danger as *A Nation at Risk* warned "what was unimaginable a generation ago has begun to occur—others are matching and surpassing our educational attainments."

The report prompted states and local districts to examine the schools' responsibility to guarantee student learning. The rhetoric of *A Nation at Risk* and reports that followed, while often contested on the basis they are exaggerated and alarmist in nature (Berliner & Biddle, 1995), energized the country's quest for educational excellence.

This report set in motion the next set of reports emphasizing account-ability. Since then, standard setting, assessments, and accountability have continued to gain momentum. At the 1989 education summit held in Char-lottesville, Virginia, President George Bush and the nation's governors focused their attention on establishing a system of accountability, stimulat-ing state and local initiatives to change schools and the entire learning enterprise, and creating an environment ripe for widespread reform and innovation. Eventually, the committee adopted eight National Education Goals. The goals stipulated that American students would be able to demonstrate competency in subjects such as English, mathematics, science, history, and geography by the year 2000. In 1991, President Bush announced *America 2000: An Education Strategy*. The long-term, national education strategy included improving current schools and making them accountable for the achievement of all students; inventing new schools to meet the demands of the twenty-first century; encouraging lifelong learning; and creating communities in which this learning can take place.

In 1994, President Clinton adopted the *Goals 2000: Educate America Act*. This legislation assisted states and local districts in reaching the eight National Education Goals adopted in 1990. *Goals 2000* again placed aca-demic standards and assessments based on those standards at the forefront of reform efforts and American ideals for public education. The reform rec-ommendations included increasing the use and scope of standards and accountability systems. The Commission on Excellence also recommended standardized tests given at various levels of schooling. State and local tests would assess student achievement, thus distinguishing areas of needed remediation and acceleration. Congress' reauthorization of the Elementary and Secondary Education Act in 1994 and 1999 reiterated national com-mitment to *Goals 2000,* educational achievement for all children coupled with greater state and district flexibility with proof of increased achieve-ment. These reforms, following in the footsteps of reforms initiated in 1983, recommended access for all children to high standards (O'Day & Smith, 1993).

Policy makers believe that the presence of standards and testing, espe-cially those aligned with state or local standards, improve teaching and learning (O'Day & Smith, 1993). Although an ambiguous understanding of standards exists among the public, educators, researchers, or policy makers (Elmore, Abelmann, & Fuhrman, 1996), Murnane and Levy (1998) con-cede that "if standards and assessments are not sufficient for higher student achievement, they are necessary" (p. 118). The National Education Goals advocate, and most states maintain, the same standards for all children. Recently, some have suggested that alternate standards should exist for students based on their program, such as limited-English-proficiency programs (Newman, King, & Rigdon, 1997).

Most states in the United States provide some form of testing. These assessments are expected to be unbiased; and the results from them should be used to improve teaching and learning (Lachat, 1999). Except for Iowa and Nebraska, forty-eight states measure student performance through statewide testing (Jerald & Boser, 1999). High school competency tests are the most frequent type of assessment currently utilized. Arguably, competency tests may provide beneficial information when aligned with the curriculum and standards. Subsequently, statewide competency tests, like their norm-referenced standardized counterparts, "need to have high instructional and curricular validity" and the "curriculum needs to drive the content of the examinations rather than vice versa" (Geisinger, 1992, p. 10).

In the late 1990s, statewide testing was heralded as an impetus to improved teaching and learning. Grissmer and Flanagan (1998) noted that statewide standards and assessments for all students, including the accessibility of student performance data, were among the key reform policies responsible for the achievement gains from 1990 to 1997 on the National Assessment of Educational Progress (NAEP) made by North Carolina and Texas. While many commend statewide standards and assessments for raising the bar for educational excellence, others argue that this may be a myth (McNeil & Valenzuela, 2000).

Most states and local districts throughout the country maintain accountability systems and use performance indicators, including scores on standardized tests, at the school and/or district level. To date, forty-nine states have established some type of academic standards and maintain an accountability or reporting system on school performance (Jerald & Boser, 1999). Many of the accountability systems today are characterized by an emphasis on student performance as determined by criterion-referenced achievement tests. This "new educational accountability" system replaces reliance upon educational inputs and processes for determining school and/or district accreditation (Elmore, Abelmann, & Fuhrman, 1996).

The evolution of accountability from the measurement of inputs and processes to the measurement of outputs holds schools and districts accountable for the ability of students and schools to meet preestablished standards. However, in an educational environment that levies formal and informal rewards and sanctions on students and teachers, we must proceed with caution. While few dispute the necessity for educational accountability, many continue to contest the nature of the accountability system, the evaluative measures, and the subsequent interpretation and results. Berliner and Biddle (1995) added that the problem with accountability is how it is exercised, not the theory.

THE TEXAS POLICY ENVIRONMENT

The increasing number of states with accountability or reporting systems is indicative of the expanding state role in educational accountability. Thirty-six states issue report cards on individual schools; nineteen states issue public ratings of schools; nineteen states reward successful schools; sixteen states maintain legislative authority to close, sanction, or reconstitute failing schools (Jerald & Boser, 1999). Texas, North Carolina, California, and Kentucky are among these examples.

In 1984, the Texas legislature passed House Bill 72. House Bill 72 directed the state to develop an accountability system focused on student performance. Consequently, since 1984–85, school districts have published annual performance reports. By law, these reports are made available to the public. Eventually, the information collected for the Academic Excellence Indicator System (AEIS) report became a tool for determining district accreditation and school ratings. Today, the AEIS includes the following:

- TAAS passing rate by grade, by subject, and by all grades tested
- End-of-Course examination—participation and results
- Attendance rate for the full year
- Dropout rate (by year)
- Graduation and dropout rates (4-year longitudinal)
- Percent of high school students completing an advanced course
- Percent of graduates completing the Recommended High School Program
- AP and IB examination results
- TAAS/TASP equivalency rate
- SAT and ACT examination—participation and results (Texas Education Agency, 1999a)

Additional information on students, staff and personnel, finances, programs, and demographics is available in the full AEIS report. AEIS provides information at the campus, district, region, and state level. Since 1994, the Texas Education Agency has assigned accountability ratings to schools and districts based on student performance on TAAS, annual percentage of dropouts, and attendance rates. Performance data are desegregated into four student groups: African American, Hispanic, white, and economically disadvantaged. Moreover, by rule the Texas State Board of Education established that all students *shall* learn the essential knowledge and skills in English, mathematics, science, and social studies. Statewide assessment in Texas has evolved from minimum competency testing to testing state curriculum standards. First, the Texas Assessment of Basic Skills (TABS) test, a criterion-referenced minimum competency test in reading, writing, and mathematics was given to students in grades 5 and 9 from 1979 to 1985.

After TABS, the Texas Educational Assessment of Minimum Skills (TEAMS) examination (also a minimum competency test), was administered from 1984 to 1990. The latest state exam is the TAAS. This testing system has been in operation since the 1990–91 academic year.

The statewide assessment program includes TAAS to assess student performance on the four core area curriculum standards. Since 1994, students in grades 3 through 8 and the 10th grade are tested in reading and mathematics; writing is tested in grades 4, 8, and 10; and science and social studies are tested in grade 8. A Spanish-version TAAS, benchmarked in spring 1996, is now available for grades 3 through 6 in reading, writing, and mathematics. Since 1998–99, students must also demonstrate satisfactory performance on end-of-course examinations in Algebra I, Biology I, English II, and U.S. History to be eligible for high school graduation.

The State Board of Education has also approved the following changes in accordance with Senate Bill 103. First, all limited-English-proficient (LEP) students will participate, taking the Reading Proficiency Test of English (RPTE) annually until English reading proficiency is demonstrated and they are switched to the English version of TAAS. All LEP students in grades 3 through 8 are required to take either the English or Spanish version of TAAS. An exception will be made for recent unschooled immigrants, who will receive a one-year exemption in grades 3 through 8, and non-Spanish speakers, who may have up to a two-year exemption in grades 3 through 6. Students labeled LEP may still opt for a one-time postponement of the exit-level examination. Those students, whose parents reject LEP services, must participate in the English version of TAAS and the RPTE annually. In spring 1999, 168,373 LEP students took either the English or Spanish TAAS. An additional 67,766 LEP students were exempt. As of spring 2000, performance for LEP students taking the Spanish TAAS will be included in the accountability system. LEP students taking the English TAAS are already included in the base indicators for school accountability.

As a result of Senate Bill 103, future statewide assessment in Texas will also change. According to proposed amendments, Texas students will be assessed in mathematics in grades 3 through 7 without the aid of technology, and in grades 8 through 11 with the aid of technology; reading in grades 3 through 9; writing in grades 4 and 7; English language arts in grade 10; social studies in grades 8 and 10; and science in grades 5 and 10 (Texas Education Agency, 1999b, 1999c). The new assessment program must be implemented no later than 2002–03.

THE SCHOOL CONTEXT

Bates Elementary School (pseudonym) serves nearly 500 students ranging from pre K through fifth grade. Located in the heart of San Antonio, Texas, Bates's student population is 99 percent Hispanic. Bates qualifies as a Title I campus with 96 percent of the students participating in the free and reduced lunch program. Over 40 percent of the students are limited or non-English speaking, and the school has a mobility rate of 22 percent. The demographics of Bates Elementary School are similar to the other urban elementary school campuses within the San Antonio Independent School District (SAISD). It differs from its counterparts, though, in that its students consistently perform well on the Texas Assessment of Academic Skills. As a district, SAISD had only 56.5 percent of its students pass all the TAAS tests in 1998. In contrast, Bates has a long history of success and, within the past several years, has been named as either a recognized or exemplary school.

The poor performance on the TAAS of so many students and the reality that 88.6 percent of the students in the San Antonio Independent School District are economically disadvantaged convinced the superintendent that serious attention to reform that could support student learning was important. He decided to steer the district in the direction of whole school reform movement and aligned San Antonio ISD with the New American Schools (NAS) movement. Each campus in SAISD, under the leadership of the principal, was asked to study the various NAS designs and select a model to implement with the support of New American Schools Design Teams. According to Richard Elmore, in his book *Restructuring Schools, The Next Generation of School Reform* (1990), the motive for restructuring schools may arise from concerns about demography, equity, and social justice or from what some perceive to be a crisis in the quality of the teaching force. The whole school reform movement in SAISD was certainly linked to concerns about demography, but it was most directly related to a sense of crisis about student performance in the district.

In contrast to its counterparts, Bates Elementary was not a campus in crisis. Therefore, it is not surprising that Bates, with the support of district leadership, chose to embrace a reform model that was not one of the New American Schools' models. Most of these models focus directly on changing organization and governance, curriculum, and pedagogy. The model selected by Bates, *Keys to Excellence in Your Schools* (KEYS), sponsored by the National Educational Association, was concerned with the conditions necessary for high quality schools. This model focused on diagnosis of strengths and weakness within the school setting but deliberately did not prescribe specific structures or teaching strategies. Thus, KEYS also allowed the campus to, in the words of one teacher, "continue with what works." Under some circumstances, the choice of a reform model that allows for continuation of current practices might reflect an apathy or unwillingness to change on the part of the school community. This was most definitely not the case at Bates. It was a school that manifested a strong commitment to students and their achievement and a well-developed collaborative culture. The data-oriented, non-prescriptive approach to improvement advocated by KEYS was a nice match for this site. In the next section, I offer a brief description of certain dimensions of Bates Elementary School that seemed to make it a good site for a reform like KEYS. I then turn my attention directly to the unfolding of KEYS at this school.

Bates: A Good Site for a KEYS-Type Reform

As a reform model, KEYS has several distinctive features. Built upon research about conditions that foster student achievement, it revolves around a data collection system designed to provide schools with information that can help them assess strengths and weaknesses. As a reform KEYS is distinctive in that it is not linked to any particular structure, curriculum, or pedagogy. Rather, it assumes that the individuals within the school are in the best position to design their own pathway to improvement and assumes that the information about conditions within the school can and will be used in this effort. In many ways, Bates was ideally suited for a nondirective reform like KEYS. The individuals in the site shared a strong commitment to learning and children, communicated easily with one another, and worked well together.

A strong commitment to learning and to children is a hallmark of the culture at Bates Elementary School. One teacher chose the following words to describe this feature:

Teachers are friendly to the children. They treat them as if they are . . . their own. This is what I felt made it unique compared to other schools where I've been. They give a lot of importance to the children. . . . Also they have a lot of things going on to keep the students interested, specializing in a lot of handwriting, reading, everything in general. . . . Teachers meet a lot to challenge and to discuss ways to improve and perfect students.

Another pointed out that the commitment to Bates and its students is demonstrated by a remarkably low level of turnover among faculty and staff:

When I came to Bates, it was very different as far as teachers making a commitment to the school. I was very impressed with the fact over three-fourths of the teachers had been here for over ten years. There is a very low turnover for teachers in every year. I was very impressed with the commitment level of the teachers in this public school. And I still hear some horror stories about other teachers. And that commitment isn't there like it is here. . . . It was not just a job for the teachers here in this school. I mean they really made a commitment to these students and to their parents. We want this school to be the best school in this district.

The words of these teachers suggest that educators at Bates believe that they can best honor their commitments to children by discovering ways to encourage high achievement. Bates's principal certainly expressed this view when he indicated that his goals for the school were simple ones. He wanted students to be knowledge producers and teachers to be problem solvers focused on student achievement. He strongly believed in the power of individual learning, but also believed in the power of the learning community (Reyes, Scribner, & Paredes, 1999). His vision for the school seemed to be shared by other administrators and by the faculty who, in many ways, demonstrated their commitment to be a place where students succeeded.

The shared commitment to children and learning contributed to a high level of collaboration among teachers and administrators. One teacher noted, "Not only was there a commitment, but we were able to work with each other." Other teachers agreed. One teacher articulated the connection between a strong commitment to the "whole" child and collaboration within and across grade levels:

My grade level [second grade] is not separate from the rest of the school. I am in close contact always with third grade, also with first grade. So if third grade is having problems when we send our kids to fourth grade, they will get together with us and say this is what we've noticed is missing. We know what is missing. So then we turn around and we work here for the students to be ready to go to fourth grade. We always have class grade level meetings. We do not see kids as separate, we see them as a whole.

Another teacher noted that "communication" and "a common goal" helped teachers to "work together" as "a real family."

Several teachers acknowledged that the principal played an important role in facilitating and supporting cooperative work at Bates. One individual noted: "the administration is great, because they set up the ground rules and everybody just follows them and makes sure that everything is getting done . . . the administration is very supportive. When we need anything they back us up and they listen to your ideas and you know they just do whatever they can to support you. They look for new things, new ways that we need." Another respondent concurred and described the principal this way:

He listens to us very well. He takes our opinions and then he sees what concerns us and works with us instead of dictating what needs to be done. He says what do you guys think and I think that has made our school what it is.

As these comments suggest, student achievement provides the centerpiece for the collaborative culture at Bates Elementary School. One teacher suggested that the fine track record of Bates in this area was a major source of pride and that it inspired a strong commitment to the school for her and other teachers:

You know, [student achievement] is one thing that I'm very proud of. I admire a lot the respect that these children have for adults, and their behavior is excellent. We don't have to hassle problems because students know what to do. . . . There has been a lot of work to get this school to where it is. I'm very proud of the fact that we have mastered student achievement, that not every school has what we have. We have a very unique school and the behaviors are excellent; and I'm proud of them.

The teachers and administrators at Bates were committed to working together to support children. They had developed good communication and were able to focus their efforts on activities that promoted student achievement. Thus, at this site, the KEYS data were introduced into a site where educators worked well together. Teachers and administrators at this site were able to use these data to sharpen and focus efforts that were already yielding results.

KEYS IMPLEMENTATION AT BATES ELEMENTARY SCHOOL

Instruction aimed at promoting student success was a central focus at Bates Elementary School. When the results of the KEYS survey were presented to Bates faculty, teachers quickly began to search for ways to use this information to sharpen and focus efforts to ensure that every child learned at a high level. As noted earlier, the faculty had opted for this type of reform because it would allow them "to continue doing the kinds of things that were already happening here." At the same time, though, teachers and administrators were not averse to change and carefully considered areas of weakness uncovered by the survey. Indeed a number of teachers lauded the fact that this reform allowed them to identify, "what our weaknesses and our strengths were so we could work on these weaknesses."

Continuing What Works

In the results of the KEYS survey, teachers and administration found affirmation of their high expectations for student success, instructional practices guided by assessments of student learning, and their supportive working relationships. These were among the practices they wanted to continue.

High Expectation for Student Success

One of the items on the KEYS survey assesses the extent to which "Teachers, education support personnel, students, and parents believe all students can learn" (KEYS indicator 5). The responses of faculty and administrators indicated that this belief was indeed present and widely shared at Bates Elementary School. My interviews and observations indicated that this belief went well beyond functioning as just a slogan at this site. One teacher summed up a shared commitment when she noted, "our goal here is that we think all children can learn." Indeed, without exception, the teachers and administrators with whom I spoke made reference to student learning and doing what is in the best interest of the children. For example, one faculty member mentioned, "I just think in a lot of our practices we try to do what's best for students." Another emphatically stated, "We are concentrating on the children and what the children can do." Other comments stressing the same point included: "We do have high expectations of our kids," "the kids, they have the potential to soar," and, "we want our kids to strive."

At Bates, impressive performance on the TAAS was one of the markers of student success. It was, however, by no means the primary focus at this site. One teacher noted that the faculty was committed to cultivating "certain skills . . . lifelong skills" that would enable students to "be successful in the real world." The counselor made several references to the importance of students' understanding that coming to school was their job: "In elementary school, kids need their foundation about coming to work. Come to school—it is your job to be on time." It is important to note, also, that student success at Bates was typically discussed as something more than simply preparing students to meet the expectations of the outside world. One educator's words summed up the prevailing sentiment: "Our children can perform and can surpass the level that most people have pigeonholed them in. . . . I think that we really believe that our children can learn and can go beyond. So if they can go beyond, then *we* [emphasis added] must go beyond."

Quality Instruction Guided by Assessments of Student Learning

One entire section of the KEYS questionnaire focuses on determining the ways educators use assessment to inform instruction. Indirectly some of the items within this section also address the quality of instruction and seek to assess the degree to which teachers and administrators are seeking to create quality instructional programs that really meet student needs. Responses to this section of the survey coupled with comments made by teachers during interviews indicated that faculty at Bates have a great deal of confidence in their locally designed program for instruction. One stated, "We have developed our own way, our own methods to teach these things. And it is working." Another noted, "The system Bates has been using to prepare their students for the TAAS exam has been in place for several years. What we have been trying and working with our children for the past four to five years has been successful."

Bates's teachers consistently referenced the TAAS exam as they discussed their instructional practices. One described their work this way: "We had reading groups, writing groups, math groups . . . we have all kinds of groups. Each grade level has a representative . . . and they make up grade level tests over TAAS objectives and teach them. I guess it's curriculum alignment; several years ago that wasn't the buzzword."

Although the TAAS examination was the primary assessment mentioned by participants in this investigation, it was by no means the only one. Teachers spoke of frequent efforts to determine if and how children learned. One, for instance, noted, "We are always assessing and trying to see where our children are." One participant did express a concern about an "over-emphasis on TAAS" and wondered if the state mandated exam and its role in shaping instruction was potentially excluding some types of student learning and experiences. Most, however, although they spoke frequently of the TAAS exam, also revealed a general commitment to "increasing student achievement" beyond the passing of TAAS.

Supportive Working Relationships

A major section of the KEYS survey addresses conditions that lead to "open communication and collaborative problem solving." In this area, Bates's faculty and administrators again found affirmation of the working relationships they had developed. During interviews, participants made frequent references to the "positive climate" at their site, and several pointed to the low turnover as both an indicator of and a contributor to the positive climate at this site. One respondent stated, "The teachers that I am teaching with have been here for many years also . . . we are also friends." Others concurred and indicated that they saw clear connections between the reality that teachers at Bates "get along real well" and the academic performance of students.

Teachers participating in this investigation indicated that they sensed support, not only from teaching colleagues, but also from administrators. Comments about leadership at this site included: "[Administrators are] supportive and very helpful," "I think administration has made it a point to really listen a great deal," and "People feel they are being listened to." Here, too, teachers saw a connection between their positive and supportive relationship with administrators and student academic performance.

Teachers and administrators certainly worked well together prior to Bates's participation in the KEYS project. Many noted, though, that the process of self-reflection that was required by KEYS brought the faculty even closer together. "I think this has built a trust among us at the grade level." One made reference to the cooperative problem-solving model presented in the KEYS training, noting, "When you work closely together and you make decisions as a group, not just as an individual, you have more perspective plus you know that you can count on someone else to help you along if you get stuck." And several reported that they believed that the already responsive administration was even more supportive. One noted that participation in KEYS had helped to create conditions where "things are more accessible" and administrators "are more flexible." Another stated that the principal seemed even more attuned to "valuing teacher input" after the KEYS survey highlighted the importance of teachers in the reform process.

Identifying Areas for Improvement Efforts

In addition to the successes mentioned, the staff at Bates identified several areas of relative weakness and targeted them for special attention. These areas for improvement included articulation between grades and parent and community involvement.

Improved Communication between Grade Levels

As noted previously, Bates was a site characterized by supportive relationships between and among faculty and administration. These relationships were long standing and predated the school's involvement with KEYS. The results of the survey and the discussions and planning that followed did, however, reveal a need to work on enhancing communication between teachers and articulation of curriculum and instruction at different grade levels. One teacher pointed out that the analysis of the KEYS data had led her and others to an important discovery. "Through that process [KEYS] we are discovering that one of the problems we seem to have is inter- or cross-grade level communication." Another mentioned the same concern and credited KEYS with prompting changes and sparking improvements in this area: "Teachers felt that there needed to be more collaborative talk between grade levels and even within grade levels—collaboratively speaking—I think there is quite a lot more of that going on this year. So, I feel that we're moving in the right direction." Other respondents agreed. Indeed, increased communication between and among grade levels was touted as one of the most noticeable outcomes of the early stages of the KEYS implementation by nearly every participant: "One of the things we do in our KEYS process is have cross-grade level meetings, and that helps with communication between grade levels about expectations. We just met as a grade level last week and went around to each other's rooms. And we feel that through communication, we're able to open up lines of communication between grade levels."

In the view of teachers, enhanced communication was linked to the development of smoother articulation of curriculum and instruction between grade levels. One, reflecting on discussions that resulted from work with KEYS, described sessions this way: "They talked about why the groups weren't ready for the next grade level." Another second grade teacher stated that conversations prompted by KEYS led her and her colleagues to work to ensure that "what we are covering in second grade is really, you know, [the kind of material that] where we leave our kids . . . where the third grade wants them." Two others made similar points. One noted that work linked to KEYS has "really helped us line up our expectations and our time lines." Another stated that in the past four years, "I've never seen quite as much integration between two grade levels and the seeking out of where students should be at the end of the year."

Parent and Community Involvement

In addition to highlighting a need for enhanced communication between grade levels, the analysis of KEYS data also assisted faculty and administration in realizing that work could and should be done to increase the involvement of parents and the community. Although some teachers seemed happy with the level of parental involvement in their classrooms, the responses to the survey reflected concern by the teachers about the lack of participation by parents in both their children's school activities and homework assignments. Comments made during the interviews confirmed that these were areas where conditions at Bates were less than ideal. The KEYS process provided a framework for planning ways to improve.

Discussions about ways to increase parent involvement focused on a number of strategies. Some teachers concentrated on structures that would bring parents into the school both as supporters and as decision makers. One respondent, for instance, noted that "Bates has no parent organization and [we] are trying to figure out how to get the parents involved and begin a PTA, which is what we are hoping for through the KEYS." Others focused on strategies for encouraging family members to support their children's academic work. Aware that many parents in this low-income area lacked academic skills, teachers focused on ways they could build both capacity and confidence. A number of suggestions were offered to accomplish these goals. Most focused on "bring[ing] parents in for demonstrations, or [to] show modeling or what we are teaching their children." One teacher pointed to the success of the KEYS sponsored workshop that had already been conducted: "Over 100 parents showed up for a program that involves a workshop where they have the parents come in and learn how to do division and simple math facts, reading comprehension—so, when the kids bring their homework home the parents can help them."

In addition to looking for ways to equip parents to help their children with schoolwork, teachers and administrators sought for ways to overcome an apparent language barrier that was inhibiting parental involvement. Although most of the Bates Elementary schoolteachers and administrators are bilingual, many teachers still cite an inability to speak English as a barrier to the parents' willingness to come to the school. One of the teachers described this problem very clearly: "I think a lot of that is because of the community—it's a poor area. Parents don't speak English, so it is very difficult for them to come into a school and feel comfortable in an atmosphere where I think they feel inadequate. A lot of them just came from Mexico and can't even help the fifth graders with their math." Even with these difficulties, most of the respondents saw much forward motion in this area, as reflected in the following comment: "I think that parents are becoming more aware of their children's progress—a parent is always the first teacher and I think because of KEYS we have made parents realize they are a big part of their child's education."

In addition to prompting attention to parental involvement, the KEYS process also sparked efforts to work more effectively with the larger community surrounding Bates. As articulated by one respondent, the problem is one of "trying to get the community involved—parents or businesses. We had a school-wide fundraiser this year that had not been done in the past. . . . Yeah, I think it will help us build community spirit centered around the school by getting the community more involved in our school." Another teacher commented: "I think that by utilizing the school community, we found that we wanted to use outside resources to augment what we do here . . . businesses are commenting about higher achievement levels and the district is aware of greater achievement. Others are noting ways to utilize our successes across the district."

The recurring strand of thought in these discussions centers on the fact that the school as a whole could improve its community interaction and impact in ways that were not specifically tied to the parents. As one teacher argued, "we wanted to also work at bringing in resources from the community and helping us with our kids," while another noted that "we have reached out to different communities, different community agencies and resources that we have brought into the school this particular school year."

CONCLUSIONS: MAKING SENSE OF KEYS AT BATES ELEMENTARY SCHOOL

Bates Elementary School was and is a tightly woven community that stresses involvement of all stakeholders working toward academic achievement. This focus clearly drives activities and practices, for there is minimal attention paid to extracurricular activities. Bates illustrates achievement can occur if academics is the focus and goal of the school. Non-academic activities can be integrated into the school day, but the focus is on learning, not on the distractions that sometimes can result when students get involved in nonacademic activities. Bates has developed an effective learning environment that enables teachers and students to be academically successful. This environment has been constructed by administrators, teachers, and some parents—all working together to develop a high performing school. It appears that the key factors that have led to Bates's extraordinary record include involvement, coordination, support, and accountability of all community members of Bates Elementary.

The factors that led to Bates's outstanding record of academic achievement were also factors that helped the Bates community find meaning in KEYS as a reform strategy. The benefits afforded from a reform such as KEYS at a school such as Bates Elementary may well be found in the words of the mid-career second grade teacher. When asked if she saw any advantages in adopting the KEYS program for the school, she responded:

Oh yes, I sure do; instruction and curriculum and special programs can be tailor-made to our community, our particular population's needs. That is something that may work in some settings and not work in others. And if you just buy into a program and plug that in, it is not going to be the best program. It may be the best program for one student but not for all. This way, we will be able to make informed choices and I think that will positively impact our students.

The KEYS reform is distinctive in that it focuses heavily on conditions that have been shown to correlate with good outcomes for children. One emphasis in the survey is on assessing the extent to which adults in the school setting share views of children's capabilities and work together to see that every child learns at a high level. Participation in this reform helped educators at this site to realize that, while they did uniformly hold high expectations for the success of all children, they did not communicate quite as effectively as they might. In this area, the reform helped to spark efforts to make better linkages across the entire school. The consistently positive feedback in the responses of the participants supports the notion that KEYS has had a major impact on promoting better linkages throughout the school and in promoting improved morale among the instructional staff. As summed up by one respondent: "It was more of a one-on-one in the past. Now we're making it more a group effort. If we need any help in fifth grade, if I get a lapse of how to solve a problem or if the kids aren't getting something, I can ask one of my co-workers and they'll give me some other strategy or way to teach something. I like that!" The linkages within the school that are being fostered as a result of participation with KEYS seem to be matched to some extent by efforts to reach out to parents and the community to bring them more into the life of the school. Efforts to create a parents' organization and to provide workshops to assist family members in understanding the work children are being asked to do represent two attempts to respond to a need in this area.

The teachers and administrators with whom I spoke actually saw few disadvantages to the KEYS program. Indeed, none of the interviewees saw any major disadvantages to KEYS and often spent much time articulating what they saw as the advantages, even when responding to a question or probe explicitly about potential disadvantages. When asked directly if they saw any disadvantages to KEYS, the majority of the respondents answered with either a categorical "No" or "None," or that they "don't see any disadvantages." Probes directed at further exploring the possibility of disadvantages usually encountered a shift back to the positive aspects of the program. As one teacher of twenty-nine years experience responded: "I don't see any disadvantages at all. I see mostly help and what we are doing is for the benefit for the children and the community and school, you know. It is the helping process, you know."

The time commitment, both in time away from instruction for meetings and the summer training requirements, was briefly mentioned by a few interviewees as a minor disadvantage or drawback to KEYS. However, only one teacher's complaint was about the need for "more time." When asked about problems with KEYS she responded:

I think for one, time. I wish that we had more time to be more in-depth as far as training is concerned. I realize that once we get into the school year our training kind of stops and it's the matters-at-hand that become more important than anything else. I think to keep something alive you've got to constantly be putting it in the forefront. I wish that there were more time in the day. I, as a teacher, know that once you start the school year the responsibilities are enormous. Sometimes it almost seemed as if it were too time consuming to be able to do one extra thing. So I wish we had more time.

In closing, Keys to Excellence in Your Schools is designed to be a process for improvement from within and is intended to be conducted over time. In its implementation, there is strong evidence that KEYS has had an impact on Bates Elementary and is making it possible for this "exemplary" school to look beyond TAAS.

REFERENCES

Berliner, D., & Biddle, B. (1995). *The manufactured crisis: Myths, fraud, and the attack on America's public schools.* New York: Addison-Wesley.

Elmore, R. (1990). *Restructuring schools, The next generation of school reform.* San Francisco: Jossey-Bass.

Elmore, R., Abelmann, C., & Fuhrman, S. (1996). The new accountability in state education reform: From process to performance. In H. F. Ladd (Ed.), *Holding schools accountable: Performance-based reform in education* (pp. 65–98). Washington, DC: The Brookings Institution.

Geisinger, K. (1992). *Testing limited English proficient students for minimum competency and high school graduation.* Proceedings of the Second National Research Symposium on Limited English Proficient Student Issues: Focus on Evaluation and Measurement. OBEMLA, 1992. Available: http://www.ncbe.gwu.edu/ncbepubs/symposia/second/vol2/testing.htm

Grissmer, D., & Flanagan, A. (1998). *Exploring rapid achievement gains in North Carolina and Texas.* Washington, DC: National Education Goals.

Jerald, C., & Boser, U. (1999). Quality counts 1999: Taking stock. *Education Week on the Web.* Available: http://www.edweek.org/sreports/qc99/ac/tables/ac-intro.htm

Lachat, M. (1999). *Standards, equity, and cultural diversity.* Providence, RI: Northeast and Islands Regional Educational Laboratory.

McNeil, L., & Valenzuela, A. (2000). *The harmful impact of the TAAS system of testing in Texas: Beneath the accountability rhetoric.* (ERIC Document Reproduction Service No. ED 443 872)

Murnane R., & Levy, F. (1998). Standards, information, and the demand for student achievement. *Federal Reserve Bank of New York Economic Policy Review, 4,* 117–124. (Transcript of presentation at the Excellence in Education: Views on Improving American Education Conference).

National Commission on Excellence in Education. (1983). *A nation at risk: The imperative for educational reform.* Washington, DC: U.S. Department of Education.

Newman, F., King, M. B., & Rigdon, M. (1997). Accountability and school performance: Implications from restructuring schools. *Harvard Education Review, 67,* 41–74.

O'Day, J., & Smith, M. (1993). Systemic reform and educational opportunity. In S. Fuhrman, (Ed.), *Designing coherent education policy: Improving the system* (pp. 250–312). San Francisco, CA: Jossey Bass.

Reyes, P., Scribner, J. D., & Paredes, S. A. (1999). *Creating learning communities: Lessons from high poverty high performance schools.* New York: Teacher's College Press.

Texas Education Agency. (1999a). *An overview of the Academic Excellence Indicator System for the state of Texas.* Austin, TX: Author. Available: http://www.tea.state.tx.us/perfreport/aeis/about.aeis.html

Texas Education Agency. (1999b). *State Board of Education meeting: Attachment I: Statutory citation relating to proposed amendment to 19 TAC §101.3, Testing accommodations and exemptions.* Austin, TX: Author. Available: http://www.tea.state.tx.us/sboe/schedule/9911/101-003stat.html

Texas Education Agency. (1999c). *State Board of Education meeting: Proposed amendment to 19 TAC §101.3, Testing accommodations and exemptions* (Second Reading and Final Adoption). Austin, TX: Author. Available: http://www.tea.state.tx.us/sboe/schedule/9911/101-003.html

11

The School and Self-Reflective Renewal: Taking Stock and Moving On

Bradley S. Portin, Lynn G. Beck, Michael S. Knapp, and Joseph Murphy

The process of examining and improving teaching practice in schools, at a time when multiple initiatives and pressures impinge on schools, creates a unique opportunity to consider both what works and the complex stories of schools as they attend to these multiple expectations. The cases in this book provide just such an in-depth look at the work of schools as they take on the challenges of educating students. The cases tell the story of schools in nine states taking stock through a self-reflective strategy—in particular, through the use of the KEYS process—and moving on, sometimes moving on with KEYS, or sometimes discarding KEYS and moving on without it.

Our work in this book is not an evaluation of a particular school improvement initiative, but rather a careful examination of the process of taking stock—of self-assessment—that many schools engage in during this time of widespread public attention to the quality of schools. The cases illuminate the many means by which school staff look at their own practice and the needs of their school community, look elsewhere for inspiration and guidance, or retreat to practices that they believe have worked in the past. The array of responses to the challenge of renewal is as diverse as the schools and communities we studied. For that reason, the cases presented in this book help us to understand a range of responses to renewal rather than proposing a single renewal recipe that may work best in all schools.

The process of self-assessment, of stocktaking, that schools go through when using self-reflective strategies is inherently incomplete. This is one of the central tenets of KEYS, which was never intended to be an end product in a school improvement process. Instead, the initiative's theory-of-action holds that school improvement can be set in motion through a reflective tool (such as the KEYS instrument) acting as a mirror, stimulating action, providing a source of important issues to attend to, and offering an organizing rubric for a variety of activities that schools might pursue. The KEYS strategy, thus, places its bets on the power of the process, one that encourages schools to begin down a path of clearer understanding of strengths and weaknesses toward a vision of what they might do to improve their service to students. KEYS seeks to create a systematic organizational learning cycle for individual schools. A similar cycle may pertain at other levels (indeed, in commissioning these case studies and other analyses, NEA as an organization is attempting to take stock of and improve its KEYS Initiative).

The cases in this book look at how NEA's initiative, a national movement, plays out in schools locally—how these schools take stock and move forward from their experience of, and participation in, KEYS. Studying any attempt at school reform, no less this initiative, is diabolically difficult. For one thing, any systematic attention paid to a school and its search of renewal is time-bound. Researchers trying to make sense of the melange of forces and capacities within this period of study do so while simultaneously recognizing that there are precursors to what they see in schools and what school personnel experience. Our attention to the KEYS initiative was focused on a particular span of time, usually the first several years during which each school first encountered the KEYS reflective process.

As does the KEYS Initiative itself, the case accounts focus on individual schools. While not the only important unit of change (the state and district systems are other appropriate targets of change efforts), there is broad consensus that the school is both an important and appropriate unit of change uniquely positioned at the intersection of teaching and learning. Mindful of this, the KEYS planners built the initiative on the assumption that the improvement processes had to be built school-by-school, with, and by, the unique configuration of people who comprised the school community. Accordingly, the case study research team selected individual schools (or a small cadre of schools in the case of Tennessee) to shed light on the story of the way KEYS engaged educators in pursuit of improvement goals. Therefore, we made a deliberate choice to probe deeply in a small sample of schools rather than survey a larger population of schools engaged in the initiative. We believed that the lessons learned by looking deeply at the experience of individual schools would tell more about the way a self-reflective process plays out in the complex work and environment of schools. However, recognizing that the state policy and union context would likely present a central set of influences on each school's KEYS story, we chose to conduct the case study work in nine different states (see Appendix A). These nine states differed from one another in terms of reform goals, union leadership, political culture, and other factors. As such, we recognize that this still represents a sample of nine states, not fifty. There will be different stories untold from states not selected. At the same time, however, it is important to note that the similar characteristics of state educational reform, operating under the umbrella of heightened accountability, are creating a number of common sets of experiences from state to state.

The power of case study as a research method lies in its ability to construct a story, a chronicle of events and experiences across a particular period of time, that seeks to account for the forces and conditions in the organization and its environment that contribute to that narrative. The case study account permits one to describe and assess subtle connections among events, and between them and the participants' experience of these events; the result is an integrated explanation of both what occurred in a community and what might explain the action that is taking place. In addition, the case study story serves to illustrate the way in which policy is lived out and connects to practice.

In the next section, we present a framework that explains the interplay of actions and conditions that we saw in the schools in these nine states. Specifically, we describe how the content of the renewal initiative and both the internal and external context of the school shape the responses of these organizations. In the following section, we describe what these cases tell us about the array of forces that shape and mediate the school's response to self-reflective renewal. In the final section, we outline lessons arising from this approach to self-reflective renewal.

SCHOOL RESPONSE TO RENEWAL: AN ORGANIZING FRAMEWORK

There is much to pay attention to when exploring, understanding, and explaining the work of schools and the attempts by school staff to change what they are doing. In particular, school renewal is always about the content and chronology of renewal activity as it unfolds in a particular context. Most often, the story of a school's renewal effort focuses on a particular set of solutions—the overt content of renewal—and seeks to capture the struggle by staff to incorporate these solutions into school routines and to document the longer-term consequences for participants and students.

As a self-reflective approach to school renewal, KEYS does not offer a set of solutions, concentrating instead on establishing the process of self-appraisal and subsequent action. As such, this kind of reform is content-free, or put another way, its *content* is the process itself, as well as the data that the process produces. The process, which we have described as holding up a mirror to the school, surfaces that which is not seen in everyday action, which might otherwise remain hidden without a deliberative process to bring it to light. The result is a portrait (however incomplete and perception-bound) that encourages school personnel to look more closely at their action, programs, culture, and capacities and how those elements influence their efforts to improve education. Akin to the reflective practice literature in teacher pedagogy (Calderhead & Gates, 1993; Clift, Houston, & Pugach, 1990; Schön, 1985), the KEYS process encourages a school to begin making sense of the tasks and challenges in front of them in terms of a set of systematic indicators and measurements about the school's functioning. This sense-making process, in some form, sits at the core of the cases.

Depending on various factors, the formal steps and features of the KEYS process may or may not provide useful scaffolding for the sense-making that school staff must do. Clearly, whether or not they internalize a KEYS-like process of self-reflection, school staff are always making sense of the often ambiguous organizational world in which they work (Weick, 1995). Whether school staff are focused on their instructional work, the interplay of interests in the immediate school community, pressures from external forces for testing and accountability systems, or the needs of the larger community they serve, they are always trying to give meaning to the demands they confront and the direction their work is heading.

Our efforts to make sense of each school's story were guided by a framework of ideas that pertains to any school-focused renewal initiative. At the center of our framework (schematically shown in Figure 11.1: The Dynamics of Self-Reflective Renewal in Schools) are the school staff's efforts to make sense of the challenges they face. These challenges are related to the central instructional and direction-setting work they are engaged in and the actions and consequences that follow their efforts to make sense of events. Surrounding that central set of interactions are three sets of driving forces. The first represents the content of the renewal initiative itself; the second, the internal context for renewal within these schools; and the third, the external context. Each interacts with the others to shape the unfolding story of renewal, and each in turn predisposes the school to receive the renewal initiative in a particular way—that is, affects its institutional readiness for renewal.

We discuss the elements of the framework in more detail next. We then consider how the elements interact to shape the schools' response to renewal. In later sections of the chapter, we use the cases presented in earlier chapters to illustrate how this conceptual map frames and accounts for events in different kinds of settings.

The School's Engagement with Renewal

At the center of the figure is the activity undertaken by school staff under the rubric of *renewal*. In our view, this activity can be productively thought of as including three distinct elements: (1) attempts by school staff to make

FIGURE 11.1   The Dynamics of Self-Reflective Renewal in School

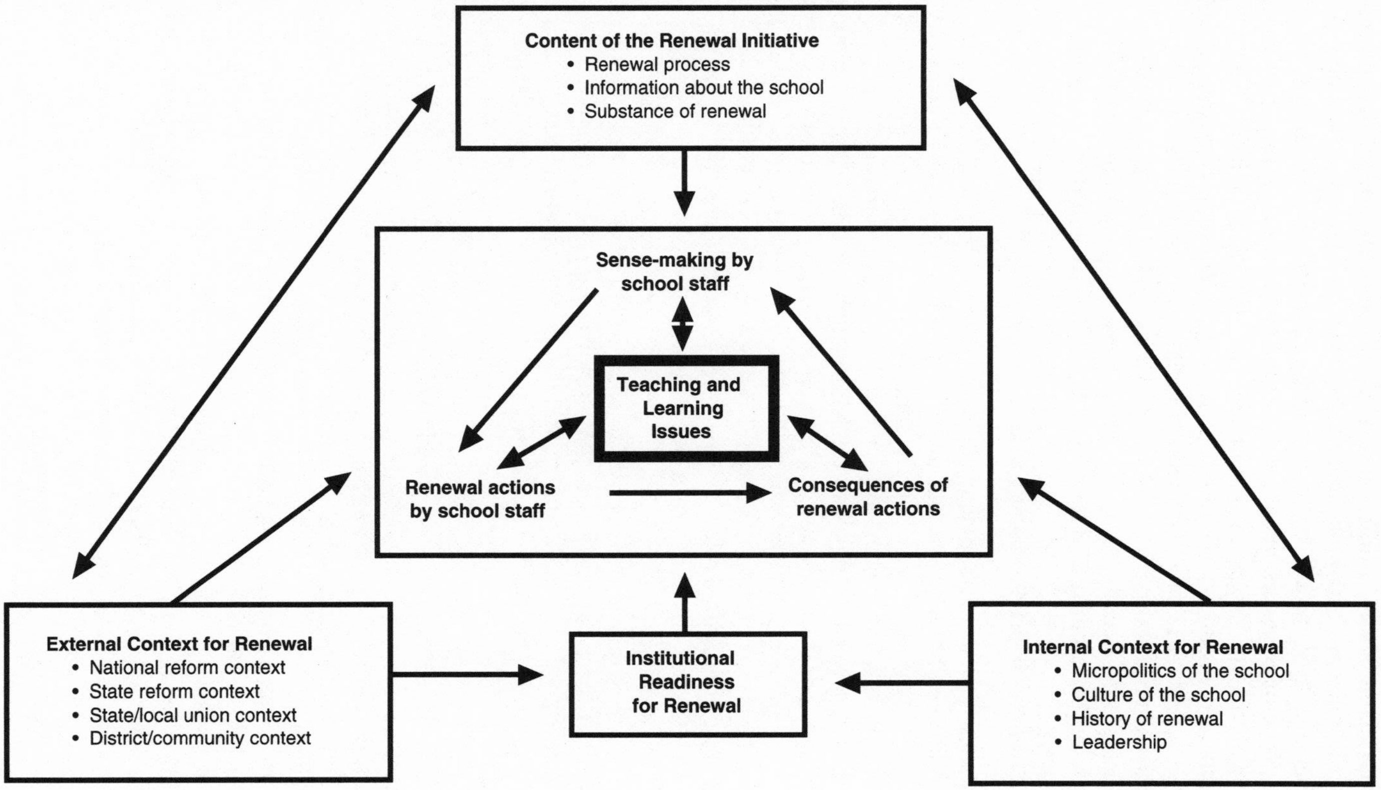

Content of the Renewal Initiative
- Renewal process
- Information about the school
- Substance of renewal

Sense-making by school staff

Teaching and Learning Issues

Consequences of renewal actions

Renewal actions by school staff

Internal Context for Renewal
- Micropolitics of the school
- Culture of the school
- History of renewal
- Leadership

Institutional Readiness for Renewal

External Context for Renewal
- National reform context
- State reform context
- State/local union context
- District/community context

sense of the issues confronting the school and the opportunities presented by the renewal initiative; (2) actions taken, in the name of renewal, or in resistance to it, based on the sense that prevails among staff members; and (3) the consequences of renewal actions for the functioning of the school, and ultimately for teaching and learning. We place *teaching and learning issues* at the center of the figure because these are so important to the working lives of all school members. Whether or not these issues are acknowledged as important, they are likely to be a primary reference point for sensemaking and renewal activity. Ultimately, the consequences of renewal activity for teaching and learning are what matter most.

Content of the Renewal Initiative

In any renewal initiative, participants respond first to the substance of the initiative—what it says about desirable practices and how to get there; what it offers or prescribes for curriculum, use of time, or organization of staff; how it envisions problem solving and the process of change; and so on. As a process approach to renewal, the KEYS Initiative offers little of this content and so school staff are responding initially to an absence of overt prescriptions or potential solutions to the challenges confronting the school. Rather, staff are invited to take a self-reflective look at the school's functioning along the thirty-five school effectiveness dimensions measured by the KEYS instrument. As such, the KEYS instrument describes rather than prescribes.

Individual participants (i.e., the design team leaders, union facilitators, or others) may offer a perspective on what to improve and how. However, the role that these various actors play is not primarily to prescribe action, but rather to explain the instrument and the ideas that inform it, to interpret the results and help the school staff fashion courses of action based on the analysis. Throughout, it is up to the staff to determine what meanings to give to the results, what action to take, and what further programs or strategies will best help them address their aims. In this way, their decisions, the deliberations that led to these decisions, and the data (formal or informal) that prompted the deliberations all become the content of the renewal initiative. The content of the initiative thus looks quite different from school to school.

To be sure, the data regarding the thirty-five indicators are not content-free. The indicators reflect judgments concerning aspects of the school's functioning that have been shown by research to be critically linked to school performance (Schneider, Verdugo, Uribe, & Greenberg, 1993). In this sense, while acting as a mirror, the KEYS instrument does not reflect all that is in the field of view, but rather focuses attention on specific features of the school related to staff interaction, assessment, expectations, and other aspects of the school program.

Internal Context for Renewal

Whatever the content of a renewal initiative, the school's response to it is likely to reflect forces and conditions within the school, which comprise an internal context for renewal. Among the many features of a school, the following four aspects of internal context appear to play an especially important role in self-reflective renewal: the micropolitics of interactions among school staff, the culture of the school, the history of renewal activity, and leadership and staff resources.

First, renewal initiatives are likely to jostle the alignment of interests that are always in tension with one another in the school. As such, the micropolitics of the school (Blase & Anderson, 1995; Hoyle, 1986) are inevitably affected, potentially altering the manner in which groups and individuals in the school exercise their influence to shape the direction of the school or what will be attended to under the umbrella of renewal. Consider, for example, the following sets of interests within a school embarking on the KEYS process: the union (seeking to represent teachers' interests and working conditions), the district (seeking to bring the school into line with its broader visions of good practice), and the community (seeking to get the school to reflect core values and expectations of community members). Add to that the interests reflected in school leadership (principals and teacher leaders seeking to maximize their own influence on practice), as well as the individual interests of staff members (who seek, at a minimum, to maintain autonomy and conduct instruction in ways they feel most comfortable with). There is inherent conflict among these interests. Whether or not it is overt, the resulting distribution and exercise of power and influence in the school will have a great deal to do with the way a particular renewal initiative is viewed and enacted.

In the case of KEYS, the initiative's attempt to mirror events in the school has the likelihood to bring the micropolitics of the school to the fore in ways that differ markedly across settings. Sometimes, reflecting local union concerns, groups within the school may put the brakes on the self-reflective process so as to protect the working conditions of the teacher. In other instances, the local union for the purpose of surveying the working conditions may advocate a self-study process. This may arise, particularly, if there are concerns about the school and its leadership. Or, with an eye on the local community, participants in a KEYS process may think carefully about whom precisely to involve in data gathering and its interpretation. Shall we open this up to parents, or classified staff, or even students? The question is likely to be answered with an eye to the way these groups might exercise influence over the outcome and over the future direction of the school. Some school staffs may see much to gain from inclusion of such groups; others see a great deal to lose.

Whatever interests (internal or external to the school) emerge in the daily micropolitics of school life, they do so within an established organizational culture, with a particular history of involvement with renewal activities. The school's culture—that is, its shared values and ideas about schooling, instructional practice, and professional work—is manifested in beliefs about "the way things are done around here" and in corresponding patterns of behavior. Renewal initiatives call into question these patterns, or at least invite staff to reconsider the assumptions on which they rest. In turn, the staff's openness to the initiative and ways of understanding it are necessarily rooted in preexisting beliefs and patterned behavior.

The culture and history of the school are generally linked, and together they color the process and outcomes of self-reflection. As school staffs reflect on their schools' attributes and accomplishments, prompted by a process such as KEYS, they do so in light of past events such as a leadership turnover, community conflict, or previously engaged projects. Veteran staff will offer, to themselves and any newcomers, a reconstructed story of these events which can affect staff motivation to engage in further renewal efforts.

Finally, the leadership and staff resources of the school are inevitably invoked in the process of renewal, as participants imagine new directions for their work (a main function of leadership) or try to create conditions that enable new ways of working (again, a role that leadership plays). Participants' capacity to carry out renewal plans reflects, in part, what staff know and are able to do, or are able to learn to do. Schools vary considerably in this regard; some have ample leadership and staff resources, others have much less to work with. School principals are in a central position to influence the fate of the self-reflective process, either by acting as the innovation champion (or opponent) or else by providing a more facilitative form of support (or resistance). Other members of staff who take on leadership roles are also likely to be significant factors in the success equation of KEYS, which depends heavily on such individuals to take on the responsibilities of a design team to carry out action steps based on the survey results.

External Context for Renewal

School staff and leaders act within a set of constraints, resources, and opportunities originating from outside the school, and these, too, can exert a robust influence on the trajectory and outcomes of self-reflective renewal in the school. This external context for renewal includes the influences of national attention on educational accountability; the environment of state reform and other state policies; state-level union activity, district initiatives, organizational conditions, local union infrastructure; and the presence and participation of partner organizations, especially the local community context. Across the nine states represented in this study, state educational reform—often manifested through accountability measures and testing—

was a clear and dominant presence in most of the school cases. State-level curriculum control, emphasis on performance testing, and the use of testing data as an accountability measure are a likely force for change from outside the school. For reasons that are both obvious and subtle, high-stakes testing was likely to preoccupy school staffs and divert or minimize energy for self-reflection.

Given the KEYS Initiative's origin in a national teacher union, personnel from the union (the state union affiliate, UniServ staff, and local association representatives) affected the possibilities for self-reflection in a given school. Union personnel might provide facilitative support and guidance for the process (as intended by the National Education Association). The form that the union influence took included direct support for engaging in the KEYS process, interpretation of the results of the survey when they were returned to the school, and a link to the school through the local association and building representation. As also revealed in the state cases, the state affiliate could make or break the likelihood that a school would consider using KEYS in their school.

Besides local union activity, two other local forces emanating from the *district* are likely to exert a powerful influence on reform. First, a school-driven renewal process might run up against a superintendent or board initiative, which may or may not emphasize self-reflective process. Second, the district conception of what school renewal ought to look like may or may not include a largely process-based strategy. In the press for immediate results, district-level leaders may opt for strategies that direct action toward content rather than process.

As noted earlier, the local community also plays a crucial role as historical watchdog, persistent critic, or source of support. Traditional patterns of school-community relations guide and shape the risk or opportunity a school perceives from engagement in KEYS. In some respects, a self-reflective process may be seen as providing fuel for critics or even weakening the school's ability to attract students to the school. "Don't rock the boat" and "keep your cards hidden" are a natural response of a school staff that is wary of possible adverse reaction from powerful community interests. By the same token, the community is not always perceived as a threat. Indeed, some school staffs can see a self-reflective process such as KEYS as a way of cementing community support and building partnership.

The School's Response to Interacting Forces

The three sets of elements just discussed—the content of the renewal initiative, the internal context for renewal, and the external context—exert influence over the school's engagement with renewal, in interaction with one another, as suggested schematically by the double-headed arrows in Figure 11.1. The story of the school's response to self-reflective renewal can thus be understood best by considering how these forces and conditions combine to explain the choice made by school staff to engage in KEYS, the manner in which they entered into the process, and the sense they made of the process.

Consider the interaction between the content of the renewal initiative and the external context. The absence of explicit content in the KEYS Initiative opens the way for initiatives by state or district actors to become the content or focus of renewal activity. One might expect this to be most true of school settings in which district or state reformers had fashioned strategies that place heavy demands on teachers and principals, as was true in cases portrayed in several of the earlier chapters. External pressures notwithstanding, the content-free nature of the KEYS Initiative interacted, as well, with forces and conditions in the school's internal context. Some configurations of internal interests, leadership, and staff resources resonated well with this process-based initiative; others did not.

Another kind of interaction merits special notice. What we term *institutional readiness for renewal* reflects the interaction between the internal and external context influenced by the content of the renewal initiative. Thus, in the same district or school context, some schools were more predisposed to make productive use of a self-reflective process than were others. What this illustrates is a differential response by the schools. In order to approach the KEYS mirror, the external and internal contexts had to align in such a way as to make sense of taking on this type of renewal activity.

WHAT THE CASE STORIES EXEMPLIFY

The story of KEYS, as represented in Figure 11.1, is one of connections. Taking on an activity such as KEYS involves a complex interaction among context, content, readiness, and the nature of the challenges in front of the school. All of the forces outlined in Figure 11.1 come into play in each case to one degree or another, but certain elements assume a more prominent role in each story while others fall more into the background. Thus, each school's experience highlights different interactions, which account for the reform outcomes in these schools.

In each of the following sections, we draw attention to different parts of the explanatory framework from Figure 11.1. The illustrations in the following three sections are a way of thinking about the dominant message, rather than an exclusive message. In the first section, we examine the cases where the content of the renewal process, and the attendant sense-making and renewal activity, was largely dependent on events and pressures in the school's external environment. In the second section, we turn our attention to cases where the content of the renewal process was more centrally shaped by the school's internal context. Finally, in the third section we look at several examples of where the interaction of external and internal contexts largely overshadowed the renewal initiative and set the tone and direction for events within the school.

Cases of External Context Dependence

In three cases (Tennessee, Minnesota, and Maryland), external forces and conditions interacted with the KEYS process to produce a focus for renewal activity, in some instances taking full advantage of the self-reflective process spotlighted in KEYS, and in other instances swamping it. As mentioned earlier, state educational reform policy played a predominant role in the choices that schools in these states made about what to pay attention to and what to work on. In one instance (Memphis, TN), active reform leadership from the district dominated the response of schools to KEYS. In this case, the superintendent of the district set the parameters of reform content by providing the schools with an approved list of renewal initiatives from which they could choose. KEYS, while initially on equal footing with other reform packages such as Roots and Wings, was subsequently given a different status: its process focus led district leaders to require that it be used in conjunction with another whole school restructuring model. With the firm support of the Memphis Education Association, thirteen of fourteen schools chose to retain KEYS alongside a second reform model. For these schools, KEYS offered a way of making sense of external expectations while simultaneously capitalizing on the support provided by the union. A data-rich environment, a district on the move, and unflagging union support set the stage for KEYS to be interpreted as a useful way for schools to approach their students' learning needs.

Similarly, in Minnesota, dynamics at the state level, both in the state education agency and in the teachers' unions, mediated the effects and momentum of KEYS in the schools. In this case, state-level union leaders initially showed a good deal of support for getting the KEYS process in place in a number of schools. Two external events overshadowed this initial support and seemed to redirect energies away from KEYS: the merger of the two teachers unions (AFT and NEA state affiliates) and the implementation of rigorous graduation requirements. In the case of the union merger, energy devoted to the state-level union superstructure drained attention away from the support for KEYS activity that the schools had initially experienced. Furthermore, the implementation of the state graduation standards quickly captured local educators' attention, in effect, shutting down the more open-ended deliberation about school needs and activities that KEYS had initiated.

In Maryland, state-level action had the opposite effect, that of solidifying and reinforcing the effect of KEYS on Shoreview High School. Here, a state association working group married the generic KEYS process to a more specific curriculum for school improvement—an initiative entitled Improving Maryland's Schools (IMS). As part of this endeavor, the state association created several professional development modules that were used to prepare the school-level team from Shoreview and other schools at leadership retreats for implementing IMS. The processes set in motion by these experiences gave school teams the tools to focus on salient issues in ways they had not previously imagined. Following deliberation about results of the KEYS survey, school staff developed several foci of renewal activity, including improving student achievement, but also strengthening school learning climate, student support services, and intra-staff communication.

Cases of Internal Context Dependence

In a second cluster of cases, in California, Washington State, and Illinois, the internal context of the school was more responsible for whether and how the school took advantage of the opportunity extended by the KEYS Initiative. The fit between the process-focused nature of the renewal initiative and the culture, history, leadership, and micropolitics of the school figured prominently in the way staff made sense of their circumstances and renewal prospects. This was despite the fact that staff worked within state and district environments that were as demanding as those in the cases noted earlier. The case of Robert Wallace High School in California exemplifies this pattern. There, a change-averse staff was drawn to KEYS because of its open-ended, flexible nature, and was helped to take advantage of the process by active leadership from a school-based improvement coordinator.

The internal context of the school could either encourage or discourage school staffs to view KEYS as a useful opportunity, as the two school cases in Washington State demonstrate. At Kirkby High School, where KEYS was eventually set aside, a change in school leadership, staff cautiousness, external perceptions of the school, and a heavy load of other internal projects seemed to prevent KEYS from being seen as a way of making sense of the core tasks confronting them. While sympathetic to KEYS, neither the outgoing nor the incoming principals advocated or championed this process. That responsibility fell to two teacher leaders, who initially carried the KEYS banner enthusiastically but succumbed eventually to a series of internal project demands. For them, and others in this school community, KEYS did not seem to provide a useful organizing rubric for the various tasks that lay before them. Rather, staff turned to other organizing rubrics, such as the structure of accreditation self-study (one of the tasks before the school), a school improvement planning outline furnished by the district, and an existing set of curriculum committees. In this instance, KEYS did not serve a catalytic function for the school.

For the second Washington school, the Essex School, the internal context propelled the school toward an opposite outcome. There, strong advocacy by both the principal and the teacher leaders led staff to view KEYS as a powerful tool for examining the changes they were hoping for their school and its unique population. KEYS, seen as a process akin to strategic planning, made sense for them, and more importantly, helped staff make sense of a number of renewal tasks on their agenda. The staff's internal cohesion and stability helped shore up the process (unlike Kirkby High School, which was also characterized by a stable staff). Also, as a correctional school for young offenders, they enjoyed a unique degree of autonomy that provided the school staff with the latitude to focus their energies largely within the confines of the school. For them, KEYS created a means for organizing the tasks and challenges confronting the school and provided a source of relevant information and structure to guide their activities.

As the story of Walter Rumsey Elementary School in Illinois dramatizes, internal forces within the school can also shut down the reform process entirely. There, a convergence of internal and external factors conspired to cut short the possibilities for the KEYS process. While the external support system afforded by state, district, and local union staff was not as strong as it should have been, thereby contributing to KEYS' demise in this instance, the churn of events in the school was clearly the major factor impacting the school's engagement with renewal activity. A rapid change in student population, combined with leadership instability, increased scrutiny of test scores, shifting staff morale, and struggles with the development of school-based decision making, made the school wary of a deliberative, open-ended change process. The school's new principal saw little direction in the data emerging from the KEYS survey. He also viewed the KEYS process as a potential threat to his desire to consolidate and exercise power more unilaterally. In such a situation, KEYS—which by its nature empowers and engages staff collaboratively in addressing the school's needs—met an early end.

Cases of Interaction between External and Internal Contexts

Whereas in the prior cases the trajectory of KEYS in each school could largely be accounted for by the interaction of either the internal or external context with the nature of the self-reflective renewal process, other cases demonstrate more substantial interaction between internal and external contexts. In several cases, this dynamic led to KEYS fading into the background. In the Mississippi case, weak internal capacity at the school and a lack of external support contributed to the failed graft of KEYS onto the Onward to Excellence initiative. Internally, it appeared that inadequate preparation and too many improvement goals overwhelmed the school's attempts to link KEYS to an already existing reform initiative. In addition, the support from local and state union personnel did not appear adequate to address the needs expressed by the school.

In both Florida and Texas, the outcome of efforts to use KEYS can be understood as the result of interactions between the internal contexts of schools and external contexts characterized by accountability pressures. In both states, the external political contexts were similar, with Governors Jeb Bush and George W. Bush respectively leading the charge for accountability, high stakes testing, and financial and public support consequences for high and low performing schools. Interestingly, in the Florida case, these pressures and the attendant policy churn overwhelmed KEYS-driven renewal while at the Texas site, KEYS took off and became a vehicle used by committed educators to encourage and sustain high levels of performance. The differences between the two sites, it seems, lay in the ways players within and, to a lesser extent, around the schools made sense of the pressures and the ability of KEYS to help address them. In Stonewall Jackson Middle School, teachers and administrators (and the association leaders who might have supported KEYS), saw themselves in a daily fight— fighting simply to stay afloat in a policy context that, in their view was "extremely antagonistic to teachers." These educators saw the Florida Comprehensive Assessment Test (FCAT) system as threatening and felt that all of their resources and energy needed to be put into coping with it. They were not opposed to KEYS and, indeed, saw it as having merit, but believed that time spent working on KEYS renewal efforts was time away from reacting to accountability pressures. The assessment system (and all of the related policies) were, in the view of educators at Stonewall Jackson, powerful enemies, and KEYS was viewed as a weak tool in their toolbox.

The Texas story offers, in many ways, an almost startling contrast. Teachers at Bates Elementary School felt that a very public assessment system provided them with an opportunity to communicate their students' performance to the community. Educators at this site did not feel overwhelmed by the Texas Assessment of Academic Skills. They believed that their students were able to meet the challenges it posed, and they were confident that they could help the students do this. For them, KEYS' lack of prescription about courses of action made it a strong, not weak, tool. They saw it as providing them with useful information about areas where they could improve but also as allowing them to continue doing what seemed to work for them—in other words, not forcing prescriptions upon them.

LEARNING FROM THE STUDY

In this final section, we turn our attention to what may be learned from this study, as well as a few of the questions that remain or cannot be determined from these cases. We aim to bring attention to what we see as the lessons and conditions for school staff considering renewal through a self-reflective, process-based strategy such as KEYS. In addition, the process of analysis spurred us to consider a number of metaphors for the KEYS process, which we begin this section with.

Metaphors for the KEYS Process

As a research team, we used a variety of metaphors to characterize the KEYS process in schools. We returned to two metaphors repeatedly, those of a mirror and a booster rocket. In the case of a mirror, the connection is straightforward and flows quite naturally from the notion of self-reflection, discussed earlier in this chapter. As a reflective strategy, KEYS presents school staffs with a means for seeing themselves in terms of the data developed by the survey and through subsequent discussion about the meaning of these data. The cases in this volume attest to the number of possible reactions to looking in the mirror. These reactions may include puzzlement over details of school functioning that attract attention, the discernment of a bigger picture into which school issues fit, or a startle reflex where the representation of the school fails to match the image in their mind's eye. School staff either like what they see in the mirror, or they turn away from it as quickly as possible to avoid seeing what appear to be blemishes. In addition, individuals and groups may find that the reflection in the mirror diverges so far from the image they had built up in their mind that looking too long and hard is troubling.

A second metaphor, that of a booster rocket, emphasizes the potential for a KEYS-like process to catalyze action and to assist with the heavy lifting of renewal. The metaphor communicates the notion that participation in a self-reflective process such as KEYS can provide a school with extra impetus to get on with renewal efforts already underway, or else to help an incipient effort get off the ground. At the same time, as the metaphor suggests, the process by itself cannot carry the whole weight of renewal. Whether the target of renewal activity becomes undertaking a mandated self-study, adopting a restructuring plan, addressing festering issues in the school's community, or fashioning a plan for boosting student achievement, the KEYS process can focus effort and build momentum toward renewal goals, given appropriate leadership and other supportive conditions. In some of the cases, the fact that KEYS concentrates energy on deliberative self-examination may explain why the booster rocket eventually runs out of fuel and the staff energy seems to focus increasingly on other matters—or on a particular solution the process surfaces. In these instances, the KEYS process appears to provide the initial direction and conditions to move a school staff down a path of restructuring and improvement in educational practice. However, without partners from outside the school and fuel for ongoing readiness, the initial energy toward renewal may run out.

Metaphors have their limits. They can help one understand essential meanings in a case story, but they can divert attention from other aspects of the story and other possible meanings. Clearly, for some schools, KEYS provided the sense-making structure to make plans and find direction for addressing difficult issues of teaching, learning, and school functioning. For other schools, the process initiated a reactive response, in which staff questioned the data and its accuracy in representing who they surely knew they were. For some of these schools, the process may have even led to shut down. In such instances, the data are simply too alarming and loaded with risk. This might encourage a retreat to familiar and isolated patterns of practice.

While our metaphors help to capture the overall character of the KEYS process in action within schools, they fail to account fully for the differences in schools' response to this renewal initiative. To do so, one must turn attention to the self-reflective strategy itself, to understand how it is or is not likely to accommodate the differences among schools.

Lessons about Self-Reflective Strategies for School Renewal

The cases we have presented, understood within the framework outlined previously, make it possible to appraise the relative strengths and weaknesses of this process-oriented, self-reflective approach to school renewal. The cases suggest a number of strengths of this approach, but, curiously, reveal that the initiative's strengths can also be the basis of its failure under certain circumstances. The power of self-reflective strategies, then, lies, in their capacity, in particular settings, to connect with other events inside and outside of the school, and offer participants an integrated picture of their work and new possibilities for it. In these settings, case study schools were ready for self-reflection, and took advantage of the opportunity afforded by the KEYS Initiative. In other schools, features of the strategy that were advantages elsewhere became liabilities; representations of the school were viewed as indictments and openness to school-initiated ideas was seen as a lack of substance.

Let us first acknowledge the strengths that a strategy such as KEYS provides, both to individual schools and to larger systems of schools within districts, states, and the nation. For one thing, the process is highly adaptable to each school's circumstances and idiosyncrasies. School staff can establish their own time line, shape the administration of the instrument to the needs and interactions with their community, and set up any kind of follow-up sequence that fits into local circumstances. In a similar way, the strategy accommodates a wide range of local ideas about problems and potential solutions. By refusing to offer a specific set of solutions for good schooling, the strategy avoids the predictable resistance by some staff whose philosophies run counter to any specific reform package.

Furthermore, the strategy engages thinking and creative work, as school staff struggle to find direction in their analysis of their school's functioning. In that struggle, the KEYS strategy offers specific anchors for the deliberative process—recognizable features of the school highlighted by each of the thirty-five measured indicators that are known to be associated with high performance in schools. The data thus give the schools a starting place that has demonstrated relevance to student learning, from which to consider a variety of actions that might improve learning opportunities and results.

By design, KEYS is also inclusive. It invites the participation of as many groups and individuals as the school staff chooses. In addition, it seeks the participation of union and UniServ personnel in a way that bridges traditional divides between teachers and administrators. (The connection with a major national teachers union has the added virtue of expanding the reach of KEYS to virtually all localities in the nation.) By its nature, the self-reflective process encourages multiple voices in deliberating the directions for renewal and thereby is likely to have an empowering effect on teachers and others in the school community.

All those features of the strategy recommend it to schools in a variety of settings in which staff have some need to engage in renewal activity of some kind. That fact heralds one of several noteworthy weaknesses. The strategy has little to offer school staff that do not feel the urge, if even covertly. Some of the neediest schools in the country, for example, are locked into patterns of functioning that do not serve students or faculty well. In such instances, a renewal process that relies on the internal will of the staff and that starts with measures of school functioning—which are likely to both look bad and convey a sense of the school's failure—has little chance of engaging staff energy and opening doors to new ways of serving young people. Add to that schools in which leadership is exercised in a non-participatory way by principals or others who have authority to guide their colleagues' work. Leaders who are not at home with participatory processes will not be comfortable with KEYS or similar approaches to school renewal and are likely to reject the process before it can get very far.

Consider, as well, schools in settings in which district or state dictates, or both together, deprive the school of any real discretion over the design or functioning of the school program, expecting instead that the school staff will implement as faithfully as possible a set of prescriptions from on high. In these cases, as noted earlier, the demands and structure of the external context may tie the hands of school staffs from initiating a self-reflective process and making decisions to restructure the school.

Beyond these obvious instances, in which the school's internal and external conditions preclude use of a self-reflective strategy, other weaknesses of self-reflective strategies are apparent in schools that do embrace this kind of approach. For one thing, the strategy turns the school staff inward—confronts them with what they are currently doing (as represented by survey measures) and invites them to imagine courses of action that will improve measures of functioning. What is there to stimulate the imagination? How does a school staff entertain new realms of possibility that, heretofore, hadn't occurred to them? Even though there is expressed or latent creativity in any group of educators, there are also collective blind spots or simply a limited range of experiences and expertise on which to draw. A wider range of possibilities reside elsewhere, and KEYS does not necessarily help educators in a particular school see these possibilities. The KEYS design does not automatically put in place partners who can push back at the thinking of the school staff, challenging them to sharpen ideas, examine assumptions, and consider different ways of construing their work.

Therein lies a second principal weakness for any school engaged in self-reflective renewal. At least as framed by its initial design, the KEYS strategy is utterly dependent on the capacities of local, district, and state-based union personnel, who form the primary support infrastructure for the individuals in schools. The union's UniServ facilitators and other union staff, for example, may be able to assist schools to engage in renewal activities, including help with interpreting data, considering program options, and the like, but their capacity to do so is likely to vary tremendously, reflecting their own working experience and expertise. Many UniServ staff came to their position through traditional union work dealing with grievances and bargaining, not through immersion in teaching, learning, and instructional program design. To be sure, as policy implementation research has been telling us for decades, local contexts have a great deal to do with the quality of any educational effort, whether it be a self-directed local renewal activity, or a state-mandated reform. But this kind of renewal activity places a premium on the expertise of available partners in the renewal enterprise. As seen in a number of the case studies, until a more intentional infrastructure is built up around the nation to support this kind of work, schools are just as likely to get bad (or no) advice as good advice—weak support as strong.

In appraising a strategy such as KEYS, one must remember that the cases in this book present experiences with the first wave of KEYS implementation, starting in the mid-1990s. Since that time, in some respects prompted by findings from these case studies, NEA has taken steps to address some of the weaknesses in the initial KEYS strategy. The lack of attention in the KEYS survey instrument to pedagogical and instructional indicators has been remedied in a new version in use over the past several years. Reporting formats have been streamlined, to maximize their ability to communicate to audiences inexperienced with data, and to deemphasize the sense of being graded or ranked. The NEA has also sponsored the development of an on-line professional development curriculum, which can be accessed by schools undergoing the KEYS process. This curriculum provides a source of provocative ideas from the outside about reform processes, restructuring, teaching and learning improvement, and other matters likely to be on the school's renewal agenda. While not eliminating the disadvantages of this kind of strategy, these steps indicate an evolution in this particular self-reflective strategy that may increase its range and impact in the years to come.

Conditions Supporting Self-Reflective School Renewal

While the cases we have examined do not exhaust the possibilities for KEYS, or any self-reflective strategy for that matter, they point to certain prerequisites for the success of self-reflective strategies. The cases also surface likely tendencies in the way different kinds of schools enter into the process, proceed with it, and make it work for renewal goals (or fail to do so).

The overriding lesson is that not all schools are ready for self-reflective renewal. Our cases would suggest that schools are most likely to benefit from this approach to change when five prerequisite conditions are in place: a sense of precipitating issues and a sense of urgency, concerted leadership, school-level discretion, access to resources, and familiarity with data (or ways to gain this familiarity). Each set of conditions arises at the intersection of internal and external forces.

To begin with, something propels a school staff to reconsider what, and how well, it is doing. Without something to reflect about, the difficult work of critically appraising the school's work and figuring out where to take it is unlikely to happen. The precipitating issues can arise from outside the school, inside, or both, as the cases in this book richly illustrate. The prerequisite condition is that these issues touch a sufficient number of staff to make them consider investing in a self-reflective process when the occasion arises (or being willing to go along for the ride, if such a process is imposed on them).

Within the school, a sufficient cadre of teacher leaders, in conjunction with a supportive principal, need to be in place. The impetus for renewal activity can come from various configurations of these leaders; not all need be actively pushing a self-reflective strategy, but if any are actively resisting such an activity, self-reflection is unlikely to flourish. Outside the school, leaders in the district and the union should be similarly supportive, or at least neutral, about the value of self-reflective renewal activity. Ideally, the state educational and union superstructure would exert positive leadership in favor of self-reflective renewal, but it is more likely that local leadership will buffer some of the contradictory messages from the state, under some circumstances.

Self-reflective strategies presume that the school staff will work out its own solution to the school's needs and that they will be given room to do so. In other words, the school is granted sufficient autonomy by the district to develop its own improvement plans and is simultaneously willing to seize the autonomy that is granted. A delicate balance of authority exists in all school districts between the prerogatives of the central office and school board, on the one hand, and those of the school leaders and staff on the other. Districts seeking to nurture school-based governance through one or another form of decentralization are likely to set the stage for self-reflective strategies. Centralizing districts, by contrast, may make it more difficult for self-reflective strategies to flourish.

While the initiative for renewal based in self-reflection lies with school staff, the full range of supportive resources is unlikely to be found within the school's walls. Chief among these are sources of ideas and help with thinking through the puzzles presented by school renewal—in short, sufficient expertise in the vicinity of the school or accessible by school staff so that deliberation over data and its aftermath can be productive and informed by a wide range of possibilities. Such knowledge resources may reside in the union, the district central office, other schools, local universities, professional associations, or combinations of these sources. The prerequisite for self-reflection is that, among these sources, there resides a critical mass of experts who can become available to the school engaged in self-reflective renewal. Other resources are also important—among them time, space, materials, and money—but the cases we have examined give little guidance about a particular level of such resources that are necessary.

Systematic self-reflection starts with data about the school. School staff are unlikely to have much expertise in working with data of this sort, but some familiarity or comfort level with data clearly helps, at least among some school members. Alternatively, having individuals near at hand who can introduce the school staff to the possible meanings that reside in data is an important condition for the success of this kind of strategy.

Putting Self-Reflective Renewal in Perspective

The lessons emerging from these cases must be understood for what they are: images of possibility in a range of instances that represent many, but not all, of the settings in which KEYS has been tried. In this regard, we should be clear about several limitations in the case study set we have presented:

- We have studied only a small number of schools and have far from exhausted the possible configurations of local conditions in which KEYS might be tried. While the patterns we have unearthed are likely to pertain to many settings, they do not capture the full range of conditions across the nation that is relevant to the implementation of this strategy.
- We concentrated our work on the early implementation of a self-reflective process. These cases concerned the first several years of the KEYS Initiative in most instances, and so we cannot comment on the continuing story of renewal in these schools or on the possible role that KEYS may have played at later stages. Our assumption that KEYS is most likely to have its strongest effects early in a cycle of renewal activity simply has not been tested. Nor can we shed much light

on the prospects for the most recent form of the KEYS Initiative, which remedies some of the deficiencies of the earliest versions.

- Our research focused on individual schools, in accordance with the NEA initiative's design and the premise that the story of renewal must, in some respects, be understood school by school. However, the focus on the individual school downplays the possible roles that the district can play stimulating, guiding, and supporting renewal activity, and fails to consider the interaction among schools within a given jurisdiction. Other analyses (Hightower, Knapp, Marsh, & McLaughlin, 2002; Marsh, 2000) suggest the district has various constructive roles to play in that regard. Though our accounts include attention to district influences, and in one instance examined a district-wide strategy (in Memphis), we have not fully explored the ways that the district can engage and support self-reflective renewal within individual schools.

In other words, there is more to learn and know about the power and prospects of self-reflective renewal. The cases we have analyzed suggest that in a variety of local circumstances, KEYS can have a useful role in helping school staffs grapple with and come to grips with some of the difficult issues confronting them. In other circumstances, this strategy appears to have less to offer, but our analysis helps to predict what kinds of conditions might bring about this result. What lies ahead is a continuing process of studying this approach to renewal, so that we help it realize the considerable potential it appears to have.

REFERENCES

Blase, J., & Anderson, G. (1995). *The micropolitics of educational leadership.* New York: Teachers College Press.

Calderhead, J., & Gates, P. (Eds.). (1993). *Conceptualizing reflection in teacher development.* London: Falmer.

Clift, R. T., Houston, W. R., & Pugach, M. C. (Eds.). (1990). *Encouraging reflective practice in education.* New York: Teachers College.

Hightower, A. M., Knapp, M. S., Marsh, J. A., & McLaughlin, M. W. (Eds.). (2002). *School districts and instructional renewal.* New York: Teachers College Press.

Hoyle, E. (1986). *The politics of school management.* London: Hodder & Stoughton.

Marsh, J. A. (2000). *Connecting districts to the policy dialogue: A review of literature on the relationship of districts with states, schools, and communities.* Seattle, WA: Center for the Study of Teaching and Policy (CTP), University of Washington.

Schneider, J. M., Verdugo, R. R., Uribe, O., Jr., & Greenberg, N. M. (1993). Statistical quality control and school quality. *Contemporary education, 64*(2), 84–87.

Schön, D. A. (1987). *Educating the reflective practitioner.* San Francisco: Jossey-Bass.

Weick, K. E. (1995). *Sensemaking in organizations.* Thousand Oaks, CA: Sage.

A Methodological Note

The case studies presented in this book began in August 1996 with the orientation meeting of the case study research team in Washington, DC. In attendance at this meeting were Joe Murphy, convener and project director; researchers Lynn Beck, Kathryn Borman, Michael Knapp, Karen Seashore Louis, Saundra Nettles, Pedro Reyes, Sam Stringfield, and Charles Teddlie; and a number of NEA representatives including Jacques Nacson, Don Rollie, Jeff Schneider, and Oscar Uribe. Although Mark Smylie did not attend the first meeting, he was in close contact with the research team and attended subsequent meetings. Linda Bol, Lisa Jones, and Bradley Portin joined the research team after the first meeting.

The first meeting opened with an in-depth discussion of KEYS and of plans for its implementation at various sites around the country. As described in Chapter 1, the association had what amounted to a strategic plan for rolling out this reform, a plan that involved promoting KEYS initially in states that represented a range of demographic, cultural, and political structures. Leaders in NEA's division of Teaching and Learning believed that KEYS could serve as a vehicle for school improvement. They also believed that association leadership and its members could learn much about conditions affecting KEYS and other reforms by looking at its unfolding in environments that differed along several dimensions.

As the members of the case study research team considered goals and challenges of their project, differences and similarities across settings, and options for collecting data that could inform their case studies, they decided upon an approach that afforded both conceptual coherence and procedural flexibility. Conceptual coherence was obtained as team members, working with association representatives, identified the theory underlying KEYS design and implementation plan and developed a set of research questions that would guide the investigation in each of the sites. Procedural flexibility was ensured as team members identified variables that were likely to affect KEYS in their states and as they agreed to use a variety of data collection and analysis techniques to enable them to pursue answers to the research questions within different contexts. In this Methodological Note, we offer a brief description of the KEYS theory of change as developed by the case study team members and present the research questions that guided the investigations in each state. We then describe the procedures used in each of the case studies. Our "Note" concludes with a few remarks about collaboration among members of the research team and about decisions regarding the presentation of results.

KEYS THEORY OF CHANGE

As noted in Chapter 1, the KEYS reform is built upon two sets of complementary research. One, typically referred to as "effective schools research," focuses on identifying site conditions that correlate with high levels of student achievement. A second concentrates on uncovering decision-making structures and leadership practices that appear to be linked to organizational health and productivity. Insights from these bodies of research contributed to the design of a reform initiative that assumed the following:

- High-quality schools are multi-dimensional environments characterized by a set of thirty-five definable factors. A positive correlation exists between these factors and the achievement of students. In this sense, the factors can be thought of as "KEYS" to excellence in schools.

- Teachers and participants in the school community can effectively determine the degree to which a particular school exhibits the thirty-five KEYS.

- Accurate information about the extent to which a school exhibits the thirty-five KEYS provides an excellent starting point for planning improvement initiatives within a school community.

- Teachers and others in the school are in a good position to plan, initiate, and implement school improvement efforts.

- Improvement efforts that lead to a greater presence of the KEYS to excellence can and will lead to higher levels of student achievement.

- Structures within the National Education Association can provide guidance and support to teachers as they take a leading role in school improvement efforts.

RESEARCH QUESTIONS

When the case study research team met in Washington, DC, in August 1996, the KEYS reform had been introduced to state-level association leadership in several states and was in the process of being adopted within individual schools. The researchers were in a position, therefore, to study the ways that dissemination, adoption, implementation, and early impacts of this reform strategy played out within the various sites. Using the KEYS theory of change as a framework, they developed the following six research questions regarding the entry and consequences of the KEYS process in a given school community:

- How do the district and state contexts influence the implementation of the KEYS process and its outcomes in the school?
- How is KEYS implemented and adopted at the state and local levels?
- How does the school engage in school improvement processes in response to the KEYS Initiative?
- How does the KEYS process affect the organizational health of the school?
- How does the KEYS process affect the core technology and teaching?
- How does the KEYS process affect valued student outcomes?

SITE SELECTION, DATA COLLECTION, AND ANALYSIS

As noted earlier, the states selected for the case studies were chosen because they represented a range of geographic, cultural, economic, political, educational, and association contexts. The selection of specific sites within the states was, to some extent, opportunistic and dependent upon decisions by schools to adopt and implement KEYS. There was also, though, an effort to be as purposeful as possible in choosing sites representing different grade, socio-economic, and demographic levels. The following "types" of schools ultimately provided the basis for the investigations:

- Tennessee—twelve urban schools including eight elementary, three middle or junior high, and one high school; eleven schools had a majority of African American students; low SES (in eleven schools the percentage of free and reduced lunch students ranged from 76 to 96 percent)
- Minnesota—one "semi-rural" elementary school; over 90 percent white, middle SES (7–8 percent free and reduced lunch)
- Maryland—one urban high school; 65 percent white, 30 percent African American, 5 percent Asian, 1 percent Hispanic
- California—one suburban high school; 66 percent white, 34 percent Hispanic, 2 percent Asian, 2 percent African American, 2 percent Filipino, 1 percent American Indian; middle SES

- Washington—one rural high school; 92 percent white, 8 percent minority; middle SES; and one rural residential school, operated dually by the State Juvenile Rehabilitation Administration and the local school district; 53 percent non-Hispanic white, 19 percent African American, 15 percent Hispanic, 7 percent Native American, 5 percent Asian, 1 percent not reported; highly transient population
- Illinois—one suburban elementary school; 34 percent white, 7 percent African American, 55 percent Latino, 4 percent Asian; 49 percent low-income families; 53 percent limited English proficient; 29 percent mobility rate
- Mississippi—one urban elementary (K–3 grade level); 63 percent white, 33 percent African American, 5 percent other; middle SES
- Florida—one urban middle school; 44 percent Hispanic, 40 percent white, 13 percent African American, 3 percent Asian; low SES
- Texas—one urban elementary school; 99 percent Hispanic, low SES (96 percent students free and reduced lunch); 40 percent of students are limited or non-English speaking; mobility rate of 22 percent

During late 1996 and early 1997, the case study team identified possible informants and data sources and assembled a set of data collection strategies to assist them in addressing the research questions within their specific sites. Throughout the entire research process (1996–1999), the team met regularly and communicated between meetings via e-mail. These meetings and communications provided opportunities to discuss research challenges and emerging findings and to review data collection and analysis strategies. Next we offer a brief description of strategies used in each site.

Tennessee

Data sources for the Tennessee case study included individual interviews (principal, KEYS coordinator, teacher, and Memphis Education Association representatives) and observations made during site visits; documents included material from KEYS training sessions, school improvement plans, articles and reports on Tennessee and Memphis educational reform, and memos and documents related to KEYS and other reform efforts in the Memphis City Schools. Interviews and site visits occurred during spring and fall 1998. Interviews with principals, KEYS coordinators, and teachers were semi-structured and focused on four major areas: (1) the process of KEYS adoption and implementation; (2) the relationship between KEYS and major school restructuring designs in use within sites; (3) perceptions of KEYS and its impact; and (4) strengths and weaknesses of KEYS as a reform initiative. Interviews with Memphis Educational Association members were informal and conversational and addressed MEA's role in KEYS implementation, compatibility of KEYS with other reforms, and barriers or challenges facing KEYS. For the interview data obtained from schools, a content analysis was used to develop topics and categories of responses for each of the questions. Data obtained from interviews with MEA representatives were organized and summarized around major themes.

Minnesota

The data sources included multiple informal interviews of key informants and stakeholders in the KEYS program at the school site (UniServ directors, the site principal, and elementary school teachers). In addition, interviews were conducted with other stakeholders with an interest in school reform in Minnesota, including state department and union officials, legislators, and community leaders. The authors and two other colleagues at the University of Minnesota conducted all interviews and analyzed data inductively.

Maryland

Data sources included formal and informal interviews with key informants (state association leaders, principal, teachers, University of Maryland faculty who worked with KEYS training), observations of association and site training/professional development activities, and observations made during site visits; documents included meeting minutes, school improvement plans, state association professional development materials, planning materials, and documents used by a visiting evaluation team. Data analysis was based on procedures described by Miles and Huberman (1994). In the early stages of analysis, field notes and documents were assigned descriptive and interpretive codes based on the major research questions for the study. Responses from the interview protocols were arrayed by respondent and coded, and open-ended interview responses were coded. As the case progressed, these coded data were grouped into themes identified in meetings of KEYS researchers. At the conclusion of major sequences of events (e.g., the adoption of KEYS by the state association) time-ordered matrices were developed. Two interim case summaries were produced, distributed to other case study researchers, and discussed in the KEYS meetings. At the conclusion of data collection, patterns in prior analyses were used to generate an effects matrix.

California

Data sources included interviews with key informants (principal, teachers, superintendent, site KEYS coordinator, parents, California Association of Teachers representatives) and observations made during KEYS training sessions and during site visits; documents included association reports and policy documents, articles and reports about California educational reform, and school and district reports (including results of KEYS survey, minutes and strategic plans, annual school "report cards," etc.). Interviews and site visits were conducted between 1997 and 1999 with follow-up telephone interviews in the fall of 2000. Data were analyzed for themes and patterns using Merriam's process of "intensive analysis" (1988, p. 127) for category construction and content analysis.

Washington

Data sources included interviews with key informants (administrators, teachers, Washington Education Association representatives) and observations made during site visits; documents included reports and articles about Washington school reform and relevant documentation from the two sites (reports of student performance, accreditation plans, district and school strategic plans, memos, etc.). Site visits occurred over a three-year period (1996–1999). Data were analyzed in two stages following a process described by Miles and Huberman (1994). During the first stage, researchers developed a within-case chronology of events and connected it with contextual conditions, interactions of key players, and their interpretation of various events. Content analysis was used to identify patterns and categories that seemed to emerge from the data. Subsequent analysis focused on the construction of cross-case patterns. At this stage, researchers assembled major categories and developed conceptual matrices to array the findings. The process of comparing and contrasting cases followed Patton's (1990) discursive logical analysis process.

Illinois

Data sources included interviews with key informants (Illinois Education Association representatives, district administrators, site-level administrators and teachers, an educational consultant from a local university, administrators from neighboring districts). Documents included school, district, and association publications; government and chamber of commerce documents; and articles and reports about Illinois and Chicago area school reform. Interview data were collected between 1997 and 2000 and were analyzed for themes and patterns that could explain the problems that prevented the successful implementation of KEYS at the case study site. These results were then considered in light of research about factors influencing school improvement processes.

Mississippi

Data sources for the Mississippi case study included individual (principal, teacher, and Mississippi Association of Education representatives) and focus group interviews and observations made during fifteen site visits; documents included materials from KEYS training sessions, NEA materials regarding educational reform in Mississippi, goal statements developed by faculty committees, results from KEYS survey (April 1997), articles and reports on Mississippi educational reform, and memos and documents related to KEYS implementation. Data collection took place between 1996 and 1999 with most site visits occurring between July 1997 and January 1999. Several strategies guided data analysis including the constant comparative method as described by Lincoln and Guba (1985), Yin's (1994) approaches to case study analyses, and Krueger's (1988) strategy for analyzing focus group data.

Florida

Data sources included individual interviews (school-based administrators and teachers and Florida Education Association representatives) and observations made during site visits; documents included reports and articles about Florida School Reform and school-level reports including those made in response to Governor Jeb Bush's "A+ Plan." In order to better understand unsuccessful implementation of KEYS at the case study site, the researcher also conducted site visits and interviews in several schools where KEYS was, in fact, implemented. Site visits occurred during 1997 and 1998. These data allowed for comparison of conditions linked to successful and unsuccessful implementation. Data were analyzed for themes and patterns that could explain the problems that prevented the successful implementation of KEYS at the case study site.

Texas

Data sources included individual interviews (administrators, teachers) and observations made during site visits; documents included reports and articles about Texas school reform, school-level reports including those related to student performance on the Texas Assessment of Academic Skills, and memos and reports related to KEYS and other school improvement efforts. Site visits occurred over a two-year period (1997 and 1998). Interview data were analyzed and coded using an "open coding" strategy as described by Strauss and Corbin (1998). This is a method using actual words of interviewees and the context of discourse to generate specific codes. The 209 codes generated during this initial coding process were then consolidated into 19 conceptual categories. These categories provided a framework for further analyzing interview texts.

COLLABORATION AMONG THE RESEARCH TEAM

As noted earlier, the KEYS research team, from the beginning, was committed to conducting a study that was conceptually coherent but flexible in the sense that approaches were appropriate to specific site contexts. During the first two years of the study (1996–1998), the team met three times, communicated by mail, e-mail, and telephone, and coordinated and presented preliminary results of the investigation at conferences. Between 1998 and 2000, the team met two times each year, continued their electronic communication, and continued to present the results of the their work at conferences.

Collaboration and communication among the team and between the team and various representatives of NEA had several important benefits. Researchers were able to discuss challenges to the investigation posed by conditions in their site. Furthermore, they were able to discuss emerging findings, engage in cross-case comparisons, and examine results in light of the KEYS theory of change. Because NEA representatives were always participants in face-to-face meetings and in most electronic conversations, the research team was also able to provide the association with up-to-date reports on the progress of the cases and to ask for information as needed.

As case studies were completed, team meetings, presentations at conferences, and so forth provided researchers and the editors of this book with an opportunity to explore insights that could be derived from the results of this project and offered chapter authors and manuscript editors the opportunity to talk about various issues related to the presentation of the data. These meetings also provided association representatives with the opportunity to interact with the research team and gave association leadership important information to assist in the refinement of the KEYS instrument and the processes for supporting this reform.

PRESENTING THE RESULTS

As noted previously, the KEYS research team created a number of in progress reports of their findings and presented these to one another and at conferences. These reports served as prototypes for the chapters included in this book. The editors worked together and with the authors to reduce redundancy, to clarify certain details, and to create stylistic consistency.

Representatives from the National Education Association read all chapters and worked with the authors and editors throughout the process, supplying them with information and support (in a variety of forms). NEA's role, however, was entirely consultative and they did not participate in any editing of the book.

REFERENCES

Krueger, R. A. (1988). *Focus groups: A practical guide for applied research.* Newbury Park, CA: Sage Publications, Inc.

Lincoln, Y., & Guba, E. (1985). *Naturalistic inquiry.* Newbury Park, CA: Sage Publications, Inc.

Merriam, S. B. (1988). *Case study research in education.* San Francisco: Jossey-Bass.

Miles, M. B., & Huberman, M. (1994). *Qualitative data analysis* (2nd ed.). Thousand Oaks, CA: Sage.

Patton, M. Q. (1990). *Qualitative evaluation and research methods* (2nd ed.). Newbury Park, CA: Sage.

Strauss, A., & Corbin, J. (1998). *Basics of qualitative research: Techniques and procedures for developing grounded theory* (2nd ed.). Thousand Oaks, CA: Sage.

Yin, R. K. (1994). *Case study research design and methods.* (2nd ed.). Newbury Park, CA: Sage Publications, Inc.

Indicators of a Quality School

I. Shared understanding and commitment to high learning goals

1. Parents and school employees are committed to long-range, continuous improvement.

2. Central and building administrators are committed to long-range, continuous improvement.

3. Goals for achievable education outcomes are clear and explicit.

5. Teachers, education support personnel, students, and parents believe all students can learn.

6. School district administrators and school board members believe all students can learn.

II. Open communication and collaborative problem solving

4. Teachers, education support personnel, parents, school building administrators, students, school board members, district administrators, and civic groups are all involved in improving education.

12. Everyone actively seeks to identify barriers to learning.

13. There is a general willingness by everyone to remove barriers to learning.

14. School staff work to remove barriers to learning.

15. Students and parents work to remove barriers to learning.

16. School and district administrators work to remove barriers to learning.

17. A cooperative problem-solving process is used to remove barriers to learning.

32. There is two-way, non-threatening communication between school administrators and others.

33. There is two-way, non-threatening communication between the school staff and district administrators.

34. There is two-way, non-threatening communication among teachers.

35. All communication takes place within a climate for innovation.

III. Continuous assessment for teaching and learning

18. Teachers assess student improvement daily.

19. Administrators assess student improvement daily.

20. The school uses teacher-made tests to assess students.

21. The school uses oral classroom activities to assess students.

22. The school uses exhibitions to assess students.

23. Assessments take into account student background.

24. Academic programs are assessed.

25. Teachers consistently rate program quality.

26. Assessment results are actually used, and classroom decisions are based on assessments.

27. Instructional materials are selected based on quality.

28. Instructional materials are selected based on appropriateness to student needs.

29. Instructional materials are not selected based on cost.

IV. Personal and professional learning

11. School is an overall learning environment for employees and students.

30. There is ongoing, consistent staff development in the areas of decision making, problem solving, leadership, and communication.

31. Staff development is an ongoing, high quality, state-of-the-art, practical experience for all school employees.

V. Resources to support teaching and learning

7. Space is adequate within the school building.

8. Supplies are adequate.

9. Support services are adequate.

10. Psychological and social work services are available.

Appendix C

The KEYS Survey

The KEYS survey,[1] *The Conditions of Teaching and Learning* (National Education Association, 1997) contains 125 items. In addition to descriptive information about the respondent and school (e.g., role, length of service, school level), the survey asks for the respondent's "professional judgments regarding the conditions of teaching and learning in [their] school." Below are examples[2] of items from the survey.

Ninety-four items ask the respondent to "indicate how accurately each statement describes the situation in their school":

Scale: True / More true than false / More false than true / False

- *My school has explicit goals for student learning.*
- *Assessment results are used to develop new programs and instructional strategies to address student deficiencies.*
- *District office administration, school administrators, and school board members work cooperatively to eliminate barriers to learning caused by conditions in the community.*
- *School administrators encourage teachers to share what they have learned from staff development activities.*

Twelve items ask the respondent to rate "quality," "quantity," and "overall adequacy sufficient for school provisions."

- Space for classroom activities
- Computers for student use
- Clerical support
- Social work services for students

Five items ask the respondent to rate the "quality" of various aspects of the school including:

Scale: Excellent / Good / Not so good / Poor
- The school environment overall
- Student performance on standardized tests

Eight items ask the respondent to rate how "satisfied" they are in various areas including:

Scale: Very satisfied / Tend to be satisfied / Tend to be dissatisfied / Very dissatisfied
- Your school administrators' professional competence
- Your salary
- Your job autonomy

NOTES

1. The KEYS survey has been revised since the case studies in this book.
2. All survey items not represented.

REFERENCE

National Education Association. (1997). *The conditions of teaching and learning.* Survey available from: National Education Association, 1201 Sixteenth Street, Northwest, Washington, DC, 20036.

Index

Dodge, Walter, 116, 119, 120, 121,
    123, 125
Dual language programs, 151, 152

Early childhood programs, 39
Eastin, Delaine, 74
Educability of learners, 8–9, 38, 69,
    169–170
Education courses, 35
Education Minnesota, 43–44, 47, 48,
    51n.3
Elementary and Secondary Education
    Act, 162
Elmore, Richard, *Restructuring
    Schools, The Next Generation of
    School Reform,* 166
E-mail, 80
Empowerment of parents and
    teachers, 4
English proficiency, 114
Equity, 9
*Essential Academic Learning
    Requirements* (Washington State), 95
Essex School. *See* Washington State
    schools, Essex School
Experimentation, 5
External assistance, 11, 13, 121–123
    Memphis, 19
    Mississippi, 129, 130, 136, 139,
        144, 145
    Rumsey Elementary School, 112,
        122, 126
External context, 186–187, 189–190
Extracurricular activities, 174

F schools, 35
Faulkner, William, 138
FCAT. *See* Florida Comprehensive
    Assessment Test
FEA. *See* Florida Education Association
Federal government, 6
Fifth Discipline Fieldbook, The (Senge,
    Roberts, & Ross), 60
Fifth Discipline, The (Senge), 60
Flexibility, 12
Florida and the KEYS, 147–159, 192,
    204, 207
    A+ Plan, 148

Bush, Jeb, 148, 149, 154
    conceptual underpinnings,
        149–150
    conclusions, 158–159
    context, 147–149
    Florida Comprehensive Assessment
        Test (FCAT), 148, 150, 154, 158,
        159, 192
    FTP-NEA affiliate, 148, 157
    policy churn, 149, 158, 159
    research issues, 150–151
    schools studied, 151–158
        Horizon Middle School,
            154–156, 158
        Oak Elementary School,
            157–158
        Stonewall Jackson Middle School,
            150–154
        Walker Middle School,
            156–157, 159
    state's high stakes test, 148, 149
Florida Comprehensive Assessment Test
    (FCAT), 148, 150, 154, 158,
    159, 192
Florida Education Association
    (FEA), 148
Focus groups, 14, 42, 54
Fragmentation, 3
Frames of reference, 93, 95
Freeman, Jill, 80–81, 88
Freshmen placement, 80
FTP-NEA affiliate in Florida,
    148, 157

Garcia, Nilsa, 156–157
Garrison, Wayne, 15n.2
Glenview (Illinois) Education
    Association, 36
Goal diffusion, 136
Goals, x, 10
Goals 2000, 17
Goals 2000: Educate America Act
    (1991), 162
*Goals and Strategies for Shoreview
    High School,* 61, 69
Graduation standards, 42–43, 47, 51
Grafted reform, 129–130, 140, 144
Grant development, 28–29, 42, 44

Internal assistance in Mississippi, 129, 130, 136, 139, 144, 145
Internal context, 185–186, 190–191
Internal interpreters versus external interpreters, 107
Iowa Test of Basic Skills (ITBS), 130
ITBS. *See* Iowa Test of Basic Skills

Jansson, Robert, 117, 118, 119, 122, 123, 127
Johns Hopkins University, 18
Johnson, Sue, 53, 55, 56, 57, 60
Jones, Lisa M., 33, 201, 214

KEYS Indicators of a Quality School, ix, 11, 61, 184, 209–210
  continuous assessment for teaching and learning, 210
  open communication and collaborative problem solving, 209–210
  personal and professional learning, 210
  resources to support teaching and learning, 210
  shared understanding and commitment to high learning goals, 209
KEYS Survey, 211–212
  ambiguity of, 157, 159
  language and useability, 46, 87–88, 89n.3
  and noncertified staff, 45
  revisions of, 212
KEYS to Excellence in Your Schools, 179–181
  confidentiality, 45
  core values, 8–10
  defined, ix-x, 7
  disadvantages seen in, 175–176
  focus groups, 14, 42
  framework of core areas, x, 10
  in Illinois, 117–118, 126–127
  instrument and process, 12–13, 57–58, 180
  longitudinal pictures, 14
  national context, 1–15
  organizational conditions, 8

potential and limits, 13–14
revisions of, 199
strategic assumptions, 10–12
strengths and weaknesses, 194–197
technical and statistical aspects, 15n.1
theory of change, 202
see also Methodological note; National Education Association (NEA); Self-reflective school renewal
KEYS Training Manual, 87
Knapp, Michael S., 1, 91, 179, 201, 214
Knowledge, nature of, 3

Language barriers, 173
Latinos, 113–114, 150, 151, 157
Leadership, xi, 110, 126, 185, 186
  building leaders, 107–108
  collaborative, 60
  distribution of, 3
  participatory, 111, 116, 195
  principal, 100, 171–172, 195, 197
  responsibility for, 36, 48–50
  teacher, 41, 50, 100–101, 108, 197
  top-down, 136, 137
  training for, 82, 83, 88
Leadership development program, 122, 126
Leadership Training Retreats, 55, 55–56, 59, 60, 63, 71
Leadership transitions, 95, 99, 100, 103, 107
Learning conceptions, 3
Learning Lab Schools, National Education Association (NEA), 119
Learning styles, 143
Legislators, xi, 5, 34
LEP. *See* Limited-English-proficiency
Lewis, Helen, 117
Lifelong learning, 38, 61, 162, 170
Limited-English-proficiency (LEP), 163, 165
Littlefield, Lee, 147, 149, 150, 158, 159
Lobbying, 48, 84
Local context, 102–103

About the Contributors

LYNN G. BECK is Dean of the School of Education at Pacific Lutheran University in Tacoma, Washington. Beck's research and teaching interests include the ethics of educational leadership, the preparation of leaders, and models for educational reform. She has authored or co-authored seven books and is also the author of a number of articles and chapters. Recent publications include *The Productive High School* and articles in *Educational Administration Quarterly* and in the *International Journal for Educational Leadership* and a chapter in the *Handbook of Research on Educational Administration* (2nd ed.).

LINDA BOL is an Assistant Professor at Old Dominion University. She teaches graduate-level courses in educational research and evaluation. Her research interests include the impact of instructional practices on student study activities and achievement, teachers' assessment practices, and evaluation of educational reform efforts.

KATHRYN M. BORMAN is Professor of Anthropology and Associate Director of the David C. Anchin Center at the University of South Florida. Dr. Borman has extensive experience in her main research interests: educational reform and policy. She is also currently the editor of two journals, *The Review of Educational Research* and *The International Journal of Educational Policy, Research and Practice*.

LISA M. JONES is a Postdoctoral Fellow in the Center for Applied Research and Educational Improvement and the Postsecondary Education Policy Studies Center at the University of Minnesota. Her research and teaching interests have focused on K–16 linkages, academic/industry relationships, and organizational behavior and educational policy. Recent publications have examined the principalship, conflict of interest and university-industry relationships, and P–16 transitions.

MICHAEL S. KNAPP is currently Professor of Educational Leadership and Policy Studies at the University of Washington, where he directs the Center for the Study of Teaching and Policy. His scholarship concentrates on the dynamics of policy and leadership, in relations to school improvement, teacher development, and the quality of teaching, especially in disenfranchised communities. Dr. Knapp has written extensively about his research, including *Teaching for Meaning in High-Poverty Classrooms* (1995), *Paths to Partnership* (1998), and *The School District and Instructional Renewal* (forthcoming).

KAREN SEASHORE LOUIS is Director of the Center for Applied Research and Educational Improvement and Professor of Educational Policy and Administration at the University of Minnesota. Her research and teaching interests focus on educational reform, knowledge use in schools and universities, and educational institutions as workplaces. Her research in K–12 education has focused on school improvement, educational reform, and knowledge use in schools. Recent publications address the development of teachers' work in schools, the role of the district in school reform, urban education, comparative educational reform policies, the changing role of the principalship, and organizational learning.

JOSEPH MURPHY is Professor of Education at the Peabody College of Vanderbilt University. He is also Chair of the Interstate Leaders Licensure Consortium. Murphy's primary interest is in school improvement, with emphases in the areas of policy and leadership. His most recent book, entitled *The Productive High School: Creating Personalized Academic Communities,* was published in 2001. Murphy has also published more than 150 book chapters and articles for leading refereed academic journals and professional outlets.

SAUNDRA MURRAY NETTLES is Associate Professor of human development in the University of Maryland College of Education and research director for the University's Consortium on Race, Gender, and Ethnicity. She researches and writes on issues relating race, gender, school, and community contexts to psychosocial resilience and success in schools. She is the author of the neurological case study, *Crazy Visitation: A Chronicle of Illness and Recovery.*

BRADLEY S. PORTIN is an Associate Professor in Educational Leadership and Policy Studies at the University of Washington in Seattle. In addition to the preparation of school administrators, he teaches leadership theory, politics of education, and comparative and qualitative research methodology. Portin's research and prior publications have included educational reform in the United Kingdom, school improvement initiatives, and changes in principal roles and preparation.

PEDRO REYES is Professor in the Public School Executive Leadership Program and Associate Dean for Graduate Studies at the University of Texas at Austin. He teaches school improvement and leadership theory. He conducts research on high-poverty schools and the effects of state-level education policy on students. He also is the author and co-author of more than fifty books, monographs, chapters, and articles related to his research interests.

MARK A. SMYLIE is Professor of Education at the University of Illinois at Chicago. He is also a Director of the Consortium on Chicago School Research and the Secretary-Treasurer of the National Society for the Study of Education. Smylie's research interests include urban education improvement emphasizing the relationships among school organization, leadership, and classroom instruction. In addition to fifty published articles and book chapters, his recent work has appeared in the *Handbook of Research on Educational Administration* (2nd ed.) and in international handbooks on educational change and on teachers and teaching. Smylie is a former high school social studies teacher.

SAM STRINGFIELD is a Principal Research Scientist at Johns Hopkins University's Center for Social Organization of Schools. As director of the systemic supports for school improvement program at CSOS, Stringfield has directed nearly two dozen studies examining the relationships among student-, teacher-, school-, and system-level effects of school reform in eight countries.

CHARLES TEDDLIE is a Distinguished Professor of Education at Louisiana State University. He has published numerous books and articles in school effectiveness research and educational research methodology. He is currently co-editing the *Handbook of Mixed Methodologies for the Behavioral, Health, and Social Sciences* (2002).